2⁵⁰

SUCCESSFUL SEWING

'Photographed at Heals, London. Furnishing by Heals. Sewing machine, sewing accessories and Venus dress form at Singer shops. Photographer, Tim Marlborough of Martin Ellis Studios'.

SUCCESSFUL SEWING

A MODERN GUIDE

by

NESTA HOLLIS

with illustrations

by

Winifred Rickwood

TAPLINGER PUBLISHING COMPANY
New York

First Published in the United States in 1969 by
TAPLINGER PUBLISHING CO., INC.
29 East Tenth Street
New York, New York 10003

SBN 8008-7490-0

Library of Congress Catalog Card Number 76-84974

Printed in the U.S.A.

CONTENTS

INTRODUCTION
Modern dressmaking and needlework–
your plan for professionalism
page 11

1. CHOOSING YOUR EQUIPMENT
The right tools for dressmaking and needlework
page 13

2. MODERN SEWING MACHINES
Their selection, use and care
page 34

3. YOUR IMPORTANT CHOICE
Choice of pattern, style, pattern size, fabric and colour
page 47

4. SEWING COURSE FOR BEGINNERS
A twelve-point plan for professionalism
page 55

5. DIRECTORY OF SEWING PROCESSES
page 72

6. FABRICS, FIBRES AND FINISHES
page 135

7. EMBROIDERY STITCHES
page 176

8. CLOTHES CARE
page 184

Index
page 191

ACKNOWLEDGEMENTS

My grateful thanks go to the many people who have given such invaluable assistance while I have been writing this book, including the illustrator, Mrs. Winifred Rickwood; Miss Helga Dawid of Viking-Husqvarna Sewing Machines, Bentalls of Kingston upon Thames; Miss E. Wildman, for many years head of the Educational Department of the Singer Sewing Machine Company and now retired; Mr. Ken Mills of Hoover Ltd. who has taught me so much about the technology of fibres and their care; Mr. James Quinlan of Elna Sewing Machines (G.B.) Ltd.; Mr. J. W. Viles of Alfa Sewing Machine Co. Ltd.; Mr. Christopher Thomson of Bernina; Mr. P. E. Cuckston of Pfaff (Britain) Ltd.; Mr. Derik Quitmann of Frister & Rossman Sewing Machines; Miss Barbara S. Briggs, H.M.I. Department of Education and Science and Mr. Ian G. Smith of Bondina Ltd.

In the fabric field the acknowledgements are too numerous to list in full detail. But my special thanks to Mr. Philip Rowe of the British Man-Made Fibres Federation; Mr. W. R. Beath of Courtaulds Ltd., Mr. A. Humberston of the Technical Department of the Textile Council for Man-Made Fibres, Cotton and Silk Industries of Great Britain; the technical staff of I.C.I. Fibres Ltd.; Mr. John Cannon of British Enkalon and Mr. Christopher Bellingham-Smith, of the Home Laundering Consultative Council.

Perhaps the chief vote of thanks should go to my husband, Robert Hollis, who has helped so much with the complex research and correspondence involved in connection with the Fabrics, Fibres and Finishes chapter. During the lengthy preparation of the book, he alone has prevented the possibility of my being submerged beyond recovery by paperwork – a possibility which has seemed very real at some moments in time.

NESTA HOLLIS

INTRODUCTION

Modern dressmaking and needlework – your plan for professionalism

A good sewing book should be your friend and counsellor–somewhere to turn when you cannot remember just how, say, to make a bound buttonhole, or complete a particular embroidery stitch.

But it should be more than this. It should also be a simple, enlightened guide to modern dressmaking and needlework–in fact a sewing course that teaches you modern methods for a professional finish, and carries you swiftly along on a wave of enthusiasm and comprehension.

It should tell you about all the most modern sewing aids which are available, from tiny time-savers costing very little to the modern, miraculous sewing machines which are proving such a revelation to new and experienced dressmakers alike.

However, the more comprehensive a sewing book is, the more difficult it becomes, unfortunately, to see the wood for the trees, or perhaps I should say 'to see the sequence for the stitches'. In order to progress from opening the pattern envelope to making up the article there seems no alternative but to wade through, say, five ways to tack, twelve ways to do seams, six ways to produce a pocket, three ways to set in a collar and six ways to turn up a hem.

I have tried to sidestep this difficulty for you by giving in Chapter 4 a twelve-point plan for professionalism–a simple, to-the-point sewing course for beginners. But as this basic sewing course will not by any means cover every small detail of dressmaking, I have made Chapter 5 a directory of sewing processes, so that when, in the dressmaking course, a certain stitch or process is referred to, you can turn to the directory for a full explanation. This, I feel, will at least ensure that you get a good look at the wood as a whole before you become lost in the trees.

You will notice that nowhere in the book have I attempted to tell you about methods of drafting paper patterns to your own designs. There are particular reasons for this.

Leading paper-pattern manufacturers produce their designs to such a high standard these days that it would be very difficult indeed for a beginner to produce anything as good as a good commercial pattern.

Pattern drafting is an art in itself, usually studied by those who wish to graduate to dress designing as a career. If you are a housewife who wishes to make satisfactory clothes at home, or a student still at school, it is unnecessary for you to learn the skill at this stage, when there are so many excellent commercial patterns, in designs which follow every whim of fashion.

It may be–and I hope it will be–that your appetite for dressmaking will be whetted once you have completed two or three really well-made garments, and perhaps you will then wish to extend your studies into other fields–pattern cutting and dress designing, for example, or possibly tailoring.

I said just now that a good sewing book should be more than your friend and counsellor. It should also be more than a basic dressmaking course. In these days of specialist knowledge it should, too, include a certain amount of technological information.

As I want this book to be useful to students taking examinations, as well as to home dressmakers, I have, in Chapter 6, taken a fairly technical look at textiles, not only at the fabrics you are likely to see when you go to a store but also at their chemical composition, their behaviour during making up—and perhaps most important of all, at the correct methods for washing by hand and by machine.

Again, you will not want to plough through this chapter while you are making a garment, but it may be helpful to know that the information is there for you, whenever you need guidance on the nature, choice or care of a fabric.

I

CHOOSING YOUR EQUIPMENT
The right tools for dressmaking and needlework

No-one would expect a man to dig over a large garden with a small coal shovel, or a secretary to type a report with two or three keys missing from her typewriter. If you had never before sat at the driving wheel of a car, you would not expect to climb in and drive unaided through busy traffic.

Yet many women, young and not-so-young, expect to take to dressmaking without the necessary equipment or training, and become very discouraged when they find it difficult, laborious and unrewarding.

Who can wonder that they find dressmaking an effort when one looks at the way they tackle the task? They hack out a dress using an old, blunt pair of scissors, used by the rest of the family for cutting paper, opening coffee-tin lids, snipping fusewire and carving up carpet underfelt.

The small huddle of rusty pins they find in the bottom of the sewing box are obviously inadequate, so they supplement them with a few stray office pins.

They expect the sewing machine to stitch every type of fabric perfectly, although they never think of adjusting tension or pressure, or using a drop of oil, or fitting a different needle.

They do not have the exact colour of thread they need, so they make do with a very bad match rather than go back to the shops. The thickness of the sewing thread does not even enter into their calculations.

They do not bother to try the pattern to see if it fits, but assume optimistically that as long as they buy one in the right bust size, it will all come out right. 'Well,' they think hopefully, 'if it does not fit when I have machined it together, I can always take a few tucks in here and there.' Yet sewing experts estimate that there are over three hundred different figure types for every bust size which comes in a paper pattern, so that the person who needs to make no adjustment at all to the pattern is very rare indeed.

No wonder that many women *never* succeed in making clothes they are pleased with. They work hard at everything they make, but use the wrong methods entirely. As a result sleeves never set quite right and retain telltale puckers, collars look slightly off-centre, hems are uneven and over-stitched, darts never quite match. Discouragement sets in, followed by the vow never to make clothes at home again.

If only these women could realise that by investing in some good (and not *necessarily* very expensive) equipment, and by unlearning their old habits and relearning correct modern methods, they could produce clothes of which they could be proud, with far less effort than before.

In later chapters we will be dealing with correct methods. But it is best to start with the basic needs–the right place to sew, the right place to store the equipment and the right tools for the job. Without the right tools it is probable that you will be a rather bad workman, whether or not you actually blame your tools.

THE RIGHT PLACE TO SEW, THE RIGHT PLACE TO STORE

Dressmaking must be one of the untidiest of occupations. We are not all lucky enough to have a special room which we can set aside for sewing and other hobbies, and often the living room would seem to be the only place we can use.

But is it the only place? Much thought has gone into the subject of sewing areas, and many people have found their own ideal arrangement.

Could you, perhaps, find some space in your bedroom or the spare-room for a cupboard, carefully sectioned off to take all your sewing equipment, and with space to store the garment you are making without undue crushing? If you could put the sewing machine beside the cupboard you would have a very convenient sewing area. Then, when you have to stop sewing, it would be a simple matter to stow everything away in the cupboard. A full-length mirror, too, is a tremendous help when you are trying on a garment, so try to site one nearby. This sort of arrangement, with a ceiling-mounted curtain, is shown in (1).

2

Two other ingenious sewing corners are shown. One of the cleverest I have seen consisted simply of a large, three-leaved screen, placed in a corner of a bedroom to conceal a sewing machine, with sewing aids arranged on the inside 'walls' (2). In another house I saw a large, built-in cupboard in the children's playroom, fitted out as a miniature sewing room complete with ready-to-use sewing machine, strip lighting and, of course, a good lock on the cupboard door to keep out the smaller children. When the children are safely tucked in bed, their mother is able to take over the 'den' for her sewing (3).

Whatever sewing corner you manage to devise for yourself, you will need to invest in a sewing box in which you can store all the small items you need. There are excellent sewing boxes available: for example there is a good one in the form of a sectioned container with a transparent plastic lid, or you may prefer one of the attractive wicker baskets which are fitted to hold the various sewing items.

If your budget is tight, however, you could adapt an old wooden knife-tray for the small sundries, and keep it in a special drawer reserved for sewing equipment.

1

3

THE RIGHT TOOLS FOR THE JOB

Unless you are a wizard with a needle you are not going to get very far without a sewing machine. I will be dealing with this subject in Chapter 2, and the question of sewing machine attachments will be dealt with at the same time.

There are certain tools which are absolutely essential for the home dressmaker—a good pair of cutting-out shears is the first item which springs to mind. Other aids are extremely helpful, but can be dispensed with if you cannot afford the outlay at this stage.

Some items are certainly not essential, but would make your task so very much easier, often at a very low cost, that you would be well advised to invest in at least a few of them sooner or later.

So great are the savings when you make your own clothes at home that if you set yourself up properly with good tools, you will probably redeem their cost with the first few garments you make.

Since no two people would agree on which items are essential and which are merely helpful aids, I will simply give you a fairly complete list from which you can make your own choice. Here it is:

GENERAL EQUIPMENT
Bodkin
Crochet hook
Darning mushroom
Dress form
Dressmaker's carbon paper
Hem gauge
Hem marker
Magnet
Needle threader
Needlecase
Needles, assorted
Orange stick
Pincushion (and, if wished, emery bag)
Pins
Ruler(s)
Seam unpicker
Sewing threads, various
Tacking thread
Tailor's chalk or chalk pencil
Tape measure
Thimble
Tracing wheel
Tweezers
Yardstick

CUTTING TOOLS
Buttonhole scissors
Dressmaker's shears
Electric scissors
Pinking shears
Pointed scissors, medium size
Ripping scissors
Scissor cutting-gauge

EQUIPMENT FOR HAND EMBROIDERY
Embroidery frame
Embroidery scissors
Embroidery silks
Stiletto

PRESSING EQUIPMENT
Iron
Ironing board
Needle (velvet) board
Pressing cloths
Pressing aids: mitt, seam roll, tailor's ham
Sleeve board
Sponge

That is a summary of 'the tools for the job'. I

will explain each item in turn so that you can become familiar with them.

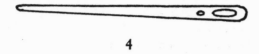

4

Bodkin (4)

A bodkin is a large, blunt needle, either flat or round with a big eye. There are various sizes and types. It is used for threading tape, ribbon, elastic or fine cord through slots or a casing. Some bodkins have a small additional round eye to take round elastic.

Carbon

See Dressmaker's Carbon Paper.

Crochet hook (5)

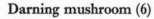

5

It is very useful to have a fine crochet hook in the sewing box. This is handy (quite apart from its conventional use for crocheting) when you are mending—for example a woollen jumper may have a hole where stitches have run, and may need 'knitting' up again before it can be mended.

Darning mushroom (6)

This is a mending aid rather than a dressmaking one, but it is invaluable for hand-darning socks and jumpers. If your eyesight is not as good as it might be, make your task easier by choosing a light-coloured darning mushroom (or painting a dark one white) which will make it easier to see the thin parts round the hole you are darning.

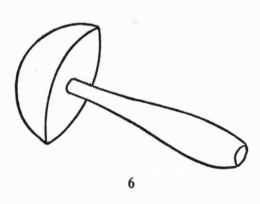

6

Dress forms (7, 8, 9, 10)

If you mean to take dressmaking seriously it will be well worth your while to invest sooner or later in a dress form—or what used to be called a dressmaker's dummy.

The best kinds are those which can be adjusted to duplicate not only your bust/waist/hip measurements but also to indicate how long- or short-waisted you are, the width of your shoulders and, in fact, every measurement which might affect the final fit of your garment. For preference choose one which includes the tops of the arms—a very important part of the body when you are fitting a garment.

It is advisable to buy one which you will be

able to adjust over the years to the changes in your figure. A dress form is not a cheap purchase, and you would not want to have to discard it after a few years because you have lost or gained a considerable amount of weight.

There is a wide range of dress forms made in a variety of materials. A browse round the sewing department of a large store will probably help you to decide which kind you find most suitable. Three useful types are illustrated (7, 8 and 9). The one in 7 is of padded, reinforced plastic, well made and fully adjustable. The wire form (8) is perhaps less durable, but it is inexpensive and good value for money. It is covered by a stockinette 'sleeve' once the correct size has been achieved. The dress form in 9 is, in fact, made from a cardboard-type material, and fits together neatly with special studs. Not as sturdy as, say, the form in 7, but reasonably priced and adjustable.

Old-fashioned dressmaker's dummies in wood or plaster (10) can still be picked up in second-hand or antique shops. But as they are mostly small-waisted and usually not adjustable, they are seldom a practical purchase (although they may have a certain decorative appeal).

8

9

7

(Figs 7 and 8: forms by A. E. Arthur Ltd
Fig 9: form by Gerda Thomson)

10

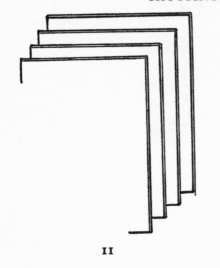

Dressmaker's carbon paper (11)

Some dressmakers like to use special dressmaker's carbon paper, usually in conjunction with a tracing wheel, as an alternative to making tailor's tacks. It is available in a variety of colours from most good department stores.

Hem gauge (12, 13)

This is used for measuring the width of the hem allowance after you have marked the correct hem length. You can buy a plastic hem gauge (12) from a shop or department which stocks sewing aids, or you can make your own in strong cardboard (13).

Hem marker (14)

Turning up a hem is a surprisingly tricky job. Even if you have someone to help you pin the hem to the correct length, the results are not always satisfactory unless your helper has a very good eye and a steady hand. It is therefore worth saving up for a hem marker which you can use to mark out a clear and completely level hemline in chalk. It can be adjusted to any hem length.

11

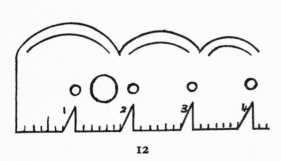

12

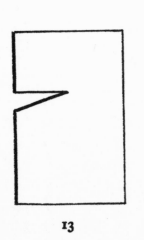

13

14

Magnet (15)

Buy a child's magnet, horseshoe-shaped, tie to it a piece of tape or ribbon, and attach it to your sewing machine or the handle of your sewing box. When you have finished sewing, the floor is quickly cleared of errant pins and needles. Keep the magnet away from scissors, to avoid magnetising them, which you might find irritating.

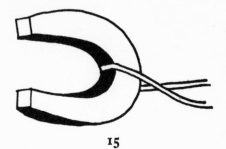

15

Needle threader (16)

Even if your eyesight is not as good as it might be, needle-threading need present no problems. A needle-threader like the one illustrated costs only a few pennies, and many home sewers find it indispensable, both for hand sewing and for use with the sewing machine. There is another type, also inexpensive, made of plastic.

16

Needlecase (17)

If possible, buy a really commodious, professional-looking needlecase, with banks of needles of all sizes neatly ranged. This encourages one to keep it replenished, and means one never has to go through the hunt-the-needle routine which can be so nerve-shattering at moments of crisis.

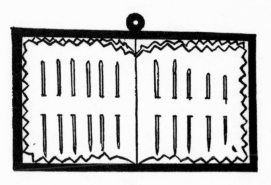

17

Needles (18)

'Sharps' of medium length are generally used for sewing, but there are at least ten sizes and it pays to stock a wide range so that you can find your favourite needle for each fabric. You will probably find that the needle you like to use most is decided not only by the fabric you are sewing, but also by your own personal preference. Some people like to use a very fine needle, with a fairly large eye, for most light and medium fabrics; some like a short, rather thick needle.

It is worth mentioning here that tapestry needles, which are thick and have a large eye and a very blunt end, can be most helpful in the sewing box, particularly for sewing up garments knitted in double knitting wool. They are also the safest possible needles to give to a small child who is experimenting with her first sewing stitches, perhaps using pieces of punched cardboard.

18

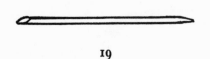

19

Orange stick (19)

Why an orange stick? This is valuable for poking out the corners of inside-outed belts, or sharp-pointed collars—a gentle and effective tool for such purposes.

Pincushion (20)

Many types of pincushion are available in good department stores, some in novelty shapes, such as pumpkins, small mice or pots of cacti, some strictly utilitarian. Most useful are those which fit on your wrist so that they are ready to hand.

You can also buy pincushions with a miniature emery bag attached. Emery bags or emery cushions are an old-fashioned idea, but a good one: if a pin or needle becomes sticky, or if it is very slightly rusted, you can plunge it into the emery bag for gentle scouring.

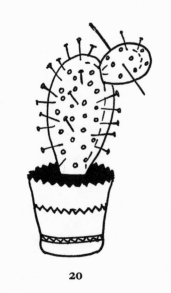

20

Pins (21)

Choose fine, sharp, steel dressmaker's pins, from a sewing shop or department. The ones which come in a tin with a dip in the lid are perhaps easiest to handle. You tip out a few pins into the upturned lid, and then instead of sticking your fingers into a prickly mass of pins as you work, you take pins from the lid, where the small 'hump' has prevented them from huddling together.

Manufacturers of good quality pins line their containers with a special paper which helps to prevent rusting.

Sizes 15, 16 or 17 pins are used for most fabrics. For sheer fabrics there are very fine pins, sometimes called lillikins, and for upholstery work one can buy very coarse pins.

Never use office pins for dressmaking. They are blunt, clumsy to handle, and make unsightly holes in most fabrics.

21

Ruler (22)

There are sewing experts who consider it essential to have a whole armoury of rulers, including wooden and plastic rulers of various lengths and even T-squares, while others

22

manage without rulers at all, confining their
needs to a good tape measure and yardstick.
However, you would probably find a 12-in.
ruler with flat, unbevelled edges very useful
(22), and perhaps also a 6-in. ruler in clear
plastic, marked to eighths and sixteenths of an
inch. If you become a dedicated needlewoman,
you can buy rules and measures (and of course
other equipment) made for the professional
garment industry, which will cost more but
last a lifetime.

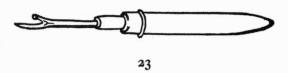

23

Seam unpicker (23)

A seam unpicker is very inexpensive and well
worth buying, as unpicking is a job one has to
be prepared to tackle from time to time. Some
dressmakers use the same gadget for cutting
open machine-made buttonholes in light fabrics.

Sewing threads (24, 25)

Most women, when they buy sewing thread,
ask for 'a reel of cotton'. The correct term,
however, is sewing thread, and this includes
cotton thread, mercerised cotton thread, machine-
embroidery thread, nylon thread, silk thread,
Terylene thread and the strong thread used for
sewing on shoe buckles and shoe-buttons. There
are also buttonhole twists (25) and embroidery
silks (44).

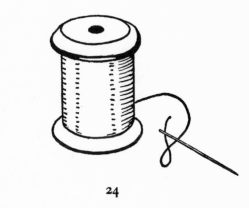

24

A good general rule is to use mercerised
cotton or silk for natural fibres, and reserve
nylon and Terylene thread for synthetic fabrics.
Sometimes a garment made of nylon fabric and
sewn with cotton thread may develop puckered
seams.

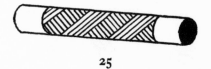

25

Tacking thread (26)

It is surprising how many people never think
of buying special tacking thread, which has
great advantages over ordinary sewing threads
for making tacking stitches and tailor's tacks.
It clings well and is easily broken or snipped
when you want to draw it out. Choose brilliant
colours which will show up well against the
fabric you are sewing.

26

27

28

Tailor's chalk (27, 28)

Tailor's chalk, preferably of the non-wax variety, is used for transferring markings from pattern to material or making alteration marks during fitting.

A chalk pencil (28) with a small brush for removing chalk traces after the job is finished is also useful.

Tape measure (29)

A good-quality measuring tape with a brass end is essential. It simply is not worth the small saving to purchase a cheap tape measure, for it may stretch in use and become very unreliable.

Thimble (30)

Anyone who has done a good deal of hand-sewing normally finds a thimble indispensable. It is worn on the middle finger of the hand used for sewing, and even if you cannot accustom yourself to wearing a thimble all the time, it is useful to keep one by you, for sewing especially strong materials. Choose a metal rather than a plastic thimble, and be sure to buy the correct size for your finger.

Tracing wheel (31)

Some find it an advantage to use a tracing wheel in conjunction with dressmaker's carbon paper for reproducing pattern markings on the material. Others prefer to make tailor's tacks or to use tailor's chalk.

29

30

31

Tweezers (32)

A strange tool in a sewing box? No—if you have tacking stitches or tailor's tacks to take out, a pair of tweezers can be a great asset.

Yardstick (33)

A yardstick may be flat like a ruler, or rounded, and may be wooden or metal. It is useful for checking grain lines when pinning pattern pieces on to fabric, and for marking out hem lengths if you have no hem marker. Look for a good-quality yardstick—a cheap one which will warp or buckle is useless.

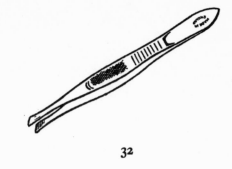

32

CUTTING TOOLS

Buttonhole scissors (34)

These are not essential, but are useful if you may be making many buttonholes, because they can be adjusted to cut exactly the button-hole length you require.

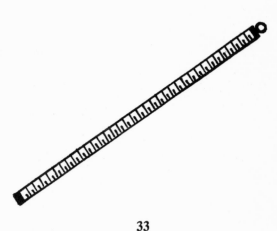

33

Dressmaker's shears (35)

Good dressmaker's shears are absolutely essential to the efficient home dressmaker, and anyone who tries to economise on them, or to make do with the household scissors, is inviting failure. If you choose wisely and give your shears loving care, they will repay you with long service and always be a joy to use.

Choose bent-handled shears about 7 to 8 in. long, with a small ring handle for the thumb and a large ring handle for the second, third and fourth fingers. It is important that they should have bent handles so that one edge of the lower blade will rest flat on the surface of the table when you are cutting out. Do not buy straight-handled scissors for cutting out fabric.

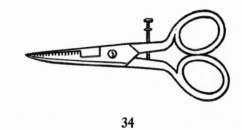

34

Shears made from steel by the hot-drop forge method, and with blades joined with a bolt or screw, rather than a rivet, are best. However, it is always advisable to try out scissors and shears in the shop before buying them—if you go to a shop which specialises in good-quality sewing aids, the assistant should not mind at all.

Never, never let the shears be used for any purpose other than cutting out fabric: paper

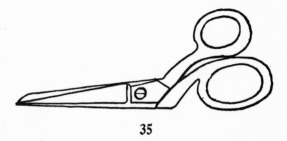

35

will blunt them very quickly, and so will anything tougher. Always store them in a dry place, and put a touch of oil on the screw occasionally.

If you have chosen wisely, your shears will keep their sharp cutting edge for a long time, but when they lose their first keenness, have them resharpened by taking them to a shop which specialises in sewing equipment, or to the sewing department of a large store. It is unwise to entrust them to the 'scissor man' who comes round the streets sharpening anything from ordinary scissors to lawnmowers.

Electric scissors (36)

36

Certainly not an essential item for the home dressmaker, but many enthusiasts are finding electric scissors a useful supplement to their dressmaker's shears. They are surprisingly light and easy to use.

Pinking shears (37)

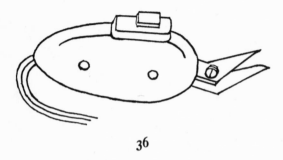

37

Some heavy fabrics can be pinked to advantage – the v-shaped cuts along the edges of the seam allowances help to avoid excessive bulkiness. However, the pinking of seams is not a practice normally recommended for good home dressmaking. If you do wish to pink seam allowances, it is a good idea to machine-stitch and pink (see page 79).

Pointed scissors (38)

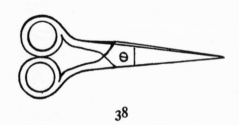

38

Important in every sewing box is a pair of good-quality sharp-pointed scissors between three and six inches long, handy for snipping threads and trimming or clipping seam allowances. The same rules apply as when choosing dressmaker's shears – always look for a high-quality pair as a long-term investment.

Ripping scissors (39)

These have rounded ends so that you do not cut the fabric when you unpick a seam. They are not to everybody's liking, however, and many dressmakers prefer a simple, inexpensive seam unpicker.

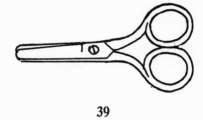

39

Scissor cutting gauge (40)

If you do a good deal of needlework or handi-craft you may find this gauge a great help. You fit it on the top blade of the scissors, adjust it to the required width, and you can then cut long strips of fabric (for example bias strips) to an even width.

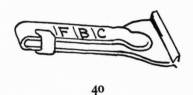

40

EQUIPMENT FOR HAND EMBROIDERY

Embroidery frame (41, 42)

The range of embroidery frames is wide, and it is advisable to go to a shop which specialises in artwork and handicraft materials in order to see a good selection. There are circular embroidery frames (41), rectangular ones (42) where the material is stretched as it is fixed on the frames, and more elaborate ones where the fabric is tightened by the turning of a screw or screws.

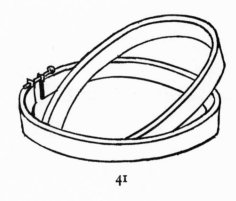

41

Embroidery scissors (43)

Small, sharp-pointed scissors are essential, especially if you will be doing any cut-out embroidery. Examine them carefully before you buy them, to see that the points meet closely, and make sure that it will be possible to have the scissors resharpened when necessary.

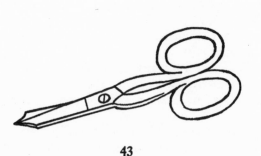

43

42

44

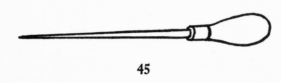

45

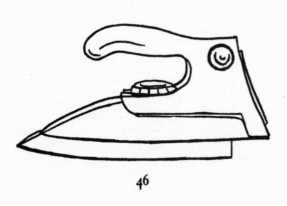

46

Embroidery silks (44)

Normally, embroidery silks are purchased in six-strand skeins and one uses three strands at a time, dividing the silk as each length is cut for sewing. Finer work may, however, require only two strands of silk, or even one.

Stiletto (45)

Not by any means an essential embroidery tool, although some needlewomen like to keep a a stiletto for making holes in fabric, in order to embroider tiny eyelet holes.

PRESSING EQUIPMENT

Pressing equipment is necessary to any home dressmaker, and a sure sign of an experienced needlewoman is an ironing board set up near the sewing machine during sewing sessions, with the iron switched on and additional ironing aids placed nearby. The iron will be in use again and again, at each stage of the dress-making process, for with only a few exceptions every seam should be pressed after it is sewn and before you move on to the next stage. It is wise to have a thermostatically controlled iron, so that you can keep the iron switched on all the time you are sewing–it will not overheat and will not consume an undue amount of electricity.

There are three types of iron available: dry irons, steam irons, and steam-or-spray irons.

Dry iron (46)

Modern irons are better designed than ever before, and the majority have thermostatically-controlled heat settings.

If you are buying a new dry iron, look for the very lightweight types (weight $2\frac{1}{2}$ to 3 lb.) which are extremely easy to use both for thin fabrics and, in conjunction with a damp pressing cloth, for thick ones.

The new irons with a cut-away handle in the Scandinavian style (46) make for very quick pressing and ironing, and are very manœuvrable.

The majority of thermostatically-controlled irons now on the market have numbered heat settings for different types of fabric. These settings have been agreed upon by the British 'Home Laundering Consultative Council', who felt there was a need for greater standardisation of iron temperatures and, after considerable research and testing, developed a method of classifying fabrics for ironing purposes. The classification is as follows:

Setting 1. COOL Suitable for acrylics (e.g. Acrilan, Courtelle, Orlon).
Setting 2. WARM Suitable for acetates, nylon, Tricel, Terylene and wool.
Setting 3. MEDIUM HOT Suitable for rayon.
Setting 4. HOT Suitable for cottons and linens.

Iron manufacturers may also include a VERY HOT setting (setting 5) for use in special circumstances at the discretion of the user. But this setting is unlikely to be used by the home dressmaker.

If you are using an iron which is more than a year or two old, it may possibly not have these settings, in which case it is best to follow the instruction book which came with the iron.

The particular value of this standardised range of heat settings is that in the next few years more and more ready-made garments will bear labels telling you how they should be washed and which iron setting to use. This should eventually develop into a sort of label-shorthand—for example, an Acrilan dress may bear washing instructions and underneath them the advice: 'Iron setting 1' or: 'Iron: 1'.

The Council also hope that in time, similar labels will be available for every length of fabric sold by the yard.

See Chapter 6 for more on H.L.C.C. and the home laundering of fabrics.

Steam iron (47)

A good modern steam iron (47) is of particular value to the home dressmaker. With some fabrics—though not all—it does away with the need for a pressing cloth. A dressmaker needs to press her work as she goes along, and a steam iron does the job perfectly, so that the fabric retains its body and does not develop a ridgy,

shiny or over-pressed look. The fact that the pressing cloth can sometimes be dispensed with means that time and trouble can be saved. Most important of all, a steam iron gives better and more consistent results.

With most types of modern steam iron you can change from steam ironing to dry ironing and back again as the need arises, and you will sometimes find these irons described as steam-or-dry irons. They work on a drip-feed principle: a measured amount of water is allowed to drop on to a part of the soleplate, where it is instantly turned into steam. The steam then travels along the steam passages, out of the soleplate and on to the fabric.

Steam irons have one temperature setting for all fabrics, but once you switch over to dry ironing you select the setting according to the fabric, in exactly the same way as described before.

I have talked to a number of people who have tried using a steam iron—in a friend's or relative's house perhaps—but who have not been very impressed by its performance.

The reason may have been that the iron was an old one—some of the very first steam irons were extremely heavy and cumbersome; or that it was of the tank type which is rarely made these days, having been almost entirely superseded by the drip-feed type. It may be that the iron was so choked up inside with hard-water deposit that little or no steam came out; or that it had been filled from a jug that was not quite clean, so that clothes were stained with pale brown marks. However a good modern steam iron,

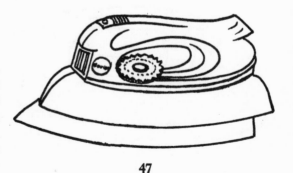

47

properly used, is an asset to anyone who has ironing or pressing to do.

There are some important points to bear in mind on the filling of the iron. Unless you live in an area where the water is very soft, it is far better in the long run to take the trouble to use only distilled water, which you buy from your chemist or drugstore at a very reasonable price. It is certainly not wise to use tap water, or distilled water from a garage (which could contain traces of harmful acids). One iron manufacturer markets as an alternative to distilled water a special bottle which converts tap water to demineralised water.

Manufacturers of irons usually suggest that water which has been boiled and cooled may be used as a substitute for distilled or demineralised water, but even this is likely to leave a coating inside the iron where water is very hard.

Many people bottle the melted ice left after defrosting their refrigerator, for use in their iron. But some manufacturers frown on this practice, because the water may not be pure: frozen food or ice cream may have thawed slightly before being placed in the freezer compartment and may possibly leak and mingle with the ice.

A steam iron should always be emptied after use, as this, too, helps to prevent the iron from 'furring up'.

Steam-or-spray iron (48)

This can be used for steam ironing but there is in addition a button on the handle which when pressed releases a fine jet of water just ahead of the iron, thus reproducing automatically the old system of hand sprinkling the ironing. It is particularly useful for thick cottons and linens which have become far too dry after washing for normal steam ironing.

There are some possible disadvantages to these spray mechanisms—for example rayon may react unfavourably to being sprayed with water and then ironed, and become permanently spotted.

If one is choosing a new iron with home dressmaking chiefly in mind, there seems little advantage in a steam-or-spray iron. A steam iron probably gives all one needs for good pressing. If, however, you are buying for the family laundry as well as for dressmaking, you may decide that the extra cost of a steam-or-spray iron is amply justified.

Ironing board (49)

Ironing boards vary from the sublime to the worse-than-useless. A really well-designed metal board with fully-adjustable height is hard to beat. One such board is shown in 49. It has two small wheels, so that once you have folded the board you can wheel it to its storing place, with no lifting.

If your house has a convenient wall space, an ironing board which folds up against the wall could be very useful. It is usually possible to buy them, but a member of the family may perhaps feel enthusiastic enough about your dressmaking activities to construct a fold-away board for your sewing corner.

An ordinary ironing board, whether newly purchased or the ancient family friend, may be adequate for dressmaking if it is wide enough, if the surface is well-padded and has a good cover, and (preferably) if the height can be adjusted. But boards which are warped like a switchback, and so thinly covered that one irons a series of fine ridges into every article,

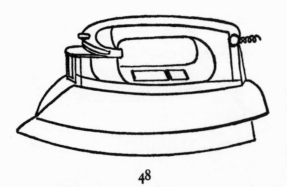

48

are quite useless. If the board you are using is old, try improving it with a new cover.

Inexpensive covers are available in most department stores. Choose one which has a thickness of foam plastic in addition to the cover fabric, to give extra smoothness to all ironing and pressing.

Various types of fabrics are used for these covers—cotton, Milium, asbestos fabric or a special type of heat-resisting plastic. Cotton covers are inclined to scorch fairly rapidly, but are inexpensive enough to be replaced when necessary. Milium gives good heat deflection and does not scorch, nor does the asbestos-type cover. The special plastic covers are guaranteed against scorching, and will remain unharmed even if you should unthinkingly leave the hot iron face down.

Whatever type of cover you choose, make sure that it is the right size and that it ties snugly to the ironing board with tapes.

49

(Wheel-away ironing board by Simplus)

Needle board (50)

This is something you will probably defer buying until you have special need of it. A needle board is used for pressing velvet, velveteen, corduroy and other pile fabrics while making them up. The fabric is placed face down on the needles so that it may be pressed without the pile being crushed or marked. Modern needle boards are made with a thick, flexible base, and may be rolled up for storage.

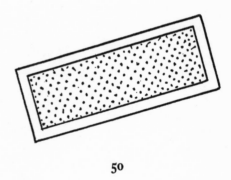

50

Pressing cloths (51)

Specially-treated pressing cloths, which look and feel like coarse paper tissues, can be bought. Not everybody, however, finds they have any advantage over fabric pressing cloths.

A cotton pressing cloth, either of fine soft cotton or closely-woven cheesecloth, is generally used for silks and rayons; a thin woollen cloth is used for woollen fabrics. A dry wool pressing cloth used under a damp cotton cloth is helpful for materials which are inclined to go shiny; it retains a matt surface and helps to avoid that flattened, over-pressed look which can give a garment such a home-made appearance.

51

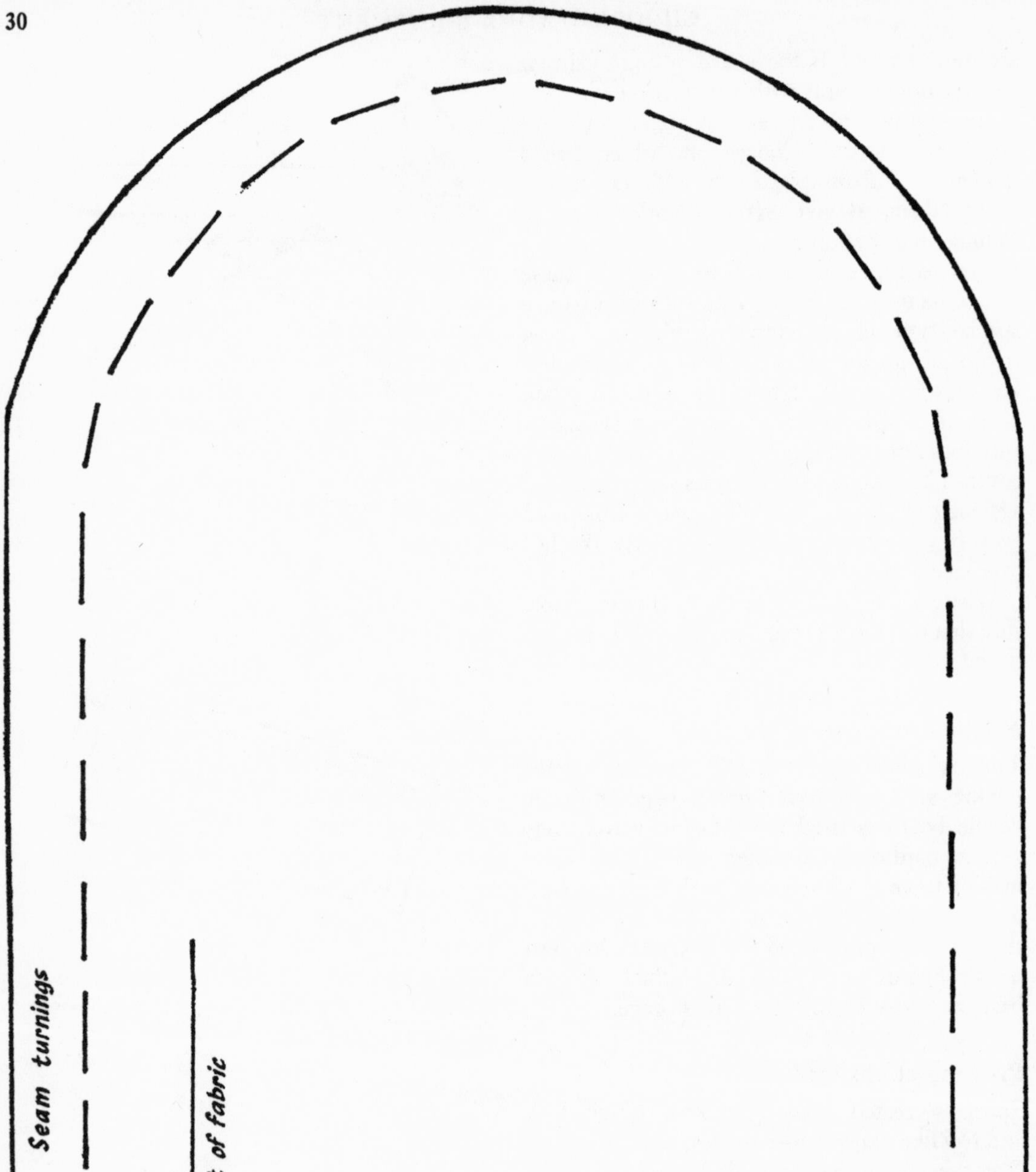

Seam turnings

Straight of Fabric

HEM EDGE

Pressing aids–a set to make yourself

There will be stages in your pressing when you will find it very useful to have a curved, padded surface over which to smooth and shape curved seams, deal with intricate gathers or small sleeves, or mould darts.

There are three pressing aids, all easy to make at home, which would answer the purpose admirably; if you make all three you will be able to select the one most suitable for each article you deal with.

The cost is minimal because the three pressing aids–press mitt, tailor's ham and seam roll–can all be cut from half a yard of strong bleached calico, and additional materials are not expensive.

The press mitt and the tailor's ham are best stitched on a sewing machine for maximum strength, although you can sew them by hand if you prefer. The seam roll is very simple to make, and is stitched by hand.

The materials for the three items together are listed below:

You will need

½ yd. white bleached calico or strong cotton, 36 in. wide

Small bag of kapok

Reel of white mercerised sewing cotton

½ yd. white cotton tape

18-in. length of broom handle or wooden dowelling 1 in. in diameter

Piece of woollen fabric about 20 in. wide. The length of this material will depend on its thickness, the aim being to roll the material around the broom handle until the roll measures about 8 in. in *circumference*. The material need not be bought specially–it may be cut from an old blanket or a discarded garment, but it must be clean and preferably white.

Cutting out

There are three pieces for the press mitt, two pieces for the tailor's ham and one piece for the seam roll.

Press mitt (52)

Trace the mitt shape on to tracing or greaseproof paper, copying all markings. Cut three identical pieces from the calico, using this pattern.

To make: Hem one of the pieces along the straight edge, making a fold for the hem at the dotted line indicated.

Place the hemmed piece between the two other pieces, and stitch the three layers together along the seamline marked, taking ½-in. seam allowances. Leave the straight end open for filling.

Turn the mitt right side out so that the seam allowances are concealed, and fill the two un-hemmed pieces tightly with kapok, ensuring that the tip of the mitt is well-padded. Turn in the raw edges, press and stitch neatly to close.

Sew a loop of tape to one side so that the mitt may be hung up if desired.

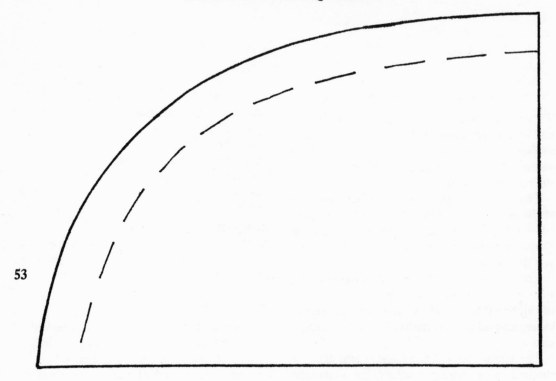

53

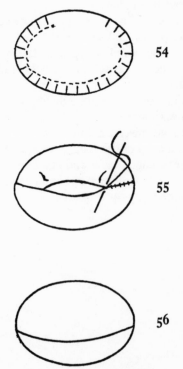

54

55

56

Tailor's ham (53, 54, 55, 56)

To make: Take a piece of tracing or greaseproof paper measuring at least 13 in. by 9 in. and fold it in half lengthways, then in half again to divide the paper into four quarters. Place the folded paper with the folds to the straight edges of the pattern (53), and trace the curved edge and seam line firmly. Cut round the line so that you have an oval-shaped pattern.

Cut two of these oval shapes from the calico.

Stitch the two pieces together along the seam line, leaving a 6-in. opening for inserting the stuffing (54). Snip the seam allowance at intervals all the way round the stitched seam line.

Turn the fabric right side out and stuff the ham firmly with kapok. The secret of success is to pack it tightly—for best results soak the scraps in clean water, then squeeze them and stuff the ham with the damp filling, packing until it is solid (55).

Finally, turn in the raw edges and oversew the opening by hand (56). Put the ham in a warm place (such as the airing cupboard) for several days to dry out.

Sew a loop of tape to one end.

Sometimes sawdust is used as a filling instead of the kapok, to give even more firmness.

Seam roll (57, 58, 59)

To make: Roll the woollen material tightly on to the broom handle (57) and stitch the raw edge down firmly. Draw together the ends of the roll to form a neat closure at each end (58).

Next roll the calico tightly round the woollen material, turning in one edge neatly and sewing it down firmly. Again, neaten the ends of the seam roll.

Sew a loop of tape on to one end (59) so that you can hang up the seam roll if you wish.

Sleeve board (60)

A sleeve board is not essential, especially if you make the three pressing aids already described. But if there is a sleeve board provided with the ironing board you use, it is a good idea to learn to use it on the more intricate parts of garments, such as the sleeves themselves. Sleeve boards can also be bought separately from ironing boards, to stand either on the board or on a pressing table.

Sponge (61)

A clean sponge, kept specially for the purpose, is useful for damping down fabrics as you press them.

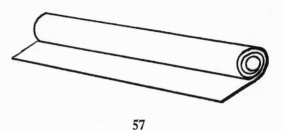

57

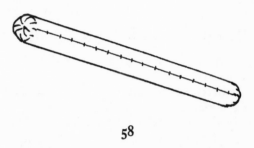

58

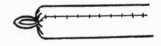

59

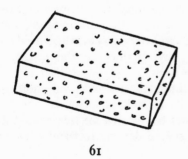

61

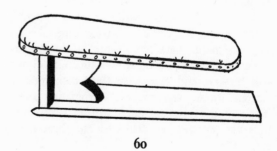

60

2

MODERN SEWING MACHINES
Their selection, use and care

CHOOSING A SEWING MACHINE

Quite the most exciting development for home dressmakers in the last decade has been the fantastic change in sewing machines available on the market. Anyone who has used only a straight-stitch machine, and is lucky enough to be planning to buy a new sewing machine, has some very pleasant surprises ahead.

If you are considering such a purchase you should take several weeks, or even months, in careful study of the market, before making a decision. Until a number of the latest makes of machine have been demonstrated to you, it will be impossible for you to imagine how useful or versatile a good modern zigzag or automatic machine can be. By taking your time you may save yourself from an expensive mistake; for although obviously you will not get the best quality at the cheapest end of the scale, price is not invariably a guide to value within the mid-price range.

What are the main types of sewing machine available?

They can be roughly divided into straight-stitch, zigzag (otherwise known as swing-needle) and automatic machines. Some of the manufacturers like to break the classifications down still further, and categorise their machines as straight-stitch, zigzag, semi-automatic, automatic and fully-automatic. For simplicity, however, we will just deal with the three main categories.

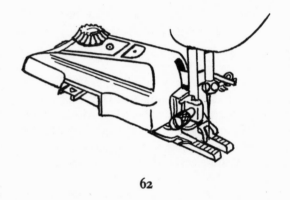

62

STRAIGHT-STITCH MACHINE
If you are *sure* you will only use the machine for plain sewing, you may find that the straight-stitch machine meets your needs satisfactorily. It may come with various attachments. Before you decide, however, be sure to try at least one or two swing-needle machines in a similar price range. It may be that for about the same cost, or perhaps only a little more, you could have the extra versatility of swing-needle sewing, without any sacrifice in the quality of the machine itself.

Straight-stitch machines will normally sew backwards as well as forwards, and they can sometimes be released for free-motion darning, using a special darning foot and a hoop attachment.

If you already have a straight-stitch machine, you can probably buy various extra attachments by the same maker. In addition, you can buy a buttonholer device (62), which will attach to most straight-stitch electric machines and enable you to produce reasonably satisfactory machine-made buttonholes. It must, however, be said that although this method is usually successful with most light fabrics, some of the heavier fabrics may prove more difficult: in which case a bound buttonhole would probably be best.

ZIGZAG OR SWING-NEEDLE MACHINE

These are much more versatile, even in their very simplest form. By moving a lever or a dial knob, you can stitch not only in a straight line but also from side to side. This means that you can produce a zigzag stitch, which widens your scope considerably.

The simplest zigzag machines will of course give a limited choice of stitches, but many medium-price to higher-price zigzag machines have a surprisingly wide range: not only satin stitch, but also blind hemming and oversewing, shell edging, making buttonholes; sewing on buttons, hooks and eyes and press fasteners; finishing off seams and raw edges; and, with some types of machine, making whipped hems on such items as sheets and pillowcases.

You may be able to produce simple decorative patterns (a small to fairly comprehensive range, depending on the model); work with twin needles, or stab needles (to produce very delicate 'holed' stitches on fine fabrics like organdie), and tackle fancy appliqué work.

Some of the more expensive zigzag machines, for example the Viking Husqvarna from Sweden, will enable you to make a stitch called 'three-step zigzag', which is valuable for finishing edges where a fabric frays very easily.

Bernina machines, made in Switzerland, offer a 'five-step serpentine stitch' which is also very satisfactory.

A warning, however, about sewing machines in the cheaper price ranges: a skilled operator can make any machine perform far more adequately than someone who is new to the task. A great many people buy the very first sewing machine they see demonstrated. If you have never watched a modern sewing machine at work before, it is very easy to be impressed by its versatility when you see it demonstrated in the shop, only to be disappointed once you have made the purchase and find that it will not perform anything like as easily as you had imagined. This applies particularly to zigzag machines.

Let me give you an example of how misleading a demonstration can be. I was talking to a friend who had bought an average-priced zigzag machine. Before the sale the demonstrator had shown her a variety of decorative patterns. She was impressed, and agreed to buy the model shown. She was also told she would be given instruction on its use, and because she was a fairly experienced needlewoman, she felt confident that all would go well. However she soon found that even with tuition it was not nearly so easy to produce patterns and embroidery as she had imagined it would be. In fact it took a good deal of skill to manipulate the controls to make a pattern.

For example, she had thought that she would be able to produce tiny leaf-shapes automatically –but not at all. The differing widths of satin stitch which filled in the shapes were achieved by manipulating the stitch-width control by hand–a trick which she found very hard to master. Her disappointment increased when she discovered that while her machine would stitch only from a central point to one side (with what is called a two-position or left-hand-position needle) another machine by the same manufacturer and costing only about £10 ($25) more, had a three-position needle–in other words it would sew from the centre point to the right *and* the left. This meant that she could have completed patterns, including her leaf-shapes, in one movement, whereas with her own machine she had to stitch one half of the pattern and then turn the fabric to stitch the other side. This may seem a trivial matter. However it applies not just to one leaf-shape but to the whole range of sewing techniques.

Most sales staff, of course, are fully aware of

what they are selling, but they may not want to jeopardise a sale by explaining the difference in cost between a two-position and a three-position needle machine. If they are untrained they may not even understand the difference themselves. However if you later decide to trade your machine in for a better one, you will probably find the resale value of a two-position needle machine very much lower than that of a three-position needle machine.

Generally speaking, the higher the price of machine, the greater the versatility. However this is not always the case: one maker's plain zigzag model may be much the same price as another maker's semi-automatic of equivalent quality.

AUTOMATIC MACHINE

This does everything that a zigzag machine can do, and more besides, including a wide range of automatic embroidery stitches.

Some fully-automatic machines can produce special stitches that stretch with the fabric–an important feature for anyone who plans to sew with stretch fabrics, like those used for stretch slacks and swimwear. Some machines, for example, offer an Overlock Stitch (used to make the seams and bind the seam allowance in one operation) and Triple Lock Stretch Stitch, and for these stitches the fabric is automatically moved forwards, then backwards while the needle stitches from side to side. This is a miraculous sight to anyone not used to fully-automatic machines, especially when the machine is switched to slow speed so that you can see the full complexity of the action. With other automatic machines the needle may move from side to side, but the fabric will only feed in one direction (unless of course you decide to reverse it manually).

Even among fully-automatic machines–the aristocrats of sewing machines–there is a surprising difference between makes. It is not so much a question of what they will do, but of how the various effects are achieved. Some models reach the end results without requiring more than the turning of a knob or two, or the setting of a lever, or perhaps the addition of a small plastic stitch selector called a cam. With others it may be necessary to set a number of levers and knobs, or to slide dials to certain settings, or to co-ordinate levers and dials with discs or cams.

Remember that one sewing machine is not necessarily better than another one because it is complicated. A large number of knobs, levers and push-buttons do not always mean more versatility. Some of the most advanced sewing machines on the market are deliberately designed to have as few moving parts and controls as possible; and one of the most sophisticated models available, with which practically every conceivable sewing variation is possible, has only two more knobs than a straight-stitch machine.

If you have a very unmechanical turn of mind you may be positively daunted by the presence of a vast number of knobs and switches and levers which all have to be co-ordinated; and if a machine *is* elaborate in its controls, you may at first need to consult the instruction book constantly for even the simplest stitch, which can be irritating.

One machine I tested, the top-price model in its range, fell down badly on the instruction book. It took two hours to work out how to sew ordinary straight-stitch, because it was necessary to wade through pages of irrelevant and disorderly information, including directions on how to use a treadle machine!

Ask to see the instruction book before you agree to buy the machine. Some instruction books, for instance, are written by experts who know their machines too well, and can no longer look at the subject through the eyes of the beginner.

Flat-bed or free-arm?

A flat-bed machine is the type which most people are used to. It has a flat working surface for the material; and if one is setting in a sleeve, or doing something else fairly intricate, one normally learns to manœuvre the work to avoid catching other parts of the article in the stitching. With a free-arm machine, however, there is no such problem because the working surface consists of a narrow rounded arm with space below it, so that you can slip sleeves or socks, trouser legs or loose-cover sections over the free-arm for sewing or darning. If you need a larger working surface, you simply clip on the extension table which is provided; and this converts the machine into a flat-bed type.

Many people consider that a free-arm machine has very distinct advantages especially as it can always be converted back to a flat-bed type. A flat-bed model, of course, cannot be turned into a free-arm machine. The choice is not so much a question of price as of make. You can get a relatively inexpensive plain zigzag machine which has the free arm. Many of the top-price automatics also have the free-arm, but some do still retain the flat-bed styling.

Sewing machine attachments

As sewing machines have become more automatic, the importance of separate attachments has become less pronounced. Straight-stitch machines in the average to higher price range usually have special attachments for carrying out a variety of specialised sewing jobs, and anyone who has bought a straight-stitch machine in fairly recent years may have purchased at the same time one or a number of attachments, such as a multi-slotted binder, foot hemmer, zipper-foot, gathering foot, edge stitcher, tucker, flange hemmer, quilter, gauge-presser foot and buttonholer. Many of the attachments popularly sold with sewing machines looked so complicated that people were discouraged from using them, and the belief grew up that it was senseless to buy a higher-priced sewing machine, because one would never use the complex gadgets.

This kind of thinking need no longer apply with modern machines, however. The fully-automatic, and to a lesser degree the semi-automatic and plain zigzag machines, can do many of the specialised jobs without any attachments. Some are still necessary of course – for example the quilter is a valuable asset with any type of sewing machine – but their fitting has been made easier by the use of a snap-on, snap-off presser foot.

This trend away from attachments seems likely to continue. What is happening in effect is that sewing machines are becoming at the same time far more complex and sophisticated in the number of operations they can perform and yet simpler to understand and operate.

Features that make sense

Here are a few of the available features, taken from among the leading makes of fully-automatic sewing machines, that seem to me to make very good sense:

* Special low-gear speed for complicated work, blind hemming, and fabrics such as PVC vinyl and leather. It is also highly valuable for anyone who is not familiar with electric sewing machines, and especially for use in schoolrooms and domestic science colleges, where students can sew at a comfortable speed until they gain confidence and skill.

A point worth making here is that low speed may be achieved in one of two ways. In a machine which incorporates a low-gear speed, the motor itself is actually slowed down because you 'change gear', and the power is increased, just as when a car changes gear. With other types of machine the process is equally simple, but the motor may continue to run at the same speed while the electricity supply is reduced.

* Simplified threading system. Most modern machines have less upper threading points than they used to have. Some, like the Bernina, do not need threading at all: the thread is simply slipped over a number of points.

* Simplified stitch selection. Where stitch selection can be simplified the whole machine benefits. One machine, the Viking Husqvarna, has a colour-coding system, where knobs with different colour markings show at a glance which stitch you are choosing (this means you do not have to consult a code number in a chart). Some machines use lever settings, some involve the user slipping on cams or discs.

* Automatic buttonholer which completes a buttonhole without your having to turn the fabric. This is especially valuable with fairly bulky garments, when turning the work can be exceedingly difficult. With some machines there

is a special dial with five digits which you turn for each of the five stages of a buttonhole. One machine, the Pfaff, allows you to cut the buttonhole without removing the fabric from the machine.

* Non-jamming bobbin. Modern machines seldom jam in normal home use although I tested one top-price machine, straight from the factory, which jammed irrevocably the second time I used it and needed a new bobbin case. Some manufacturers have bobbins which they guarantee will never jam, because of the basic design. This is a very important feature for schools or colleges, where machines are more likely to be misused.

* Pull-down light, which gives bright direct light for working on dark fabrics.

Making your choice

Only you can know what your ideal machine would incorporate, and you will only learn this by looking around at what is available. So as I said before, do not buy the first machine you see demonstrated. Visit dealers in your area and ask for a demonstration (or visit an exhibition where demonstrations are going on all the time); consult consumer reports and give intelligent but not slavish consideration to their findings. Ask friends and neighbours who have recently purchased a sewing machine for their views on it. As you narrow the choice down, see whether the demonstrator is willing to let you try the machine yourself, under supervision.

Before you make a final decision run through the following check list:

1. If you plan to buy a simple straight-stitch or plain zigzag machine, are you sure that you will not later regret being without some of the refinements which you could obtain by paying a little more? On the other hand, if you plan to buy a top-of-the-scale fully-automatic machine, are you sure that it is not *too* elaborate for your requirements, too complicated for you to cope with happily?

2. Do you find difficulty in threading the machine, or understanding how to set the tension?

3. Is the machine so complicated that you have to consult the instruction manual constantly? Is the instruction book adequate, taking you from the first stages of threading up the machine and making simple straight stitches through in logical order to more complicated stitches?

4. Are you sure that you know the difference between a flat-bed and a free-arm machine, and that the model in which you are interested offers what you require?

5. How will you store the machine? If there is a carrying case, is it strong and pleasing in design? If you plan to buy a machine table, is there one in a style which would fit in with your taste in home furnishings?

6. Is the manufacturer a reputable firm of sound standing?

7. Check that servicing, if necessary, will be prompt and adequate. Ask what period of time the guarantee covers. Sewing machines do not often go wrong, but they can. There is a surprising variation in guarantee periods between manufacturers, and guarantees may cover, say, one year or two, three, five, ten, or even twenty-five years. One manufacturer agrees to replace faulty parts free 'at any time'. Motors are usually covered by guarantee for a shorter time than the main guarantee—normally for two years.

Dealers' service—the period when you can expect to go back to the shop to ask for service without incurring labour charges—may vary between six months and five years or more, depending on the dealer.

USING YOUR NEW SEWING MACHINE

Having made your purchase, be sure you will get value for your money by taking instruction on the use of the machine. Sewing machine dealers usually offer buyers a good after-sales service, either sending a representative to the customer's home to demonstrate the use of the machine, or inviting the customer to come along to the shop premises for tuition. Some manufacturers may offer one lesson, others two or more, and one manufacturer I spoke to said that if the customer was having difficulties, which was unusual because in this case the automatic machine was a particularly simple one, she could come back to the London show-rooms whenever she wished and a demonstrator would gladly give her advice.

As with all modern equipment, it is absolutely essential to read the instruction book carefully, not once but many times. If small troubles do develop they are usually caused through misuse of the machine. So get to know your machine thoroughly, work in exactly the way the demon-strator and instruction book advise, and enjoy your sewing.

A good start with a good sewing machine can bring a lifetime of pleasure.

Sew a fine seam

The following notes are directed to those who are not experienced in the use of a sewing machine. If you *are* a skilled machinist, skip the next few pages – they will seem like a primer.

Before you begin to sew a garment:

1. **Practice sewing straight.** If you have never used a sewing machine before, it is a very good idea to start by sewing practice lines, angles and curves. One sewing machine manufacturer, Viking Husqvarna, produces practice sheets (domestic science teachers and college lecturers can make block applications for classroom use)

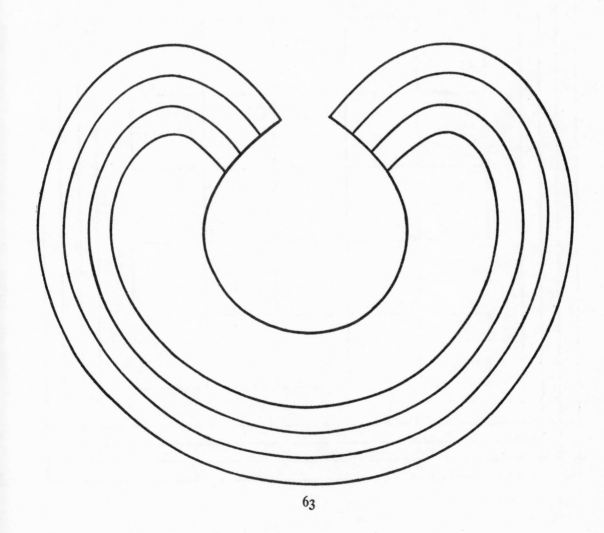

and they have given me their permission to reproduce two of them here (63 and 64).

To make up your own practice sheets for home or classroom use:

(a) Trace the designs on to squares of tracing paper. Be very careful to copy the lines accurately, using a good ruler for the straight lines.
(b) Starting with the first design, sew along the lines keeping as accurate as possible. Do not watch the needle but keep your eyes on the sewing line. If you wish you may sew without thread on these practice squares, though it is perhaps more encouraging if you do use thread. Repeat with the other practice square.

2. **Make a fabric test piece.** After cutting out the garment or article you are making, always use some of the scraps left over as test pieces.

64

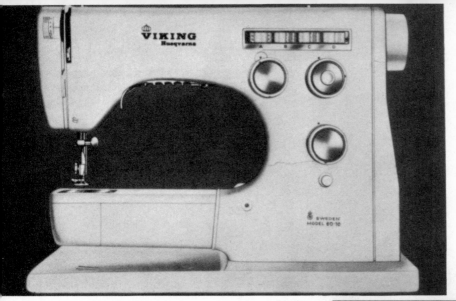

1. The near-noiseless fully-automatic Viking Husqvarna free-arm machine looks – and is – extremely simple to use. You select from a wide range of embroidery stitches simply by turning colour-coded knobs. The non-jam bobbin and the smooth-running slow speed feature make it ideally suited for school use as well as in the home.

2. The fully-automatic Elna Supermatic free-arm machine. Shown here are a few of the magnificent range of automatic patterns it can produce using a selection of built-in and interchangeable pattern disks.

3. A model from the famous Singer range. With the latest models the bobbin stays in position for rewinding in seconds, while the top thread stays threaded. Buttonholes can be made automatically with some models, or, as here, a buttonholder attachment is quickly fixed.

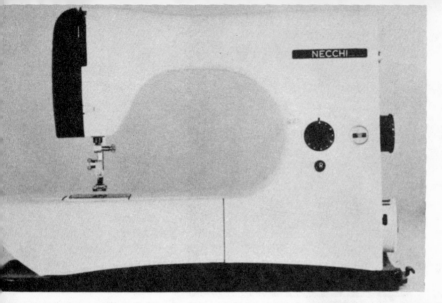

4. The Necchi free-arm fully-automatic machine; simply turn the pattern knob on the side to select from a range of automatic patterns. A special feature is the Golden Needle giving long basting stitches which are easy to pull out when necessary.

5. The Frister and Rossman Model F lightweight free-arm fully-automatic swing-needle machine weighs only 20 lbs, packs away in a neat carrying case, and produces 26 different patterns including three-step zigzag.

6. Machines in the low-priced range, like this Novum straight-stitch model with flat bed, give stitch length adjustment and a forward and reverse sewing control lever.

7. Moderately-priced automatic sewing machines are obtainable – this Brother/Jones flat-bed machine has a number of noteworthy features. Servicing should be no problem if you buy from a reputable dealer.

8. The tiny Bernina Minimatic free-arm machine is not a toy but a fully-automatic sewing machine of unusual sophistication. Special features: tiny enough to keep in a cupboard, versatile enough for all sewing. Bernina demonstrators are famed for magnificent appliqué pictures produced on their machines.

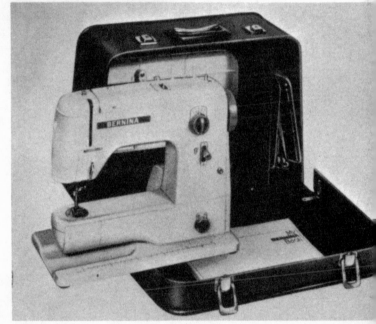

9. The automatic Pfaff flat bed machine has 'Dial-a-Switch' feature for fancy embroidery, plus attachments which include a rug maker. The carrying case includes a roomy built-in sewing box.

10. The robustly-constructed Alfa machines have a good reputation in the commercial sewing machine market, and the domestic ones, like this fully-automatic flat bed model, are also well worth enquiring about.

11. Today's sewing machines are almost magical – they stitch from side to side at great speed, often while guiding the fabric forwards and backwards to produce intricate effects. Look closely at this model and you'll see twin needles, which produce embroidery patterns simultaneously in two colours.

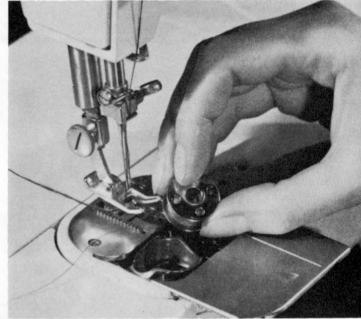

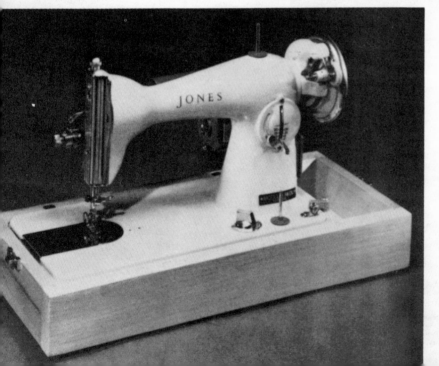

12. Not everyone looks for a fully automatic machine – an inexpensive model like this Jones flat bed machine may be preferred by someone who is looking for a means of plain sewing at minimum cost.

Cut a left-over scrap into a rectangle, fold it double, and then machine-stitch in a series of straight lines to assess the treatment it needs. Always work with two layers of material. Check the following:

(a) Stitch length–is it suitable for the fabric? As a general rule shorter stitches are needed for finer fabrics, longer ones for thicker, firmer fabrics. If there is any tendency to puckering, the stitch length may be too long. Consult the machine instruction book for guidance on stitch length.

(b) Tension–is it even? The threads should lock at the point where they pass through the fabric, and there should be no pulling either on top or underneath (see 65, 66 and 67). Refer to the instruction book for guidance on adjusting tension. Normally only the top-thread tension will need correcting. Adjusting of the bobbin thread is best left to an expert.

(c) Needle–is it suitable for the fabric? Is it sufficiently sharp or is a new needle necessary? A modern sewing machine should have its needle changed to suit the fabric. One should not follow the long-established practice, or perhaps I should say malpractice, of always using the same needle year in, year out. Changing a needle is simplicity itself on a modern machine.

(d) Pressure–is it correct for the fabric? Extremely fine or very thick fabrics may call for a change in pressure. Consult your instruction book on this point.

3. Keep to the seam line. Most patterns which you buy in this country provide for a ⅝-in. seam allowance on most turnings (exceptions are hems and cuffs). Your sewing machine may have guide lines marked on the throatplate to help you to stitch straight and at an even distance from the fabric edge. If it does not, you can buy a special seam-line attachment, or use coloured adhesive tape to mark a line ⅝ in. from the needle point (be sure that you get the tape straight!).

If your sewing machine has guide lines but they are only in centimetres, you have two alternatives. One is to get used to thinking of seam allowances in centimetres (most printed

RIGHT

65

66

WRONG: Bobbin tension too tight

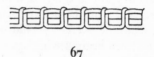

67

WRONG: Top tension too tight

paper patterns give the centimetre measurement in brackets). The other is to fix a strip of coloured adhesive tape as already described.

4. Beginning to stitch. (a) Set the needle on the seam line exactly, turning the balance wheel by hand to pierce the fabric. If the machine has a reverse action, it is a good idea to begin sewing about ½ in. from the end of the fabric, stitch backwards to within 1/16 in. of the end of the fabric, then stitch forwards again over the same line. When you begin to stitch forwards again, it is good practice to hold the ends of the threads behind the presser foot, to ensure that they are not entangled in the stitching or pulled down the needle hole.

(b) Stitch gently at first, increasing the speed gradually; you can use the special slow speed if one is available on your machine. Keep your eye on the presser foot and follow an edge or seamline–do not watch the needle.

(c) Let the fabric feed through at its own pace–do not pull it through. The only exception to this is when you are sewing very bulky seams, when the pressure can be slackened (consult the instruction book on the way to do this) and the work carefully fed forwards.

5. While you are stitching. If you wish to turn a corner, or to rearrange the work, be sure that the needle is down in the fabric before you raise the presser foot.

6. When you reach the end of the work. Most sewing machines have a thread cutter behind the presser foot. Stitch to the end of the fabric, lift the take-up lever and draw the work backwards away from the presser foot. Cut the threads to leave about 6 in. of thread on the end of the seam for tying, and about 6 in. projecting from the needle eye and needle hole (so that when you begin sewing again there will be no hold ups because of the needle becoming unthreaded or the bobbin thread not operating).

Most machines will sew in reverse so that you can reverse back over the stitches at the end of a seam, to avoid the need for fastening off thread by knotting.

Whichever method you use for finishing ends of seams, you should be sure to snip off loose ends before going on to the next piece of sewing. Get into the habit of doing it and it will never seem an irksome task. Leaving all the ends hanging until the garment is almost finished is lazy dressmaking practice.

The 'difficult' fabrics

There are some materials which present certain difficulties to the home dressmaker, but usually they are easy enough to sew with a modern sewing machine if you go about it the right way. Here are a few hints which may help you:

LEATHER

Obviously you will not use a fine needle for leather, but make sure it is not too thick either, or the needle may tear the leather. Use long stitches. Very thick leather may need a special cutting needle which has a small knife in the point, but most normal thicknesses of leather and suede, and most imitation leather, do not need this special needle.

FOAM-BACK FABRICS

These may prove difficult to sew unless your machine offers a special roller presser foot which is designed to allow the fabric to glide through. It is also possible to buy a silicone spray for treating the surface over which the fabric will slide. Both these help to prevent the foam plastic from clinging to the presser foot and feed plate.

PVC (VINYL FABRIC)

Use large stitches. Some home dressmakers advocate the use of a fine smear of oil or vaseline on the bed (or sewing surface) of the machine to help the fabric to slide through easily; others recommend the use of talcum powder sprinkled around the sewing area. Curves are difficult to sew on PVC unless they are very gradual, and shaping, too, should be avoided as far as possible.

STRETCH FABRICS

As indicated elsewhere, stretch fabrics present few problems if you have a zigzag machine, and even fewer if you have a fully-automatic machine which allows you to use special 'stretch stitches' which will stitch and overcast seams simultaneously. A synthetic sewing thread should normally be used.

OTHER SYNTHETIC MATERIALS

Use a fine needle and fine sewing thread. Most experts recommend the use of synthetic sewing thread. Loosen the thread tension slightly. Use a long stitch.

More about fabrics and fibres, together with sewing notes, can be found in Chapter 6.

DECORATIVE WORK WITH A SEWING MACHINE

Hand embroidery is an art form which goes back thousands of years, and countless generations of women have taken pleasure in creating embroidered articles. However, since sewing machines have become more sophisticated, machine embroidery has become for many people a hobby every bit as satisfying as hand embroidery, with an almost limitless range of effects possible.

There are basically three ways of making designs with a sewing machine:

(a) By the use of 'free-hand' embroidery.

(b) By the use of the zigzag stitch in appliqué work.

(c) By the use of the patterns produced automatically by the sewing machine.

Free-hand embroidery

Once you have learned the knack, free-hand embroidery is possible with most machines– even the older, straight-stitch ones. Consult your instruction book to see what adjustments must be made. Usually the 'feed dog' which pushes the fabric through the machine is disengaged. This may involve the feed being dropped out of the way, or there may be a special cover plate which disengages the feed dog.

The fabric is stretched over an embroidery hoop, and the operator manipulates it while the needle sews. If you wish to produce anything elaborate, it is obviously easier to do so with a swing-needle machine.

All sorts of effects can be achieved in free-hand embroidery–it is possible for example to produce a stitch very similar to the long-and-short stitch used in hand embroidery, and if multicoloured embroidery thread is used the result is most attractive. But like any other art, free-hand embroidery is a technique which must be learned by watching a skilled demonstrator, and then practising with diligence.

Appliqué work

This can be one of the most attractive forms of machine-sewn decoration, and when sewing machine manufacturers have sample work on display at exhibitions or in prominent stores, it is often the appliqué work which catches the eye. It is frequently used for pictures and framed fire-screens, cushions and table mats, and decorated garments for children.

However, it is worth remembering that appliqué is the *least* practical decoration for washable articles, and is especially impracticable for children's clothes. Bibs, aprons, dresses and so on have to be washed so regularly that the appliqué work may fray, particularly if, as is sensible, the mother likes to machine-wash as many garments as possible. The same reasoning applies to appliqué for table linen–it is pretty but impracticable, as the sort of washing which will remove food stains will also, very probably, dislodge the appliquéd fabric pieces, not to mention the colour bleeding which may result from washing in very hot water.

There are different methods of using the sewing machine for appliqué work. One involves cutting out shapes from different fabrics to form the design, then pressing them and tacking and stitching them in place, one at a time, on the main fabric (or fixing them with adhesive, depending on the thickness of the materials used). This is the traditional way of doing appliqué, except that instead of hand-finishing, the zigzag satin stitch on the sewing machine is used to secure and conceal all raw edges. Often a machine-embroidery hoop is used. The other way is to mark the design outline on the *back* of the main fabric and then to place the appliqué pieces on the right side. The pieces are cut larger than the shapes they are to occupy, and are zigzag stitched *from the wrong side* of the main fabric. The excess fabric is afterwards cut away on the right side very carefully, with fine scissors. The whole appliqué design is built up piece by piece.

Any scraps of fabric, from sheer organdie to thick tweed, can be used to form delightful designs. If you wish, you can ornament the appliqué pieces themselves with one or more of the automatic embroidery stitches if they are available on your machine. For example the petals and leaves of a flower formed from various pieces of fabric may be further embellished with a decorative stitch to form veining and shading. This, incidentally also helps to strengthen the work further.

Automatic embroidery

If you are going to have automatically embroidered patterns on a garment–for example a blouse or a child's dress – it will be much easier if you do the embroidery before you make up the garment (unless you plan to use the automatic pattern to embroider decorative seams).

Experiment first using odd scraps of the same fabric, folded double, to see which pattern or combination of patterns would best suit the purpose, and to check tension, stitch width and stitch length.

Before you start to stitch it is advisable to mark very precisely the lines along which you will be sewing, using faint pencil on fabrics that are washable, and tailor's chalk on thicker and darker fabrics. If two sides of a garment are to be embellished, measure carefully to ensure that the pattern runs symmetrically, and meets exactly where necessary.

Always use identical embroidery thread for top threading and bobbin threading.

Machine-embroidered patterns look better on double fabric, and if the material is fine, slip a sheet of typing paper under the fabric too, before you stitch it, to prevent the design from puckering. The paper is afterwards torn off, and any that remains will be washed out when the article is laundered.

When you begin a line of pattern, do not begin right at the edge of the fabric, or the raw edges at that point may be drawn down into the needle hole and thus flaw your work. Instead begin at least $\frac{1}{4}$ in. from the edge of the fabric.

Make sure, before you begin sewing a long line of automatic pattern, that there is enough embroidery thread on both the spool and the bobbin. If the thread should run out before you have finished, however, it is possible to blend in the continuation in the following way:

Remove the work. Take a matching strip of material, re-thread the machine and sew the pattern until you come to the exact place where the stitching ended before. Stop there, raise the needle and remove the material. Put back the original work, making sure that the needle is positioned on the correct side of the pattern so that it will take up the design again, and continue to sew. Some machines have an automatic indicator which enables you to connect up the pattern instantly, and the procedure described will not then be necessary.

When you finish a line of pattern, always draw the thread through to the back of the work and tie carefully, making sure not to pull as you make the knot. Snip off the ends.

Machine-made patterns can be useful as well as decorative. A number of automatic patterns are ideal for finishing off edges of tablecloths and napkins, and seams can also be finished with embroidery stitches for a pleasing effect— a particular advantage because it avoids the need for seam-finishing.

To sum up: advice on the sort of embroidery which is possible with each type of machine should be sought before you make the purchase, as some models are more versatile than others. It is almost always best to have a machine with a three-position needle (see page 35).

I would suggest you ask the demonstrator for special tuition on the kind of embroidery in which you are interested. Many machine manufacturers make a particular point of training their demonstrators in advanced techniques of decorative work.

Once you have the knack yourself, you will probably find that your enthusiasm increases and you will want to find new designs to make up. It may be possible to adapt designs which were intended for hand embroidery: the transfer is ironed on to the fabric in exactly the same way. The specialist needlework magazines include designs for machine embroidery from time to time, and the Embroiderers' Guild (or the Embroiderers' Guild American Branch Inc.) also produce designs suitable for machine embroidery.

CARE AND MAINTENANCE OF THE SEWING MACHINE

When you use a sewing machine you should give it the care and attention which are essential to keep it in good running order at all times. Here are the main rules to follow.

1. Cleaning: Keep the machine clean, by dusting off lint and fluff which collect around the moving parts of the machine. A small lint brush

does the job perfectly and is usually provided with the machine, but you can buy one separately. The instructions which come with the machine will give guidance on exactly how and where this dusting should be done.

Many of the more modern machines are very simple to clean. It is a good idea to keep a piece of soft cloth, such as a piece of cheesecloth or soft cotton muslin (the sort used for babies' muslin diapers) specially for the sewing machine, so that you can dust the machine each time you use it.

2. Oiling: Consult the instruction book to find out how often you should oil the machine and which parts should be oiled. Always remove dust, lint and threads before oiling. A good rule is to oil little and often. Some manufacturers recommend very frequent oiling if the machine is used continuously. If it is used only now and again, occasional oiling is sufficient. If the machine is in a centrally-heated atmosphere, it may need oiling more frequently because of the drying effect of the heating.

After you have oiled the machine and before you put it away, slip a double thickness of fabric under the presser foot, release the foot and move the needle to its lowest point so that it penetrates the fabric. Any excess oil which drains down is thus mopped up and will not spoil your work next time you use the machine.

3. Lubrication: Consult the instruction book to see whether you need to lubricate the motor or gears of the machine. Lubrication will normally only be necessary with the older types of machine; the more modern machines are almost always factory-sealed.

4. See that the machine is kept covered whenever it is not in use.

5. If you have a second-hand machine but no instruction book, you should be able to obtain one by writing to the manufacturer, quoting the serial number on the machine. Of course, if the machine is very old they may not be able to help.

6. It is a good idea to keep handy a spare electric light bulb of the correct size. If the light fails, it is sure to do so at an awkward moment—perhaps when you are in the middle of a big sewing job and cannot get to the shops.

MINOR BREAKDOWNS

Major breakdowns obviously need professional attention, but not every breakdown is so drastic: the majority of faults are minor, and caused, very often, by misuse.

The following check list gives a selection of causes for failure. Run through them before calling in the service mechanic. You may be able to put the trouble right yourself.

If the machine will not work at all

* Check whether the electricity supply is getting through (does the electric light on the machine work?). If not, check the wiring of the electric plug, and if this is in order change the cartridge fuse (2-amp. cartridge needed).
* Check whether the lead plug is properly connected with the machine—press it home fully.

If the machine will not move the fabric, but stitches on a single point

* Check whether the feed dog is disengaged (as though for darning or free-hand embroidery).
* Check whether a loose thread is caught on the presser foot.

If the needle breaks

* The needle may have been bent or blunt.
* The needle may have been inserted wrongly. It may for example not have been pushed into the needle clamp as far as it could go.
* You may have been pulling the fabric through instead of letting it pass under the presser foot at its own pace.
* You may have used the wrong size needle for the thread and material you are sewing.
* You may have machined across too thick a seam (for example an intersecting seam on thick fabric), using too small a needle.
* The needle may have struck a wrongly-fastened presser foot or attachment.

If the bobbin thread breaks

* The bobbin thread may have been threaded incorrectly.
* The bobbin thread tension may have been too tight, and out of balance with the upper tension.
* There may have been a knot in the bobbin thread.
* The bobbin may have been wound unevenly so that an overlapping thread trapped the free end.

If the needle thread breaks

* The needle may have been blunt or bent.
* The machine may have been threaded wrongly; look again at the threading guide.
* The upper tension may have been too tight.
* There may have been a knot in the needle thread.
* The needle may not have been inserted fully into the needle clamp.
* The needle thread may have been too thick for the needle.
* The needle thread may have been too fine for the fabric.

If the top of the work looks normal while the back is a mass of tangled thread

* The bobbin was probably inserted wrongly. Re-thread, carefully checking the threading sequence and the position of the thread end. Use a seam unpicker to remove the tangled threads.

If the whole machine jams, and needle and bobbin become immovable

* Do not attempt to force the machine to work, either by operating the foot control or manipulating by hand. Disconnect the machine from the electricity supply and if the fabric is still in the machine, gently extricate it if possible by removing needle and fabric together. Then try, gently, to remove the bobbin case from the machine. There may be a piece of cotton jamming it. Clean out the area as much as possible, following the manufacturer's instructions for cleaning, and re-thread the machine carefully. Re-insert the needle and re-connect with the electricity supply.

   If the trouble cannot be righted, or persists, the fault will probably need professional attention.

If the machine misses stitches from time to time

* The needle may be in backwards.
* The needle may be inserted wrongly in the clamp; position it as high as it will go.
* The machine may be threaded incorrectly.
* The needle may be the wrong type for the machine—perhaps too short. Always use the recommended needle.
* The thread may be too thick for the fabric.

If the machine is sluggish

* It is probably dirty, or needs oiling, or both.

3

YOUR IMPORTANT CHOICE

Choice of pattern, style, pattern size, fabric and colour

To anyone deeply interested in dressmaking, a visit to a really good dress fabrics department can be one of the great pleasures of life. Certainly it is for me. I go from one gorgeous length of material to another, busily visualising all the beautiful clothes I could make with them; and I can sit happily for an hour or more browsing through the paper pattern books, forgetful of time and the jostling shoppers around me. Even if you are only mildly interested in making clothes, yet need to do so for economy's sake, I am sure that just looking at the superb fabrics available will be enough to boost your enthusiasm.

This length of wool—what a beautiful suit it would make . . . this shimmering cotton—what an inspired choice for an evening dress . . . these glowing man-made fibres—what marvellous fabrics for summer dresses, flowery housecoats, stunning ensembles. The inexpensive fabrics can often be just as exciting as the costly ones in colour and texture.

To let one's imagination run riot like this is a good thing—new fabrics, new colours can give one new ideas about ways of dressing, and stop one's fashion sense from getting into a rut. But having said this, I must stress that once your enthusiasm is aroused, you must come down to earth before you actually buy a length of material.

When you become your own couturier, you have a number of important choices.

(a) For your first attempt, it is important to choose a paper pattern which is simple to make.

(b) It is important to choose the right style for your figure type.

(c) It is important to choose the right size of pattern.

(d) It is important to choose the right fabric for the garment.

(e) It is important to choose the right colour of fabric.

I will take each of these points in turn:

SIMPLICITY OF DESIGN

It is absolutely vital that you do not choose a paper pattern which is too complicated. For your first attempt at dressmaking look only among the 'easy-to-make' styles. Pick an easy-to-sew pattern and you will sail through it; pick a difficult one and you will be discouraged from sewing for years, or perhaps even for ever.

STYLE

How many times have you read fashion articles on choosing the right clothes to suit your figure? Again and again, I am sure, and perhaps it has not always meant a great deal to you because the advice ranged over so many figure types. Maybe you were not even sure what your figure type was. Maybe your figure type was not included. Perhaps you have no figure problem, and are lucky enough to be a well-proportioned 'stock size'. You may have read that if you are tall you should wear this, if you are chubby you should avoid that. If you are neither tall nor chubby, you are still none the wiser on the styles to choose.

Firstly, therefore, I would like to suggest a very simple way of assessing the styles which suit you. I am sure you have found that some garmenst you already own make you feel well-dressed, while others fill you with gloom because they hinder rather than help your figure. Have a look at the clothes in which you feel at your best. Are they slim-fitting or loose and straight? Are they in shiny, thin fabrics or in thick, rough ones? Is the waist belted, or is there a jacket which falls straight to hip level? Look in a full-length mirror, and see whether there is any predominant direction of line. Generally speaking, lines or bands across the dress will add width, while straight up and down lines will give apparent height and slimness. What about the skirt width?—is the skirt straight, bell-shaped or full? Now try on the least favourite item in your wardrobe, something which you only wear as a last resort. What is it that makes it all wrong for you? If you can analyse the reasons why one garment is a success while the other just does not suit you, you will begin to have a good idea of the sort of styles to look for when you choose a pattern.

Just one cautionary tale, however, about choosing 'your' styles. I know a girl who discovered a few years ago that the sheath dress suited her better than any other style. It flattered her petite, trim figure.

She bought a sheath dress pattern, sleeveless and shaped to the waist, and made it up, most successfully. The next time she made a dress she used the same pattern, but this time a different fabric. When autumn came, she made up the same style in a woollen fabric, with wrist-length sleeves. Now, some years later, she is still using the same basic pattern for every dress that she makes. The only things she adapts are the fabric and the hemline. The result of this basically monotonous wardrobe is that even when she wears a new dress, hardly anybody notices because the style is always the same. Her skilled workmanship and the beautiful fabrics are, in a sense, wasted because of lack of variety.

Variety is, after all, the great attraction of dressmaking—you can be adventurous without necessarily ruining the budget. And because of the skill of the pattern manufacturers, you can,

once you have become proficient at the task, be wearing copies of high-fashion models within weeks of their being shown by the couturiers or boutiques. If your fashion tastes are more moderate, you can still experiment towards styles which you had not thought would suit you.

In a schools programme on careers broadcast some time ago one contributor, only eighteen but in her third year with a top dress house, spoke with great enthusiasm about her job as a seamstress, and of the advantages of learning her skill to such a high standard: 'I can make all my own clothes in the very latest fashions,' she said, 'and for every garment I could buy in an ordinary retail shop I can make three for myself, in equally good or even better-quality material. If I marry and have children, my skill will still be of benefit to me. And apart from all that—I just love sewing.'

SOME GENERAL GUIDANCE ON FIGURE TYPES

Here are a few pointers on figure types, and I suggest you read only the comments which apply to your own figure—if you read them all, you may be more confused than before.

If your figure is perfect. Obviously there is no such thing as the one perfect figure—many people have well-proportioned frames that could not be improved upon, yet they do not all conform to the same standards of measurement and weight. There is not really an 'average' figure either. But if you are of medium or slightly-above-medium height, slim but not too thin, and can find a pattern size which suits you exactly in every detail, you can count your blessings. With a figure like yours you can afford to ignore the rules and simply wear the styles you like.

Be careful, though, that you do show your good figure to advantage. When loose, waist-concealing garments are in fashion they can be a godsend to some of us, but if *you* have a good slim waist and a midriff with some shape to it, try to bend the fashion rules a little and choose styles which flatter your figure.

If you think you are too short and too thin. Slim, petite girls should count themselves lucky but usually they do not, and spend all their time wondering how they can make themselves appear taller.

Vertical lines are the ones to favour if you want to 'add height'. For example princess lines with narrow front panels, coat dresses with a line of buttons down the front, collars with narrow lapels leading from shoulder to waist-line–all these will help to add an illusion of height to the figure.

Jackets should be fairly short, even waist-length, and it is preferable for an outfit to be in one colour (skirt and jacket in different colours may make a small figure seem less well-proportioned). If you need a contrast of colour, keep it high–a dark suit with a touch of white at the collar will give the right effect.

Try to avoid horizontal lines unless there are compensating factors which restore the balance. For instance a small person can often get away with a garment with a predominantly horizontal line, either because the colour is light, or because of the cut of the jacket or skirt, or the fact that the fabric is fine and smooth.

Coarse, heavy fabrics, on the other hand, may overpower the tiny figure, and if the lines of the garment give a horizontal effect in addition, the result can be really disastrous.

If you feel you are too short and plump. Here you have the same kind of problem as above, only more so. All your efforts must be directed towards giving your garments a vertical or diagonal line. Separates do not usually suit this type of figure, especially separates in different colours. Fabrics should be smooth rather than heavy and rough, and jackets or overblouses which just tip the hip-bone may help to camouflage a thick waist. Straight skirts are often preferable to bell-shaped ones for this figure, and flared skirts are rarely suitable even when they are in fashion.

If you are of normal height, but heavy-hipped. Choose skirt shapes which are smooth over the hips but not tight and not too straight. A bell-shaped skirt can be flattering. An attractive, eye-catching neckline will often draw attention away from the hips; for instance a wide-lapelled or shawl collar, or a deep decorative collar.

If you are of normal height, but have a thick rib-cage and large waist. Concentrate on camouflage. If hips and legs are well-proportioned, a straight skirt topped by a fairly long jacket or overblouse will conceal much of the thickness, and a slim outline below the jacket will make the whole effect slimmer. Garments in one colour are preferable to different colours for top and skirt–separates such as tuck-in blouses and skirts rarely suit this type of figure, as they draw too much attention to the rib-cage and waist.

If you are tall and too thin. Bright colours tend to add an appearance of fullness to the figure, and rounded, soft lines will help to avoid the angular look. Different colours for top and skirt will divide the figure and make it appear wider and less long. If you have thin arms, avoid long, thin sleeves. If your arms are long, three-quarter-length sleeves are perhaps the most becoming.

If you are tall and heavy. Simple clothes are best, but the lines should not be too severe–gentle curves, draped effects, diagonal lines will all help to slenderise without adding apparent height. Fabrics with a large pattern should be avoided, and those with a high lustre will generally tend to give a 'large' effect. Some large figures will take a fairly straight (though not tight-fitting) skirt, with a softly draped top. If arms are heavy, avoid sleeveless dresses, and be sure that sleeves are not tight by measuring the pattern carefully and comparing with your actual arm measurements (see page 57).

SIZE

The third point to remember is the importance of using the right size of pattern for your figure. If the store is out of the size you need, do not be tempted to buy the nearest size to it. It may save you from waiting a few days before beginning the garment, but it certainly will not save you time in the end, because adjustments will have to be made to the pattern which may throw out the line and style completely. Unless you have much experience of dressmaking it could take you many hours to achieve your correct fit. Chapter 4, page 55, deals with size in greater detail.

Modern paper patterns are one of life's technical miracles. Hundreds of thousands of patterns, in a vast range of top-fashion designs, and in a wide range of sizes, are sold every week, and yet each pattern is accurate to a degree which is quite amazing.

The pattern companies spend a great deal of time and trouble in analysing the many figure types. The large pattern catalogues which they print always include pages of instructions on the way to choose the correct size of pattern. It is well worth studying these pages carefully.

Many home dressmakers believe that one only has to choose a pattern in the correct bust size for the made-up garment to fit perfectly. Yet this is not so. Just as no two people look alike facially, so no two people have exactly the same figure. As I have mentioned already, there are hundreds of basic figure shapes to every bust size in the range.

As you will soon see the pattern companies usually divide figure types into various categories, for example you may find a pattern book with the following descriptions: Pre-teen, Teen, Junior Misses', Women's, Junior Petite and Half-size. These do not refer to age-groups, but to figure types. A Junior figure, for example, usually corresponds to the measurements of a young girl, but a middle-aged woman could have exactly the same measurements and proportions. Similarly it is quite possible for a school-girl to need a pattern from the Women's range. Now another sizing range has been introduced, called 'New Sizing'.

What is new sizing?

There are certain changes, agreed by the Measurement Standard Committee of the Pattern Fashion Industry, and adopted by all the major pattern companies. The changes were introduced jointly so that patterns correspond more closely with standard ready-to-wear sizing. All patterns which are based on the new sizing

bear the distinctive 'New Sizing' mark, with white lettering in a red rectangle.

The following pattern companies are adopting the new standard body measurements:

The Butterick Publishing Co. Ltd.
Blackmore Pattern Service
Le Roy/Weldon Pattern Service
Maudella Patterns Co. Ltd.
The McCall Publishing Co. Ltd.
Practical Fashions Ltd.
Simplicity Patterns Ltd.
Style Patterns Ltd.
Vogue Pattern Service

The Measurement Standard Committee of the Pattern Fashion Industry have prepared answers to a number of questions which may come to mind in connection with the new sizing. They have kindly allowed me to reproduce a condensed version of these Q's and A's.

Q. How do the measurements of the 'New Sizing' patterns differ from the former type?
A. As a general rule, one buys a pattern one size smaller in 'New Sizing' than in the former sizing. For example:

Former sizing	*New sizing*
Bust 34	Bust 34
Size 14	Size 12

The waistline in 'New Sizing' is slightly smaller in proportion to the bust and hips than in the former sizing.

Q. Do all patterns have the new sizing?
A. No, some patterns remain with the former sizing.
Q. How does one know which styles in the pattern catalogues are based on the new sizing?
A. All patterns using the new standard body measurements are clearly marked with the distinctive 'New Sizing' symbol, both in the pattern catalogue and on the pattern envelope.
Q. Are the measurement charts for both the former and the 'New Sizing' measurements included in the pattern catalogues?
A. Yes.
Q. If one is buying a pattern marked 'New Sizing', does one purchase the same size pattern

Body Measurement Chart

Approved by the Measurement Standard Committee of the Pattern Fashion Industry

NEW Sizing

(Red chart in Catalogues)

MISSES'

Size	6	8	10	12	14	16	18
Bust	30½	31½	32½	34	36	38	40
Waist	22	23	24	25½	27	29	31
Hip	32½	33½	34½	36	38	40	42
Back Waist Length	15½	15¾	16	16¼	16½	16¾	17

WOMEN'S

Size	38	40	42	44	46	48	50
Bust	42	44	46	48	50	52	54
Waist	34	36	38	40½	43	45½	48
Hip	44	46	48	50	52	54	56
Back Waist Length	17¼	17⅜	17½	17⅝	17¾	17⅞	18

HALF-SIZES

Size	10½	12½	14½	16½	18½	20½	22½	24½
Bust	33	35	37	39	41	43	45	47
Waist	26	28	30	32	34	36½	39	41½
Hip	35	37	39	41	43	45½	48	50½
Back Waist Length	15	15¼	15½	15¾	15⅞	16	16⅛	16¼

NEW Sizing

(Red chart in Catalogues)

JUNIOR PETITE

Size	3	5	7	9	11	13
Bust	30½	31	32	33	34	35
Waist	22	22½	23½	24½	25½	26½
Hip	31½	32	33	34	35	36
Back Waist Length	14	14¼	14½	14¾	15	15¼

YOUNG JUNIOR/TEEN

Size	5/6	7/8	9/10	11/12	13/14	15/16
Bust	28	29	30½	32	33½	35
Waist	22	23	24	25	26	27
Hip	31	32	33½	35	36½	38
Back Waist Length	13½	14	14½	15	15⅜	15¾

GIRLS'

Size	7	8	10	12	14
Breast	26	27	28½	30	32
Waist	23	23½	24½	25½	26½
Hip	27	28	30	32	34
Back Waist Length	11½	12	12¾	13½	14¼

as in ready-to-wear clothes, for example size 14 or size 16?

A. You *may* find you will be purchasing the same size. However this may not always be true, so be sure to check the red measurement chart in the catalogue to determine your pattern size.

Q. How does one determine one's correct pattern size?

A. Pattern sizes are based on body measurements. These are the actual measurements in inches of *bust*, *waist*, *hip* and *back waist length*, taken over the foundation garment you normally wear. (These measurements should be checked periodically.) From the body measurements you can select your correct size, by comparing them with those on the charts in the pattern catalogues. Your bust measurement is the key to your correct size for all garments except skirts and slacks.

Q. How, then, does one decide on the right size for skirt and slacks patterns?

A. By waist measurement. But if your hip measurement is larger than the size allowed for in the pattern, select your size by the hip measurement and then adjust the waistline.

Q. Have the names of the figure types changed in the new sizing?

A. They remain the same except for a new Young Junior/Teen figure type which replaces the Teen, Pre-Teen and Sub-Teen types. All patterns within this new figure type are marked on the envelope.

Q. How do I determine the figure type I should use?

A. By comparing your body measurements with those shown on the chart. A description and diagram of each figure type is found on the measurement chart.

The height and back waist length measurements are probably the most important measurements in determining your figure type. If you select a pattern marked 'New Sizing' refer to the new sizing chart.

Q. Are there any changes in the size *ranges* within the different figure types?

A. Yes, most have been extended to correspond more closely to ready-to-wear sizes.

Q. So far we have been discussing body measurements. What is meant by pattern measurements?

A. They are the actual measurements of the pattern pieces, from seamline to seamline, and consequently, they are the measurements of the finished garment.

Q. Is there the same amount of ease in all patterns?

A. No, the amount of ease depends on the style of garment. In a Misses' basic style with fitted bodice, set-in sleeve and a waistline seam, the ease at the bustline is about 3 in. A bodice with raglan sleeves will have more ease; kimono sleeves still more. A strapless evening dress will have less than the normal ease.

Q. Does one buy the same size pattern for a coat or jacket as for a dress or blouse?

A. Yes, you still select the pattern according to your bust size, since the pattern is made to include the amount of ease necessary. The average suit jacket is sized to wear over a light blouse, and the average coat to wear over a dress.

Q. What size does one buy if a pattern includes more than one type of garment such as a blouse and slacks pattern?

A. Purchase by bust measurement.

Q. Has the sizing for Toddlers', Children's and Girls' patterns changed?

A. There have been minor changes in the measurements, but these do not affect the pattern size you choose. However, it is always best to check the measurements on the back of the pattern envelope.

Q. Have any changes been made in the Men's and Boys' sizing?

A. No, the sizing remains the same.

The body measurement charts reproduced on p. 51 with the various measurements corresponding to each figure type, may serve to show

you how important it is that you choose the correct pattern.

Let me give you an example. Perhaps your bust size is 34 in. and you have always been in the habit of choosing a Misses' pattern. This provides for a 34 in. bust, 26 in. waist, 36 in. hip and 16¼ in. back waist length. (Or in the 'New Sizing' range the measurements would be the same except that the waist would be 25½ in. instead of 26 in.)

Perhaps you have slimmer-than-average hips and are short-waisted, and have automatically had to alter the pattern pieces with every garment you make for yourself. Perhaps it has not occurred to you that by choosing a pattern in the Junior Petite range, in the 'New Sizing', you could find a pattern with the following measurements: 34 in. bust, 25½ in. waist, 35 in. hip and 15 in. back waist length. If these correspond to *your* measurements, there will be no alteration at all to do.

So the moral is: whatever your bust size, if you find you always have to make pattern alterations, check first to see whether there is another figure type pattern which would suit you better. If you can find the style you like in the pattern size you like, you'll save yourself a considerable amount of time and trouble.

Once you know how the pattern company rates your figure, you can be careful when selecting a style to choose one where there is a pattern available for your figure type. For instance, you may be attracted by: 'Misses' one-piece dress with belted waist, choice of long or short sleeves', but if your figure bears no relation to the Misses' range you will need to look for another style.

Later I will be dealing with the method of taking a complete record of your measurements. But for the moment, the important measurements you will need in order to select your pattern size are:

Bust	
Waist	
Hips	
Back Waist Length	

These measurements, and the method of arriving at them, are described on pages 56-7 (items 1, 2, 3 and 4, figs. 68, 69, 70 and 71) and are marked with asterisks for quick reference.

FABRIC

Having chosen your pattern, you must be guided by the pattern manufacturer on the best type of fabric for the garment.

On almost all paper pattern envelopes there is a section headed 'Suggested Fabrics'. Do not ignore this—it is the product of experience, and usually the choice of fabric is wide.

Many of the rigid views about the right garment for the occasion now no longer hold good. Girls go dancing in slacks and boots, wear their smartest 'Sunday-best' clothes to the office, and their most casual leisure wear at the weekend. At one time conformity in dress and a sense of occasion were very important; now the aim is to be different and adventurous. Consequently rules of dress are difficult to define, and one can only offer a brief guide to the different fabrics used for different purposes.

Plain garments for day wear in town or office

Smooth wools, flannels, light-weight tweeds, firmly-woven woollen dress materials, cotton/wool mixtures, knitted or woven Courtelle, Orlon, Acrilan, Crimplene and other synthetic fabrics. For blouses: cotton, rayon, nylon, Terylene, etc.

Country wear

Usually heavier cloths, such as Harris and other heavy tweeds, and the heavy-quality linens, are suitable and durable.

Day dresses

Many different fabrics are suitable including fine wools, heavier linens, synthetic fabrics containing Courtelle, Crimplene, etc., jersey fabrics, crêpes, and so on, the choice depending on the season. Cotton fabrics, especially those with special finishes, and dresses of Terylene or Dacron, Tricel or Courtelle, make ideal summer wear.

Evening wear

Virtually any of the fine fabrics—cottons, linens, silk, and many of the fine synthetic fabrics—are used for evening wear. Rayon is widely used for evening dresses, from sheerest rayon georgette to heavy rayon velvet, and Tricel is a popular and very practical fabric. The material you choose will depend to some extent on the nature of the occasion: a formal dinner may call for a sheer, luxurious fabric which drapes well, while an informal dance for a teenager may call for nothing more elaborate than a simple cotton dress or skirt and top.

Leisure wear and sports wear

Many of the new stretch fabrics are proving ideal for sports and leisure wear—more about them in Chapter 6. They may require a new approach to sewing techniques, but with care you can make such outfits with flair and style.

Many of the fabrics you see in your local store will be blends or mixtures of fibres, either natural or man-made, or the two together. The skilled blending or mixing of different fibres normally imparts to a fabric the advantages of each, for example a wool/Terylene mixture will have the warmth of wool yet the strength of Terylene.

Fabrics and fibres are dealt with in detail in Chapter 6.

COLOUR

Having advised you to take notice of the pattern manufacturer's comments on choice of fabric, I must stress that this rule does not apply to colour. Never be so slavish to the picture on the pattern envelope that you only consider buying a fabric in the same colour. The dress may look outstanding in, for example, emerald green, but this does not mean that it is automatically right for your colouring and figure type.

Nowadays there is almost no bar to the colours

one may wear. At one time it was almost taboo for a red-headed woman to wear shocking pink, or for colours such as blue and green or pink and orange to be mixed. Today, however, if you mix colours which shout at each other, you are right in the fashion. No doubt this will change again all too soon. But the point to remember, whatever fashion decrees, is that there are bound to be some colours which suit you better than others. The great advantage of making your own clothes is that you can afford to make mistakes occasionally without wasting too much money.

4

SEWING COURSE FOR BEGINNERS

A twelve-point plan for professionalism

1. ASSESS YOUR MEASUREMENTS
2. BUY YOUR MATERIALS
3. BUY THE EXTRAS
4. DEAL WITH PRELIMINARIES
5. EXAMINE THE PATTERN
6. ADJUST THE PATTERN
7. TRY ON THE PATTERN
8. PLAN THE PATTERN LAYOUT AND PIN
9. CUT OUT THE GARMENT
10. TRANSFER THE MARKINGS
11. ASSEMBLE FOR FIRST FITTING
12. MAKE UP THE GARMENT

1. ASSESS YOUR MEASUREMENTS

The basis of every well-made garment is the fit. As we have already seen, it is essential to choose the correct pattern size. Some women find one make of pattern suits them better than another because it conforms more nearly to their figure type. Some find that the average paper pattern needs no alteration. But most of us, even when we have chosen the best size of pattern, have to do a little adjusting.

The time to do this is on the paper pattern, and *not* once the garment is cut out. So let us begin by drawing up a complete measurement sheet. Many people taking dressmaking lessons for the first time are amazed to find how many measurements there are to take, far more than the simple bust, waist, hip and back waist length which determined the pattern size.

Taking measurements is one job where it is best to have some help. If there is no-one at home who can give it, you may find that you can ask for assistance in the paper pattern department, or in a shop specialising in sewing aids. Often the sewing machine representatives are highly-trained in home dressmaking, and some can be very helpful.

I cannot stress strongly enough how important it is that the measurements which are taken should be accurate down to the last detail, for on this depends the success of the finished garment.

You could use the personal measurements chart that follows to form the basis of a sewing notebook. Buy a child's strong scrapbook, copy the complete chart into the front of it, and follow it with details of each garment as you make it. For each one you could include the pattern envelope, leftover scraps of fabric for future matching or patching, odd buttons left over, perhaps notes of the accessories you wear with the garment.

If your measurements change radically, you can write out the chart again, filling in the revised measurements.

It will be a fascinating record of your hobby.

YOUR COMPLETE MEASUREMENTS CHART

68

Name...

Date...

INCHES

*1. BUST (68)
This measurement is taken by your helper, standing behind you. It should take in the fullest part of the bust and go slightly higher at the back to include the shoulder blades.

....

69

2. WAIST (69)
To locate your natural waistline, tie a cord round your waist at the narrowest part. Then measure:
(a) the entire waist.
(b) across front of waist, from side seam to side seam.
Leave cord in place for the rest of the measuring if you wish.

....

....

70

*3. HIPS AT FULLEST PART (70)
You can establish which is the fullest part of your hips by trying the tape measure at various distances below the waist. Having found where your hips are widest, use the other end of the tape measure to find the distance from your waist down to the tape measure. Thus in future you know how many inches below your waistline your hip measurement should be taken. (The average is 7–8 in. below the waistline.)

....

....

(inches below waist)

71

*4. BACK BODICE LENGTH (71)
(A) centre back bodice length. This measurement is taken from the neckline down the centre back to the waistline.
(B) shoulder to waistline, right side.
(C) shoulder to waistline, left side.
This measurement is sometimes referred to as 'back waist length'.

C.............
R.............
L.............

72

*5. FRONT BODICE LENGTH (72)
(A) centre front length. This measurement is taken from the neckline straight down to the waistline.
(B) shoulder to waistline, right side.
(C) shoulder to waistline, left side.

C.............
R.............
L.............

73

*6. SIDE BODICE LENGTH (73)
Measure underarm to waistline, right side and left side.
These measurements are taken while you stand with your hand resting lightly on your hip. The top of the underarm seam is taken from a point 1 in. below the armpit. Measure both sides of the body to check any differences.

R.............
L.............

Height................ft...........................in.

Weight with minimum clothes...................................

INCHES

7. SHOULDER (74)
(A) shoulderline, right.　　　　　　　　　　　　R..............
(B) shoulderline, left.　　　　　　　　　　　　 L..............
Measure each shoulder as if along a shoulder seam, i.e. from the base of the neck (on the side) along the shoulder to the point of the shoulder. Take particular note of any difference in the two measurements.

8. SHOULDER TIP TO SHOULDER TIP (75)
Your helper should measure straight across the top of your back, from shoulder to shoulder, while you clasp your hands together in front, at waistline level, with arms forward and slightly raised.　...............

9. BACK WIDTH, ARMHOLE TO ARMHOLE (76)
Your helper should measure from armhole seam to armhole seam, 4 in. below neckline. Hands should be clasped and arms forward as above.　...............

10. SLEEVE LENGTH (77) (Check both arms)
(A) point of shoulder to point of elbow (arm bent).　...............
(B) Point of elbow to wrist (arm bent).　...............
(C) inside arm from underarm seam, 1 in. below armpit, to wrist. This measurement is taken with the arm stretched straight.　...............

11. ARM (78) (Check both arms)
This measurement is taken round the bare arm in three places, with arm straight:
(A) wrist. Measurement should include wrist bone.　...............
(B) lower arm, about halfway between elbow and wrist.　...............
(C) upper arm, about halfway between shoulder and elbow.　...............

12. SKIRT LENGTH (79)
(A) neck to floor.　...............
(B) waist to hem.　...............
You will know which hem length you like to wear, and naturally this will fluctuate from time to time.

Note: If you make clothes for various members of the family, write out and complete a chart for each. If updated regularly, it can give you a useful year-by-year record of the sizes of growing children.
* These are the four measurements most crucial in your choice of pattern size—see page 52.

2. BUY YOUR MATERIALS

Never buy fabric until you have checked the exact yardage specified for your size on the pattern envelope. Buy exactly the amount of fabric called for.

It may seem to you, as you make more and more garments, that the pattern companies are over-generous with the amount of material they specify, and you may feel sure that you can manage with less. Do remember, however, that pattern layouts have been worked out by experts, and that they take into account many factors including the 'grain' of the fabric and the cut of the garment. It is quite possible that if you devised your own pattern layout you could save half a yard of fabric, but it simply is not worth making such a small saving when you might ruin the whole look of your garment and so waste all the hours you have put into making it.

Most of the reputable manufacturers include a paragraph headed 'Suggested Fabrics' on their pattern envelopes. If home dressmakers always took the advice given, quite a few costly mistakes could be avoided. On some you may find statements such as 'Do not use fabric with a diagonal stripe or a decided diagonal weave' or 'The above yardage does not allow for shrinkage or for matching stripes or plaids'. *Never* ignore them. It takes extra fabric and extra expertise to cope with matching up plaids and stripes.

Fabrics, fibres and finishes are dealt with in more detail in Chapter 6, and there you will find sewing notes, details about the properties of the various fabrics and fibres, and notes on their washability.

3. BUY THE EXTRAS

When you have bought your pattern and a suitable length of fabric, turn to the pattern envelope again to see what 'sewing notions' you will need.

On any good pattern these will be listed quite specifically: for example hooks and eyes, interfacing, zipper and seam binding. It is sensible to choose these when you choose your fabric, in order to ensure a good match. In addition, of course, you will need sewing thread—cotton, mercerised cotton or a synthetic thread, depending on the fabric. It is best to buy it in a shade slightly darker than the fabric itself. You will need two spools to complete the average garment.

4. DEAL WITH PRELIMINARIES

Once everything has been purchased, you will probably be in a hurry to get back home and start cutting out the new garment. But before you do so, check the following.

EQUIPMENT
Make sure you have at least the essentials for good dressmaking. Sewing aids are described in detail in Chapter 1.

You will certainly not be able to manage without dressmaking shears, a tape measure, dressmaker's pins and an iron for pressing. If you have a wider selection of equipment, the work will be much easier.

FABRIC PREPARATION
You must find out whether it is necessary to pre-shrink the material you have bought before making it up. Most good cotton fabrics are pre-shrunk, and more and more woollen fabrics are too, but if you are in any doubt at all, make a shrink test.

Lay the pattern out loosely on the material, following the layout guide on the pattern's instruction sheet (see step 5, p. 60). Cut out a square of fabric about 3 in. by 3 in. which you are sure would be wasted after the cutting-out proper. Do not cut the square too near any pattern piece. Now cut a piece of paper—ordinary writing paper will do—exactly the same size as your square.

Soak the square of fabric in water, roll it in a towel, and then press it lightly with an iron, using a damp pressing cloth and choosing a suitable iron setting for the fabric. This is important, for if you use an excessively hot iron on some fabrics, they may shrink for the wrong reasons.

Next, compare your fabric sample with the paper square. If they are still identical in size

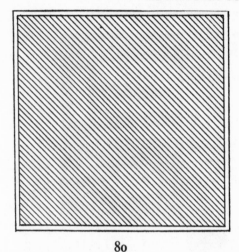

80

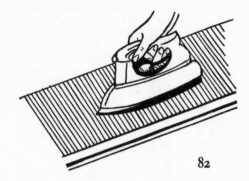

82

the fabric for pressing and refold it afterwards for positioning the pattern pieces.

you have no cause for concern, but if the fabric sample is now appreciably smaller (80) there will be no alternative but to remove the pattern pieces from the material and shrink the whole length of fabric, snipping the selvedges first (81) to ensure that the fabric finds its correct dimensions. Selvedges, incidentally, are the narrow woven borders on the lengthwise edges of the fabric.

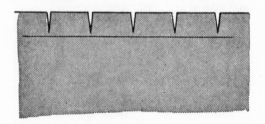

81

How do you shrink the fabric in the piece? If it is cotton, you can immerse it in hot water, and hang it to drip-dry before ironing it with a steam iron, or with a dry iron using a damp pressing cloth (82). If it is a wool fabric, simply press it all over, using a very damp pressing cloth and a steam iron if available. Work over each section slowly and carefully, pressing the iron down and then lifting it, rather than sliding it along.

Do not press-in the lengthways fold of the fabric. Whatever its type, it is best to open out

5. EXAMINE THE PATTERN

When you have opened the pattern envelope, the first thing to turn to is the instruction sheet. If you have chosen a pattern made by a reputable manufacturer, the instructions will be an indispensable help to you in making your garment. Cheap patterns may contain thoroughly inadequate and sometimes even misleading advice.

However, even the best instruction sheet cannot give a complete sewing lesson. The pattern company has to assume that the customer already has a basic knowledge of sewing and sewing language. Which is, of course, what this book aims to give you.

When you first look at the back of the pattern envelope, and then at the instruction sheet, you may feel overwhelmed by the diversity of instructions. But there is a simple way to make things easier for yourself.

Take a pen, or a brightly-coloured crayon or felt-tipped pen, and mark on the back of the pattern envelope details which apply to you (83). Ring round the version you are making, and the yardages, both for fabric and interfacing, which apply to your size. Ring round the body measurements which apply. Underline or ring round any sewing notions you will need.

Now turn to the instruction sheet. With the help of the diagram it includes, check that none of the pattern pieces is missing from the packet.

While you are doing this, sort out the pieces which apply to the version you are making, and

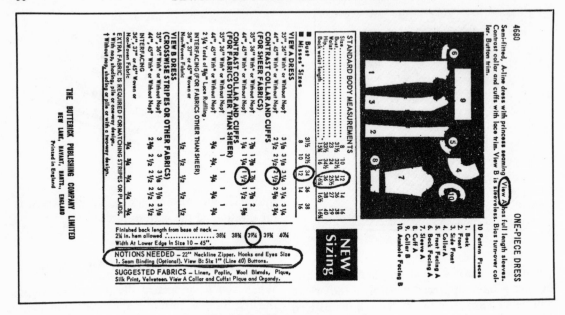

83. Marking the pattern envelope

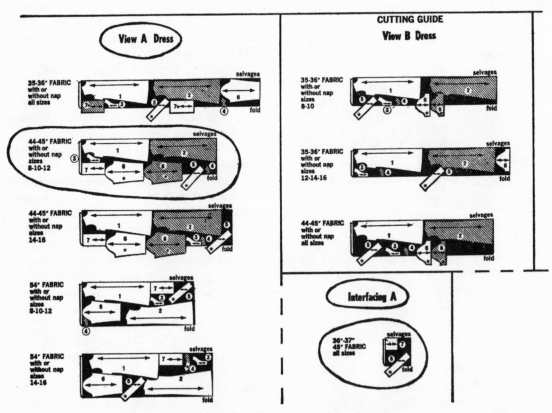

84. Marking the instruction sheet

put all the others away in the pattern envelope to avoid confusion.

Next turn to the cutting layouts on the instruction sheet. If there is more than one version of the pattern there will probably be a separate cutting layout for each version. There will almost certainly be different cutting layouts depending on the width of fabric chosen (it may be 36 in., 45 in. or 48 in. width fabric for example). There may, moreover, be different cutting layouts for different pattern sizes. Work out carefully which cutting layout applies to you and put a ring round it (84); then look to see whether there is another layout for linings or interfacings for your version. If there is, put a ring round this (or these) too.

It really is worth taking a few minutes to do this marking up. It makes cutting out seem a much less formidable task to the beginner. When you have done it, you are ready to begin making any necessary adjustments to the pattern to fit your figure.

6. ADJUST THE PATTERN

When you have a complete log of your measurements you will be able to tell whether you need to make any adjustments to the pattern.

If your *main* measurements correspond exactly with the pattern you have purchased, you may, possibly, not need to make any adjustments. However this cannot be taken as a foregone conclusion, for it may be that not *every* measurement corresponds. If you are above or below average height, or vary from the standard pattern measurements in one or more respects,

some alteration will be essential, even though you have chosen the correct pattern size for your figure.

Your next step, therefore, is to check the measurements of the main pattern pieces against your own body measurements, to see whether or not they correspond.

Always remember that the measurements denoting the size of a pattern are standard measurements, not actual measurements of the pattern pieces. Take for example a pattern described on the envelope as 34 in. bust. This does not mean that the bodice when made up will measure exactly 34 in. at the level of the bustline. If it did, the garment would be very uncomfortable, pull across the figure, strain and possibly split with every movement of the body. Pattern manufacturers allow for a certain amount of 'ease' in every garment, so that the actual size of the bodice for a 34 in. figure may be 36 or 37 in. or more, depending on the style of the garment. Similarly a certain amount of ease is allowed for waistline and hipline. So when comparing the actual measurements of the various pattern pieces with your actual body measurements, you must always remember to allow for the extra inches given for ease by the pattern manufacturer.

Here is a general guide to the ease which the leading pattern manufacturers allow. Do not, however, rely on it: check with the pattern book if the actual paper pattern does not give any guidance. Ease allowance can vary not only from one manufacturer to another, but also from garment to garment.

I would stress that these ease allowances

APPROXIMATE EASE ALLOWANCE

Bust	$3\frac{1}{2}$ in. over the bust measurement in most dresses. Evening dresses designed to fit tightly in the bodice may have less ease allowance–as little as $\frac{1}{2}$ in. in a strapless dress.
Waist	$\frac{1}{2}$ in. approximately.
Hips	$2\frac{1}{2}$ in. approximately on slim skirts.
Back waist length	$\frac{1}{4}$ in. to $\frac{3}{8}$ in. approximately.

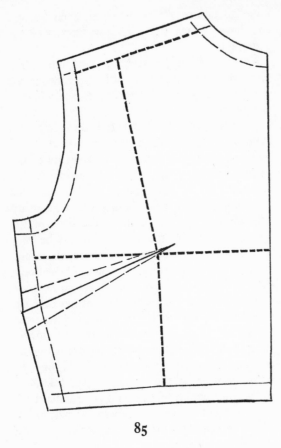

85

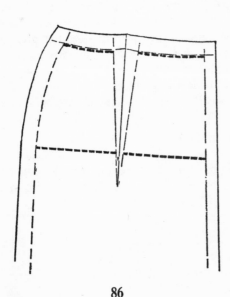

86

should not in any way affect your thinking when you select your pattern size. If your bust size is, say, 34 in. then you choose a 34 in. pattern. The only time you need to think about ease allowance is when you are checking a paper pattern against your own body measurements.

HOW TO CHECK THE MEASUREMENTS AGAINST EACH OTHER

Sort out the main pattern pieces for the bodice, skirt and sleeve.

Turn to item 1 of your personal measurement chart and copy down your bust measurement on a spare piece of paper or a clean page of your sewing notebook. After it write 'Plus ease allowance of . . .' (see notes on previous page with regard to amount of allowance for ease).

Now measure the actual paper pattern measurements. Take all the pieces which go to make up the bodice. In the average pattern there will probably be only two—the back bodice piece, which may be a half-pattern only and require you to place the centre line to a fold of fabric when cutting out, and the front bodice piece, where you will probably be instructed to 'Cut two'.

Whatever form the pattern pieces take, the object is to find out what the garment will actually measure at various points when made up (85 and 86). So when you, say, measure round the bustline of the pattern piece, be sure you do *not* include seam allowances, darts or any other pieces of fabric which will be missing when the garment is made up.

If you are keeping a dressmaking notebook, note it down neatly like this.

Pattern No......by.............size.......

Bust
Actual measurement (taken from
    personal measurement chart)   ......in.
Plus ease allowance of   ......in.

                 Total   ......
Paper pattern measurement, actual   ......in.

Adjustment needed: Add (or
    deduct as the case may be)   ......in.

To do the job properly you should go through all twelve items in your personal measurement chart, checking each measurement carefully.

Just to recap, do not forget, when measuring the pattern pieces:

(a) To allow for the standard seam allowance widths—normally ⅝ in.

(b) To allow for any darts if they intersect the line which you are measuring.

(c) To allow for the extra inches given for ease in the paper pattern.

ALTERATIONS

When you have checked all the items in your personal measurements chart you will know whether or not you need to make alterations to the pattern pieces.

Sort out any pattern pieces which need altering.

Many good paper patterns provide clear instructions on each pattern piece, showing you where to make any increase or decrease in size. There will be lines to show you where to take a tuck in a pattern which is too long, and where to cut the pattern piece if you need to insert extra paper to increase the size.

What do you do if the pattern gives you no guidance? To help you make the necessary adjustments I have taken a selection of typical figure problems and given the way to alter the pattern to find a solution (87 to 92). Glance through the sketches and you may find a way to adapt the pattern to your figure

If you have to increase the measurements of a pattern piece you will need some spare paper—tissue paper or greaseproof paper is suitable—to reinforce the altered pattern. Even if you have to make the measurements of a pattern piece smaller, you may still need spare paper,

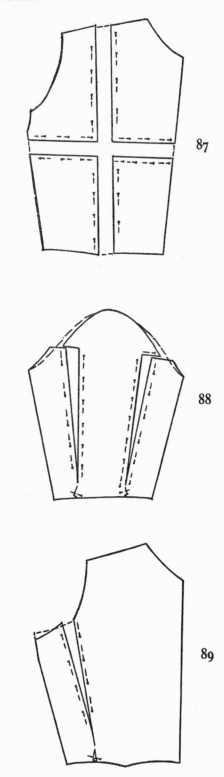

87. FULL BUSTLINE: Cut pattern from shoulder to waist and straight across bustline. Put tissue paper underneath and pin to give the extra measurement needed. Take in extra width at waistline and underarm by increasing size of darts, and form a shoulder dart so that shoulderline corresponds with back bodice.

88 and 89. HEAVY UPPER ARM: Slash bodice as shown (88) and spread to give extra width round armhole opening; pin tissue paper underneath to secure. Slash sleeve piece (89) on each side and open out to correspond with armhole opening. Pin to tissue paper. Remember that sleeve cap will still need to be larger than armhole opening to allow for correct setting-in.

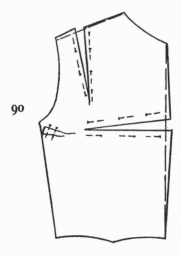

90

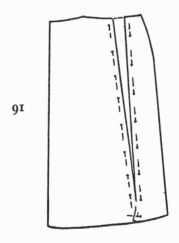

91

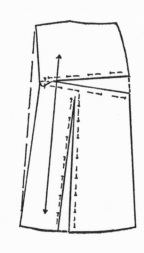

92

because the outline of the pattern piece may need neatening after the piece itself has been slashed.

Whatever the alterations, make sure that the pattern piece is still completely flat when you have pinned it. If there is a hump in it, the surplus paper must be folded into a tuck and pinned flat.

When you have finished altering the pattern pieces, check the measurements again to make sure that they correspond (apart from deductions) with those on your personal chart. Then to make sure your alterations are permanent, secure them firmly with adhesive tape.

7. TRY ON THE PATTERN

After any alterations to individual pieces have been made, give yourself a pattern fitting. To do this you pin together the main pattern pieces so that you can try them against your figure.

First pin the bodice sections together, remembering to pin in place any darts or tucks, and to make allowance for the seams.

Then pin together the front and back skirt sections, again remembering to take in darts and gathers. Finally pin bodice and skirt together. You will, of course, have only half a paper 'garment' but it will still be a very good guide.

Try the 'garment' on. Stand in front of a full-length mirror, relaxed and in a natural position, and examine the fit carefully. If possible enlist the help of someone able to give constructive criticism.

Look carefully at the shoulder line and the neckline. They are crucial to the fit of the garment, especially if the neckline is a fairly low one.

90. ROUNDED SHOULDERS, STOOPING POSTURE. Cut pattern as shown to give extra back bodice width; pin to tissue paper. Redraw centre back line clearly, to keep it straight with grain of fabric. Try on bodice pieces before making up, and use darts to accommodate any excess fabric at the shoulderline.

91. THICK WAIST. Slash skirt pieces as shown and open out to give extra width needed. Increase bodice pieces to fit.

92. FULL SEAT. Cut pattern and open out as shown. Pin tissue paper underneath to make new centre back line, still straight with grain of fabric. If you do not wish to make skirt fuller at hemline, lay a fold in pattern midway between lengthwise slash and side seam, tapering it towards hipline.

Look at the bustline. Does the point of the part finish below your bust, giving you a droopy look? Try re-pinning the pattern piece so that the dart finishes just below the point of the bust, and if this makes a noticeable improvement mark the change on the pattern with pencil or pen.

If, on the other hand, the point of the dart finishes too high, giving the bodice pattern piece a taut, flattened look, re-pinning the dart lower down may bring about a great improvement.

Look at the waistline. It is most important that it should fit snugly into your natural waistline. Check that there is enough width in the hips and waist, and re-pin if necessary.

Only when you are really satisfied with the pattern should you take the sections apart, marking the alterations clearly with a crayon or felt-tipped pen.

You may consider that you can dispense with the foregoing, quickly cut out the garment, and make it up in an evening. Some of the guidance I am going to give on pinning and tailor's tacks may seem over-cautious, too. Indeed, some people do work very speedily with very few preliminaries. However it is only fair to say that these people usually fall into one of two categories. They are either so experienced after years of making their own clothes that they automatically know when to allow a little here and there, or else they are by nature inclined to cut all possible corners. The result in the latter case (and sometimes, alas, in the former too) is that their clothes never have a professional finish: they fit badly and look home-made.

If you talk to anyone who has worked in a top couture house you will discover that a staggering amount of care is lavished over every inch of a couture garment. They may be among the most highly-skilled seamstresses in the world, yet they would never dream of trying to cut corners in their work, and they would never rush to complete a garment in a couple of afternoons. Think of this when you are next in the middle of dressmaking, and find the attention to detail a little tiresome. Become your own couturier, be a perfectionist. Once you have acquired the routine, the preliminary work will seem a matter of course. You will hardly notice it.

8. PLAN THE PATTERN LAYOUT

Now take your fabric and begin pinning out the prepared pattern pieces, carefully following the sections of the layout guide you have circled (see page 60).

Find out whether any of the pattern pieces should be placed to a fold, note how many pieces should be cut from each pattern, and make sure that each piece follows the grain of the fabric (arrowed lines on the pattern pieces will guide you). Place pins at right angles to the outside edge of the pattern, and use plenty of them to keep the pieces firmly in place.

Do not cram the pattern pieces on to the material so closely that you lose a little of the seam allowance in places. On the other hand, do not spread them out so much that you run out of fabric. You should not take pattern pieces right up to the selvedge edge or you may spoil the hang of a garment. Once the whole garment has been pinned out, it is best to cut off the selvedge edge–but not before then, or you will not be able to check the grain lines.

How do you check the grain lines? Every pattern piece bears a line which shows you the way the piece should be positioned on the fabric if the garment is to hang correctly. You can check that a pattern piece follows the correct grain of the fabric by making sure that the grain line on the pattern is parallel with the selvedge edge of the fabric. Pin the pattern piece in position, then measure the distance from the grain line, first from one end, then from the other, to the selvedge. The measurements should be identical: if they are not, unpin and start again.

Be sure you do not cut a single strand of fabric until every pattern piece is firmly pinned in position, all directions have been carefully read, all grain lines checked, and you are certain you have not planned for two right sleeves, for example, or facings that face the wrong way, or a skirt with one panel using the wrong side of the fabric.

Try forming a mental picture of each piece as it will be when made up and in position. It is so easy to make mistakes. Errors spotted at this stage will save you a cartload of frustration, not to mention expense.

9. CUT OUT THE GARMENT

When everything has been checked, begin cutting. Hold the scissors with your thumb in the smaller ring and your first three fingers in the larger ring, and cut in long, smooth strokes with the full length of the scissors. The lower blade should rest on the table while you cut, and your other hand should rest firmly on the pattern.

If the cutting out is being done properly the shears will make a satisfying scrunchy noise of metal sliding smoothly against wood–a noise, I may say, that never fails to give me a thrill of delight at cutting into new fabric.

Take care not to lift the fabric and pattern from the table, or you may distort the shape of the piece you are cutting out.

In sorting the pattern pieces you will have noticed the v-notches which occur at frequent intervals round the edges. These are to enable you to match up the different pieces of the garment with precision. These notches will have to be transferred from the pattern to your fabric, so that they act as guides once the paper pattern has been removed. I will be dealing later with the transferring of markings, but there is a special point to make about the v-notches: it is best not to cut the 'v' inwards, into the seam allowance. This could seriously weaken the seam, especially if you accidentally cut too far. A much better way is to cut the 'v' *outwards* into the waste fabric (93) so that the piece

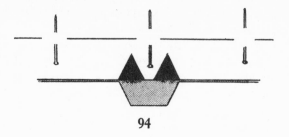

94

appears to have v-shaped tabs. When the garment has been seamed up, you can if you wish snip off these surplus v-shapes.

Incidentally, if there is a double v-notch marking, it is not necessary to cut two tabs close to each other. Instead cut one long tab shape, as in 94. It is much quicker and just as accurate.

If a pattern piece is to be cut on a single thickness of fabric and has to be repeated, remember that it must be turned over so that the pattern is cut for both sides of the body (otherwise you may find yourself with, say, two left sleeves or two right skirt panels).

As you cut the pieces out, lay them neatly in a pile. *Do not take out the pins yet.* Next cut out any facings and interfacings, linings and trimmings required.

When you have finished, gather up all the waste pieces of fabric and sort out and throw away all those which are too small to be useful. Other pieces can be kept. A few could be reserved for your sewing notebook (page 55), the rest rolled up in a bundle, tied with a strip of material and saved for test pieces for machine stitching and perhaps practice buttonholes.

One good piece can be put into the pattern envelope, in case a spare piece is needed for repairing the garment or matching up accessories.

Clear away everything which will not be needed before you begin the next stage.

10. TRANSFER THE MARKINGS

Many home dressmakers who are self-taught have become so used to thinking that pattern marking is a waste of time that they auto-

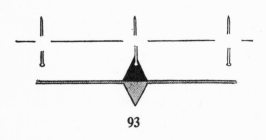

93

matically ignore the circles, v's and diamond shapes which are included for guidance.

If you do this, now is the moment to think again. The markings have been put there by experts, and it is most unwise to ignore them. Never before have paper patterns been so clearly marked to guide you away from pitfalls.

I personally find that the best method of pattern marking is to make tailor's tacks with special tacking thread, but many people like to use a tracing wheel in conjunction with dressmaker's coloured carbon paper, or a small device which transfers the markings with chalk. If you have a sewing machine of the latest type you may be able to make special tailor's tack stitching with this.

It is best for you to try as many methods as possible and then make your own choice as the need arises, for sometimes one marking method is better than another for the particular fabric with which you are working.

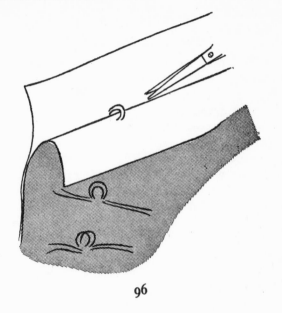

96

TAILOR'S TACKS

If you do decide to make tailor's tacks, use one colour tacking thread for the seamline markings and the centre back and front, and a different colour for marking darts, pleats and button-holes. This will mean that once the paper pattern is unpinned and the pieces of fabric are separated, you will still be able to tell instantly what the markings mean.

To make a tailor's tack, thread your needle with tacking thread, using a length sufficient for sewing comfortably with the thread doubled. Do not make a knot in the ends. Now take a small stitch right through the centre of the pattern perforation or the centre of the dot,

depending on the type of pattern. Make another stitch through the same spot, but leave a loop and two long ends (95). If you are using a perforated pattern it will be possible, when you are ready, to lift away the tissue from the fabric, leaving the tailor's tack in position. With a printed pattern, however, you will have to snip the loop of thread before the pattern can be removed.

Leave the pattern in position until all the tailor's tacks have been made. If you wish, you can sew more than one tailor's tack with the same length of thread, provided you take care that the pattern is not pulled out of position. The threads linking different markings should be snipped before the pattern is removed.

Once the markings have been transferred, put the pattern piece and fabric aside, laying them out flat, and turn to the next piece. When all the marking has been done, it is time to begin to remove the paper patterns, and then separate the layers of fabric. Do this carefully, one tack at a time, clipping the threads between the two layers (96) in order to leave a few strands of tacking thread in each layer of fabric.

Now put all the pattern pieces back into the pattern envelope, folding them carefully.

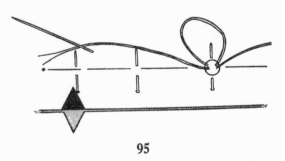

95

MARKING WITH CHALKED THREAD

Some dressmakers who use tailor's tacks like to chalk the thread beforehand by drawing it round a block of tailor's chalk, or even a piece of white blackboard chalk. This leaves a small deposit of chalk on the fabric and should the tacking thread be accidentally pulled out, the chalk ensures that the mark is still visible.

MARKING WITH CHALK ALONE

This is not a reliable method for the home dressmaker. Accurate transfer of the markings is difficult, and the chalk marks may easily be rubbed away during the making up of the garment.

USING A TRACING WHEEL

Some fabrics react better than others to this method of marking. It works particularly well on taffeta, linen and plain materials, but should not be used on white or pastel-colour fabrics, or on sheer fabrics.

The tracing wheel is used in conjunction with dressmaker's carbon, which can be bought from any good department store. Choose the colour closest to your fabric colour, and test it on a scrap of the fabric before marking the whole garment, to make sure that the markings do not spoil the right side of the fabric.

To transfer markings, slip the carbon paper underneath the pattern piece, face down, so that the markings will transfer on to the wrong side of the fabric. If there are two thicknesses of material to be marked, as there normally will be, place another piece of carbon paper with the marking side upwards, beneath the lower layer of fabric, so that these markings will also transfer on to the wrong side of the fabric. You will probably have to remove a few pins in order to put the carbon paper in position.

Place the garment piece on a smooth, hard surface, and using a ruler as a guide run the tracing wheel firmly along each marking. Do not press the wheel down too heavily, but just enough to make the markings clear. Where circles are indicated, use two short lines crossed at right angles.

As with tailor's tacks, when all marks are transferred, fold up the pattern pieces and put them back in the pattern envelope.

11. ASSEMBLE FOR FIRST FITTING

Now comes the moment when you find out whether or not your work has been accurate: the moment to tack the main parts of the garment together and try it for fit.

First carefully tack any darts or tucks which are indicated in your pattern, working on a flat surface to avoid stretching or over-working the fabric. If you have made alterations to darts in your paper pattern these should, of course, have been marked up on your pattern and transferred to the fabric and you will be able to make the dart in just the same way as usual.

The correct way to deal with darts is given in Chapter 5, page 73.

Some patterns will indicate that a section of a seam—for example part of a sleeve seam—should be 'eased'. See Chapter 5, page 81, for the correct way to do this.

If you are working with a stretchy, loosely-woven fabric, or have chosen a style which has many pattern pieces with seams on the cross, stay-stitching or taping any bias edges will help to retain the shape of the garment.

Now you are ready to tack together all the main sections of the bodice and skirt, making the tacking stitches strong enough to keep the garment in one piece during the fitting. Be sure to tack along the exact seamlines.

Owners of one of the sewing machines on which a tacking (basting) stitch is possible, may prefer to use their machine for tacking the pieces together.

Now try the garment on over a slip and a good foundation garment if you wear one. Wear the sort of shoes you will wear with the finished garment. Take another critical look in a long mirror, and again try to enlist an enlightened second opinion.

If you have done the groundwork correctly, your creation will fit perfectly, but if it does not,

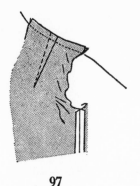

97

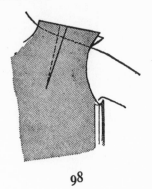

98

now is the moment to make the necessary final adjustments.

Perhaps the bodice fits badly, with crumpled parts where the fit should be smooth. It could be that you have a sloping shoulderline—sometimes one shoulder slopes more than the other—and you may need to increase the seam allowance on the shoulderline (97 and 98) to correct the fault.

Perhaps you feel the waistline is a little too loose—in this case you can increase the amount taken in by the dart, or make a second dart, to produce the right effect (99 and 100).

Perhaps the neckline fits badly, hanging away instead of fitting into the neck snugly. Darts may be the answer here too (101 and 102), but take great care that they are smooth and absolutely evenly spaced.

When you make an alteration of this nature, pin it first until you think you have the right effect, then tack and try on again, this time right side out. You may of course prefer to mark the changes with tailor's chalk, rather than pins—and then tack them in place when you have taken the garment off.

At this stage alterations are usually necessary only because of slight irregularities in the figure, which should have been picked up earlier in the pattern-fitting stage.

When you are happy that all is as it should be, you will be almost ready to assemble the garment. Just take the pieces apart again—a moment's job if you have a small unpicking tool (see fig. 23). Be sure to retain any alterations made, and carry the adjustments through to the finished garment.

99

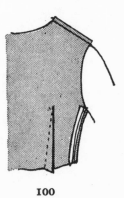

100

101

102

If you are lucky enough to own a dress form you can, once you are sure that the fit is perfect, delegate fitting duty to this, and thus avoid the constant hopping in and out of a half-made dress.

The dress form, if exactly adjusted to your size, will hold the garment correctly and smoothly in place until you near completion. When you have to stop sewing for the day, put the garment on the dress form and slip a large plastic bag over it to keep it dust-free. If you have small children it would be best to use instead two large sheets of brown paper, pinned over the garment, since plastic can be extremely dangerous where there are young children about.

12. MAKE UP THE GARMENT

Generally speaking, if you have chosen a pattern produced by a reputable pattern company it is wise to follow the order of making up which they advise. But if you find the pattern sheet is inadequate or unintelligible to you, try this order of making up. It is not by any means the only 'order of work'–for that will always depend on the garment–but it gives a good general outline to making up a dress, and you can adapt it to other items.

1. *Darts*–pin, tack, stitch and press (see page 73).

2. *Bodice*–pin, tack and stitch facings, centre front and back seams if any, shoulder seams, side seams (see page 74). Press. Do not remove tacking stitches down centre front and centre back until garment is finished.

3. *Special details*–make buttonholes if any, set in the collar if any (see page 95). Deal with pockets if any (see page 89). Press as you work.

4. *Sleeves*–stitch, press and set in carefully (page 102). Press again.

5. *Try on the bodice*. Check the following:
   * That the waistline seam falls at the natural waist.
   * That the centre front and centre back coincide with the centre of the figure.
   * That shoulder seams are straight and set on top of the shoulder.
   * That bodice darts are pointing directly to the fullest part of the bust.
   * That the neckline fits smoothly, without gaping or pulling.
   * That there is sufficient ease, especially across the back, for comfortable movement.

6. *Neaten the armhole seams*, and finish the sleeve ends or cuffs. Press as necessary.

7. *Skirt*. Complete the darts (see page 73), then join the skirt pieces. If the skirt is gathered, take in the fullness.

8. *Join the bodice to the skirt* (see page 109). Press and finish raw edges.

9. *Zipper or other closure.* Set in the zip fastener or other fastening (see page 110).

10. *Hem.* Measure, pin, tack and stitch hem (see page 119).

11. *Neaten the garment.* Neaten the inside seams and trim any loose threads; remove any remaining tacking stitches.

12. *Add any finishing touches*, for example buttons (see page 130), hooks and eyes (see page 132), pockets if not already added (see page 89). Give a final press if necessary. Sew in a wash-care label if wished (see page 138).

5

DIRECTORY OF SEWING PROCESSES

This 'directory' is not in alphabetical order. Instead I have planned it to follow the usual sequence in which a garment is made up, from the first moment when you start with the darts to the finishing stages when you complete the hem and sew on any buttons, fastenings and trimmings.

The previous chapter–'Sewing course for beginners'–should be used in close conjunction with this chapter, for in effect Chapter 4 sets out the landmarks of the journey while Chapter 5 details the route.

Obviously the sequence given will not apply detail for detail to every garment; for example, you may need to complete the whole bodice, including collar, before working on machine-made buttonholes. Nevertheless, you will find that it follows roughly the order in which you are working.

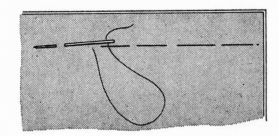

103

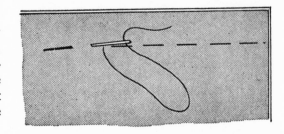

104

BASTING (TACKING) STITCHES

A basting or tacking stitch is a temporary stitch to hold pieces of fabric in a certain position until you can stitch them permanently.

There are various ways of basting or tacking and these are shown in the diagrams:

Even basting or tacking (103): in which the needle enters and is drawn back out of the fabric at exactly regular intervals.

Uneven basting or tacking (104): in which longer and freer stitches are used.

Diagonal or upright basting or tacking (105): used mainly for securing interfacings.

Slip basting or tacking (106): for temporary pleating or folds.

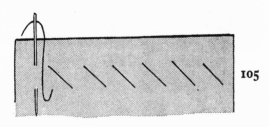

105

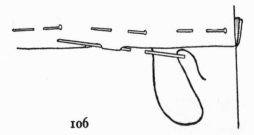

106

DARTS

A dart in dressmaking is one of the chief means of producing a third dimension–it moulds the fabric to fit the curves of the figure, and great care should be taken with darts to sew them carefully and press them meticulously in order to achieve a smooth, rounded effect.

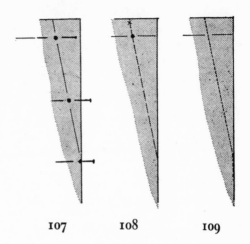

107   108   109

The right way to sew a dart is as follows. Fold the dart on the fold line, matching dart markings and ensuring that the point of the dart is exactly on the fold. Pin in position (107), placing the pins across the stitching line at right angles to the fold line. Tack alongside the stitching line (108), beginning at the wider edge and ending at the point. Remove pins, then machine-stitch along the stitching line (109), again stitching towards the point, taking the last two or three stitches directly on the fold, and taking two stitches past the point, almost off the fabric. This detail is very important indeed, for if you approach the point of the dart at too sharp an angle, the dart will look puckered when completed, and no amount of pressing will make it look smooth and moulded.

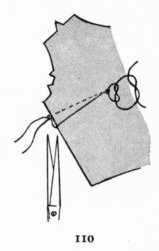

110

Remove the dart from the sewing machine, and to make sure the stitching is not puckered, draw your thumb and first finger along the seam so that the fingernails draw out any puckering. Tie the threads and then snip off the ends (110). Press the dart wrong side up over a curved surface, preferably your curved tailor's ham (see page 31). Press along each side of the stitching, then press the dart to one side (normally the pattern will advise on this).

Darts on heavy fabrics such as woollens should be slashed before pressing. Cut along the fold line to within ½ in. of the point, then press open using a wool press cloth. Finish the edges by overcasting by hand or pinking (111). Or if you have a zigzag machine, you can use it to finish these raw edges.

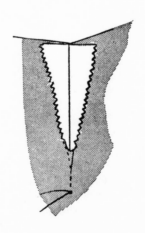

111

Double-pointed darts should be stitched and pressed just as carefully, and if you want to be sure of achieving a really smooth, even line to each point you can sew the dart in two stages (**112**), again taking two or three stitches on the thread of the fold and two or three stitches beyond the point.

tionist in seams and seam finishes. Puckered and badly-finished seams will proclaim your work as that of an amateur, and no matter how beautifully you embellish the work with embroidery or trimmings, nothing can disguise those seams.

A seam may, of course, be sewn by hand (see page 177), but most women would agree that a machine-sewn seam is much more satisfactory for general dressmaking.

There is, incidentally, a correct direction in which to sew seams. You should always work in the direction of the grain of the fabric, which normally means from the wider part of the garment to the narrower part (see **113** and **114**). In some printed patterns the direction of

112

113

SEAMS AND FINISHES

'Seam' is a general term for the joining together of two pieces of fabric. It may be a constructional seam, where one aims for the smooth, invisible fusion of the two pieces, or it may be a decorative seam, where the fact that two pieces of fabric join is made obvious, and the seam is intended to give the garment design and line.

If you are going to produce well-made garments you must determine to become a perfec-

114

stitching is indicated by arrows on the seam lines–you may have missed them on previous occasions, so look closely at your next paper pattern.

Sew a fine seam–some simple rules

Be sure to check the seam allowance given in your paper pattern (normally ⅝ in.).

Be sure you have learned to stitch straight (see Chapter 2, page 39–40).

Be sure you have selected the correct thread and the correct stitch length for the fabric you are sewing. See that the needle is suitable. Test first on scraps of material left over from cutting out the garment. Adjust the tension and pressure if necessary, following the instruction book for your sewing machine.

Be sure you pin and tack before stitching seams. It is particularly important to do this if you are a beginner to sewing or are unfamiliar with your sewing machine.

Do not dismiss these preliminary steps as unnecessary; if you get into the habit of preparing every seam carefully you will get a far better result and avoid the irritation of unpicking incorrect work. Remember, too, that if you unpick seams on some synthetic fabrics, the needle marks may still show and spoil the work.

Here, then, is the pin/tack/stitch/press/finish routine step-by-step.

(a) PIN (115). Place the two pieces to be joined on a flat surface, edges together, right sides together. Match the v-notches which have been cut to stand out on the seam turnings (see page 66). Insert pins at right angles to the seam line, pinning the v's, then the ends of the seams before pinning the remaining sections. There should be a pin every three or four inches.

(b) TACK (BASTE) (116). Use a hand sewing needle and special tacking thread. Tie a knot at one end of the thread. Rest the fabric flat on a table and carefully tack a line of stitches following the seam line but not exactly on it. This makes it easier to remove the tacking stitches after machining. Make two or three

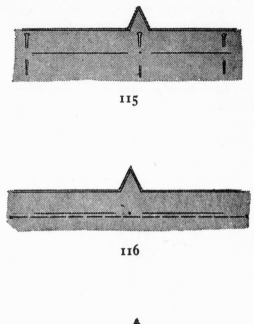

115

116

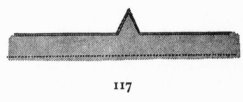

117

large stitches at the end of the seam, large enough to be pulled out easily but secure enough to stay in position until you wish to remove the tacking thread. Snip the end of the thread. Tacking stitches are illustrated in 103 and 104.

As you become more experienced you may find it possible to use your sewing machine to tack because the latest machines have a special tacking stitch, though one or several adjustments may have to be made (which some home dressmakers might consider a bother if they have to make frequent switches from machine-tacking to permanent stitching).

Remove all pins after tacking.

(c) STITCH (117). Now stitch the seam, making sure that you follow the seam allowance provided for in your paper pattern. Stitch in the direction of the grain. This normally means that a seam should be stitched from the widest to the narrowest part of the garment, as indicated in 113 and 114.

Keep the stitching straight. Modern sewing machines are designed to help you with this—some have engraved lines on the throatplate so that the edge of the material can be kept to the line. You can also buy a seam guide which fits on many makes of sewing machine. Use it to practise straight stitching (118).

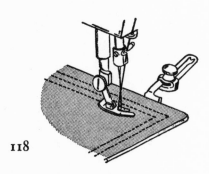

118

It is important that the ends of a seam should be properly finished. This can be done in one of two ways.

(i) at each end of the seam the threads may be knotted together and the ends snipped off. To do this, take an end of thread, tug it gently until the other thread loop is pulled through the fabric, then draw the thread right through. Run your thumbnail and the first finger along the stitched line before knotting, to make sure that you have not accidentally puckered it. Tie the threads securely at each end (119).

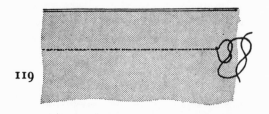

119

After knotting, snip the loose ends of thread immediately with your trimming scissors. Do not get into the habit of leaving all the ends to trim off when the garment is finished.

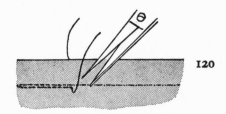

120

(ii) If your sewing machine will sew in reverse, seam ends may be finished by sewing back over the same seam line for about ½ in. You will not need to tie the thread ends, but again you should snip off the ends as soon as each seam is finished (120). Correct tension is essential if you use this method of finishing.

(d) PRESS. Next press the seam open, using a steam iron or a dry iron with a pressing cloth. Some fabrics mark easily and take the imprint of seam turnings, so if the fabric is suspect in

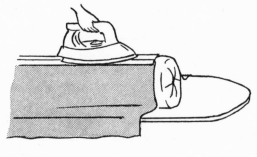

121

this way, press lightly over a seam roll (121) or make shields of white cardboard to insert under seam edges while you press.

It is essential to press every seam lightly after completion, but obviously if you have a number of plain seams to sew, you can wait and press a few at a time rather than pressing each one straight after stitching.

(e) FINISH. Now finish the seam edge in the way most suitable to the type of fabric and the article you are making. Listed below are the main ways of neatening the edges of a plain seam. You will see from the diagrams how each is done.

Bias-bound seam (122)

This is a useful way of completely enclosing the seam allowance; a valuable finish where it is important to avoid chafing in wear–for example in small children's slacks or winter dresses. The bias binding is machine-stitched along the seam, the seam allowances are trimmed, then the bias binding is folded over, pressed, tacked and stitched.

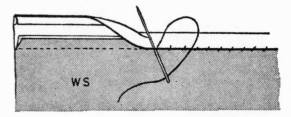

WS

122

Bound seam edges – machined and hand sewn (123)

First stitch and press open the seam. The bias binding is then machine-stitched to each seam allowance, then turned over the raw edge and pressed, and hand-sewn to finish.

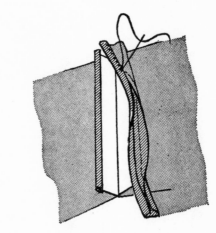

123

Bound seam edges, by machine attachment (124)

This is an effective seam allowance finish once mastered. Instructions are always provided with the binding attachment, which is fitted to the sewing machine quite easily.

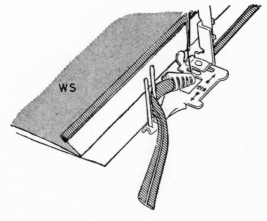

WS

124

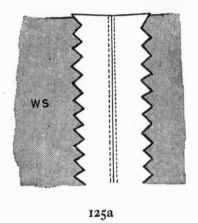

125a

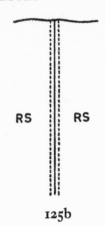

125b

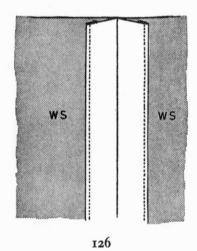

126

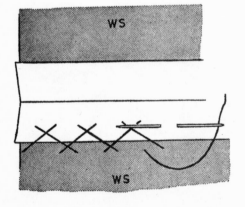

127

Double-top stitched seam finish (125a and b)

The seam is stitched and pressed open, pinked if wished with pinking shears (125a), and then top-stitched as indicated (125b) to give a neat, very secure seam.

Edge-stitched seam finish (126)

The seam is stitched and pressed open, then the seam allowances are folded $\frac{1}{4}$ in. from the edge and pressed under carefully. Finally the edges are machine-stitched as indicated. When you press and stitch, keep the seam allowances free of the garment itself to avoid catching the fabric.

Herringbone-finished seam – hand-sewn (127)

Useful for very heavy coatings and suitings where a flat seam is imperative. The seam is pressed open and you work as shown in the illustration, from left to right.

Overcast seam edges–hand-sewn (128)

Oversew the raw edges of the seam allowance, working neatly and from right to left. Do not pull the thread tightly or the edges will pucker.

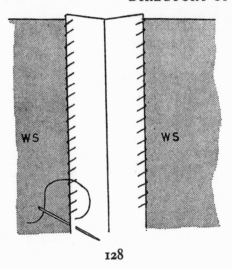

128

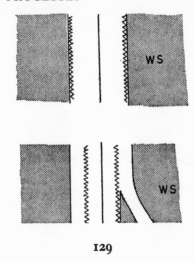

129

Overcast seam edges – sewn by machine with zigzag stitch (129)

There are two ways of doing this – either machine-stitch a line of zigzag stitching on the edge of the seam allowance, or do a closer zigzag stitch ¼ in. from the edge and then trim off the excess fabric.

Stayed and pinked seam finish (130)

Here the seam is stitched and pressed open, then the seam allowances are stitched as shown. But the stitches should go through the seam allowances only (do not stitch them down on to the fabric). Finally the raw edges are pinked with pinking shears.

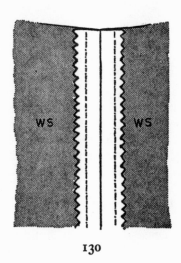

130

SPECIAL WAYS WITH SEAMS

Welt seam finish (131)

This finish is often specified for garments made from the heavier materials. Sew the two pieces of fabric together the 'wrong' way, with wrong sides facing and raw edges showing on the right side of the garment. Allow ⅝ in. seams. Press both seam allowances in the same direction. Trim the lower seam allowance to ⅜ in. Turn under the raw edge of the top seam allowance to conceal all raw edges, and press. Tack and then stitch from the right side of the fabric, to create a neat, strong and very flat seam finish.

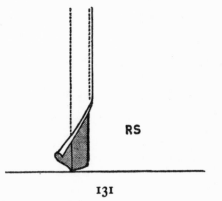

131

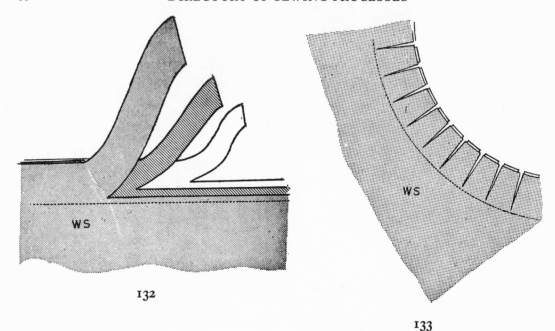

132

133

Trimming (grading) a seam

Often the instruction sheet accompanying the paper pattern will tell you to *trim* or grade a seam instead of finishing it. This happens where a seam has to be turned, in a collar for example–bulkiness must therefore be reduced as much as possible. Trimming can be done in one of two ways.

You may have to cut away both seam allowances to an even width–say ¼ in. This is likely to be specified at edges which are to be topstitched.

Alternatively, you may have to trim away the seam allowances to different widths (132). This is called 'grading', and it is usually specified where interfacing is joined in the seam. Here it is particularly necessary to avoid a ridge being formed by the bulk of several layers of fabric. Normally you will trim most fabric off the interfacing material, less off the facing material and leave the widest seam allowance on the main fabric.

Curved seams

Curved seams must flow evenly and accurately or the finished garment will have an unmistakably home-made look. Work *into* the curve, allowing it to twist round as you stitch; use the seam guide attachment if you have one.

It is wise to set a smaller stitch for a curve than for straight seams. This will give the curve greater elasticity, and also greater strength once you have trimmed the seam allowance.

Curved seams are not treated like a plain seam, because it is obviously impossible to finish off the raw edges in the same way. The seam allowance must be either clipped or notched to within about ⅛ in. of the seam line. An inward curve is clipped (133) and an

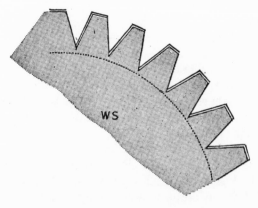

134

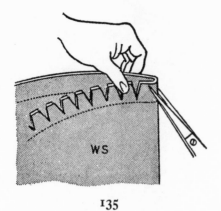

135

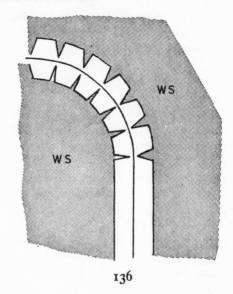

136

outward curve is notched (134) so that when the fabric is turned and pressed the seam will not be either unduly taut or unduly full but lie absolutely flat. The clipping or notching is done at about $\frac{1}{4}$ in.–$\frac{5}{8}$ in. intervals along the curve. When you cut notches, it is easiest if you hold the work as shown in 135, to prevent your cutting into the seam line.

Curved seams which will be turned to the right side and pressed together again—a collar section for example, or the curve of a neck facing—must obviously look as smooth as possible, with no bumpy or bulky parts. You achieve this smoothness by grading – see Trimming (Grading) a Seam, above.

If you are going to grade the seam allowances it is easier if you do this *before* clipping or notching.

If the curved seam is to be opened out flat (136) it is notched and clipped only, and not graded. Press the seam open under a damp cloth. If you wish the curved seam can then be top-stitched by machine.

It is of paramount importance to press a curved seam correctly. If the fabric is likely to mark easily, cut a piece of cardboard to the exact shape and size, and slip it inside the fabric when you are pressing a collar or curved cuff. If the curved seam is to be opened out to give

shaping to a garment, it is important to press over a curved surface to give the maximum moulding effect. A press mitt or tailor's ham is ideal for this job (see page 31). If the fabric is particularly delicate, slip strips of paper or light cardboard under the seam turnings to avoid pressure on the fabric underneath.

Eased seams

You will often find you have an 'eased seam' to deal with when you are making up the shoulder or the underarm of a sleeve. It means that the two pieces to be joined together are slightly unequal in length (by design and not by accident) and this must be adjusted smoothly.

This is a perfectly simple job if you gather the extra fabric beforehand either by hand or by machine, preferably with two rows of stitching. The pattern will almost certainly give markings between which the easing should be done, and these should be marked clearly on your fabric.

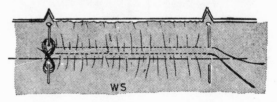

137

Stitch along the seam allowance, $\frac{1}{8}$ in. and $\frac{1}{4}$ in. from the seam line with a loose tension setting, or hand-gather. Place together the two pieces of fabric to be joined, right sides meeting and notches matched; and pin at notches and at each end of the seam.

Pull up the gathering threads of the two rows of stitches until the seam edge of the longer piece is the same length as that of the shorter one (137).

Distribute the easing evenly, and secure the thread ends on a pin at each end, as shown. Pin and tack the two pieces of fabric together. Press the gathering with a steam iron to shrink out any fullness on the seam line. Then stitch the seam, keeping the eased seam on top as you stitch, and remembering the directional rules (113, 114).

Intersecting seams

Where four pieces of fabric are to be joined with an intersecting seam the first two seams

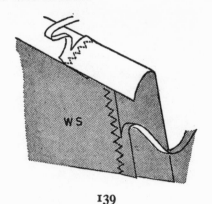

139

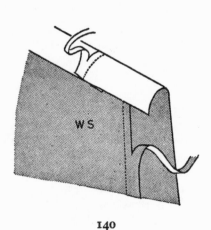

140

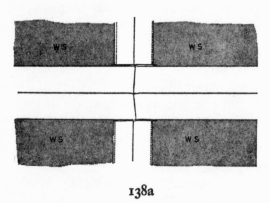

138a

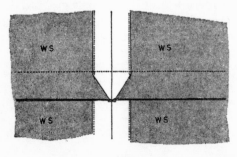

138b

are sewn in the normal way, pressed open and finished if necessary. Next pin together the two pieces to be joined, with the seam lines matching exactly. Tack and stitch the intersecting seam (138a). Turn both seam allowances first in one one direction and then the other while you snip away the spare corners of material at each side of the intersection as shown in 138b, then repeat the other side. Press the intersecting seam open. Finish the intersecting seam edges if necessary, preferably with a zigzag stitch or similar machine finish so that there is no added bulk.

Lapped seam

This is a smooth flat seam for joining interfacing or interlining. Overlap the seam edges, matching

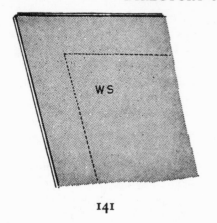

141

First measure how much cord your article will need, then cut enough bias strip or braid for the first seam. Fold the covering over the cord, pin and then tack close to the cord (142a). Stitch along this line.

Place the covered cord between the two layers of fabric, positioned right sides of fabric together, and pin and tack the four thicknesses of fabric together as shown in 142b. Finally stitch, keeping as close to the cord as possible (142c). If the fabric is very bulky an alternative method is to stitch the covered piping to one layer of fabric only, then put the two layers of fabric right sides together and stitch. There is less risk of an untidy seam if you use this latter method.

Finally, cut off the cord at the seam end, and deal with the next seam in the same way.

The strips of fabric to cover the cord must be cut on the cross, otherwise the fabric will wrinkle and the article will look unprofessional. The method of cutting bias strips is shown in

the seam line carefully, and stitch along it. Trim excess width from seam edges. If you have a swing-needle machine you could use a zigzag stitch or a three-step zigzag (139) or a serpentine stitch, all of which will give a flat, strong join. However a simple straight stitch (140) will also be suitable for most purposes.

Seam on a corner (141)

If you are stitching a seam on an outward or inward corner, stitch along the seam line to within ¾ in. of the point, then stop and change the stitch length to a very short stitch (14–16 to the inch). Stitch to the corner point, raise the presser bar, pivot the fabric and continue to stitch with the small stitch length for a further ¼ in. Stop sewing again, return to normal stitch length, and stitch on. The added strength will be a great advantage when you trim and clip the fabric and turn it right side out.

Corded or piped seam (142)

This is used as a decorative finish for cushions, bed covers and loose covers. The secret is to pin and tack at every stage before you machine-stitch, and then to use the special cording foot which is usually supplied with every sewing machine.

Choose the cord best suited to the weight of the fabric—a fine cord for cotton and light linen fabrics, a heavier cord for thick fabrics like corduroy, heavy linens and bulky woollen or worsted fabrics.

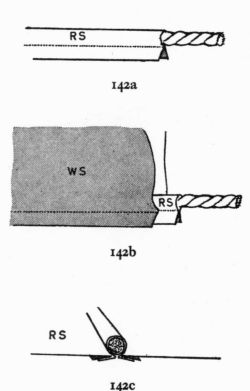

142a

142b

142c

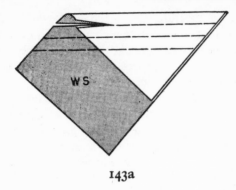

143a

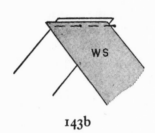

143b

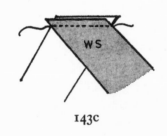

143c

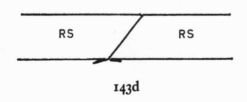

143d

143a, b, c and d. If the thought of cutting bias strips is a little daunting, you can buy wide bias braid in a toning or contrasting colour, and use this in exactly the same way. Be sure the braid is strong enough for the purpose.

Saddle-stitched seam–hand-finished (144)

This is a useful decorative seam for, say, a child's washable garment in a thick fabric. It has the advantage of securing and finishing the edges of the seam allowance without being too complicated or bulky. Make up the sleeve in the usual way, but instead of pressing the seam allowances open, press both of them to one side and tack neatly. Turn the sleeve right side out, thread a needle with three strands of silk in a colour which matches the fabric, and sew a line of very neat, even running stitches $\frac{1}{4}$ in. long through the three thicknesses of fabric. If the seam allowances are $\frac{5}{8}$ in. you should position the line of running stitches about $\frac{3}{8}$ in. from the seam line.

Flat fell seam

This is very similar to the welt seam finish (131) but is the seam used when you are sewing fine garments such as lingerie and baby clothes. It is sewn with the wrong sides of the fabric facing each other, so that the turnings come on to the right side of the garment. Stitch along the normal seam line. Trim one seam allowance to $\frac{1}{4}$ in. Press both seam allowances to one side, with the trimmed seam

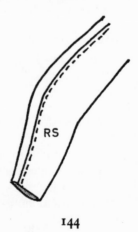

144

allowance underneath. Turn under the raw edge of the other seam allowance about ¼ in. and press. Pin, tack and stitch down by machine or by hand to conceal all raw edges.

This is quite a useful seam for fine fabrics with edges which tend to fray or curl up unless properly secured.

French seam (145)

This is the traditional seam for fine, hand-sewn lingerie, but whether sewn by hand or by machine, a French seam can also be extremely useful for other garments, and especially for fine garments for babies and young children, where frequent washing might cause an un-finished seam to fray or unravel.

Like the flat fell seam, the French seam is produced the 'wrong way'—the wrong sides of the fabric are placed together for stitching, so that the raw edges appear on the right side of the article.

Instead of stitching on the seam line, stitch nearer to the raw edges of the fabric—say about ⅜ in. from the edge of the fabric. Trim the seam allowance slightly; turn article to the wrong side. Fold along the stitched seam line so that the right sides of the fabric are touching. Press along the fold, and make a line of tacking stitches (145) ⅜ in. from the fold. Then stitch. No raw edges should be visible on the right side of the fabric; nothing looks worse than a French seam where strands are trapped in the seam, and there is almost no way of getting rid of these untidy ends once the seam has been stitched. Finally, open and press.

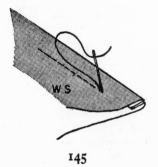

145

BUTTONHOLES

When you are choosing a paper pattern do you, consciously or unconsciously, avoid styles with buttonholes? It is true that if badly made they will be glaring proof of a beginner's work or of lack of attention to detail.

However, there is a simple way to ensure that buttonholes will not let you down in future, and that is to practise beforehand with scraps of material from the garment you are making up. The latest patterns will help you, too, for some have a drawing of the button and buttonhole actually printed on the paper pattern piece.

There are a number of different methods of making a buttonhole, some of which are des-cribed here. Choose the type which appeals to you most and which seems most suitable for your garment. Your choice will depend to a certain extent, too, on your sewing machine and its capabilities, and in the case of hand-worked buttonholes, on your skill with a needle.

All areas containing buttonholes will, without a doubt, be faced but they should also be inter-faced before working, and even if you are making a lightweight summer dress, say, from a pattern which does not call for interfacing, you should slip in a square either of bonded inter-lining or of self-fabric, i.e. pieces of fabric left over after cutting out the garment.

You should stitch the interfacing into position and then tack it down firmly so that it does not slip or slide during making up.

Bound buttonholes are made through the garment and interfacing, before the facing is stitched down.

Worked buttonholes are made after the garment is finished, through all three thick-nesses of fabric—the main fabric, the interfacing and the facing.

Whichever type of buttonhole you choose to make, there are certain basic rules to follow:
1. The spacing of the buttonholes and, as already mentioned, on good patterns their size as well, will be indicated clearly on your paper pattern, and it is imperative that you transfer these

markings on to your fabric immediately after cutting out, preferably using tailor's tacks in a tacking thread of a different colour from other markings.

2. If you want to adjust the size of the buttonholes to suit the size of the buttons, allow the diameter of the button plus ⅛ in., and make adjustments to the buttonhole width on the side away from the garment edge. It is best to test the size of the opening first on a scrap of spare fabric if the button is at all bulky or irregularly shaped.

3. If you have lengthened or shortened the pattern section in which buttonholes occur, you must re-space the buttonholes so that they are equidistant. On a bodice there should be one buttonhole in line with the bustline, and those occurring above and below it should be lined up carefully. If you need one buttonhole less or more, precise measurements should be taken to ensure that the top and bottom buttonholes are correctly placed, and that all buttonholes are equidistant.

4. Ensure that the markings for all the buttonholes are perfectly aligned. Using a ruler to ensure precision, chalk two parallel lines, one to follow the tailor's tacks marking the position of the buttonholes, the other running parallel with it to mark the exact width of the buttonholes.

Next tack along these lines, either by hand or, if the fabric is fairly substantial and will not show needle marks, with your sewing machine. You can either use the special basting stitch available with some modern machines, or use a very large machine stitch, checking tension to ensure that you do not draw up the fabric. Do not remove these guide lines until the garment is completed.

5. Now tack across each actual buttonhole line, again checking that all lines are square with each other and with the grain of the fabric.

6. Proceed, following appropriate directions for bound or worked buttonhole.

Bound buttonhole

146. Turn to the wrong side of the fabric, and, using a ruler, draw pencil lines on the interfacing ⅛ in. above and below each buttonhole line as stitching lines.

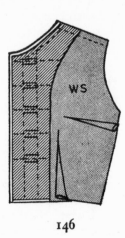

146

147. Cut a rectangular 'patch' of matching fabric for each buttonhole, measuring 1 in. more than the buttonhole opening in width and 2 in. deep. Experts differ on the question of whether it is best to cut the patch on the straight of the fabric or on the cross: the answer is that it depends on personal preference. Try both ways on sample pieces of fabric before you tackle the buttonholes on your garment.

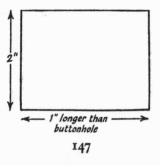

2″

← 1″ longer than → buttonhole

147

148. Fold the 'patch' in half as shown, and lay the fold along the line you have marked for the buttonhole. Open out the patch, so that the right side of the patch now faces the right side of the garment. Pin it carefully in position.

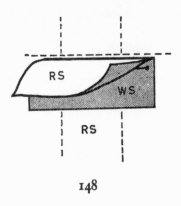

148

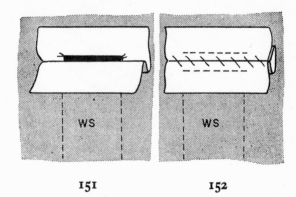

151   152

149. Turn the garment inside out, tack along the pencil lines you have already drawn (see **146** above), stitching firmly through the fabric, the interfacing and the patch. Next, machine-stitch along the same lines, using a small stitch and working in this order: Start in the centre of one long side, pivot at the corner, and as you stitch across the first short end, count the number of machine stitches carefully. Pivot again, sew along the second long side, and when you pivot and sew again, repeat exactly the same number of stitches on the other short end of the buttonhole. Finally pivot and stitch until you overlap the beginning of the stitching.

It is all-important to pay attention to every detail as you stitch round the rectangle of the buttonhole, for unless this stitching is accurate it will be impossible to achieve a perfect finished result.

150. Slash along the centre of the button-hole, taking the cuts to the corners of the stitching as shown. You will need to take your courage in both hands here, for unless you cut right up to the stitching line, you will find it difficult to achieve neat corners; but you must, of course, be careful you do not actually cut the stitching.

151. Pull the fabric patch through the hole to the wrong side of the fabric, tug gently to reveal a neat rectangular opening, and press carefully on both sides of the fabric, using a pressing cloth. Next, fold a tuck (to accommodate the excess fabric) into one side of the fabric patch as shown, and pin, then tack in position.

152. Fold a tuck on the other side of the patch as shown, and pin, then tack the tuck in position. The two folds of fabric should meet exactly. Press gently, using a damp cloth.

To hold the edges in place, oversew them together loosely. These stitches need not be removed until the garment is completely finished.

153. The view of the right side of the button-hole should be as shown–neat and symmetrical and with the tacking stitches holding the work evenly together. Press again gently if there are any wrinkles or imperfections.

RS

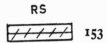 153

154. Finally, on the wrong side secure the patch at each end of the buttonhole by machine-stitching as shown, keeping as close to the end of the buttonhole as possible, and taking in the small triangle of fabric which is left at each end.

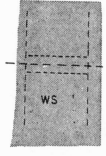 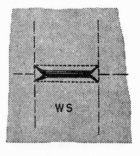

149   150

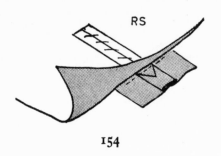

154

This is probably as far as you will go with a practice buttonhole. But when you are making a garment the final stage, after all the buttonholes are complete, is to deal with the facing or lining material. Press it and tack it in position, and cut neat matching holes to correspond with the buttonholes. Make these holes the same shape as the cut shown in **150**. Turn under the raw edges of the facing and sew down neatly by hand round the edge of the buttonhole.

Machine-worked buttonholes

If your sewing machine is equipped to make worked buttonholes, you will find full directions in the instruction book. Detailed instruction would be impossible here, as machines vary so much. There are modern machines that make a buttonhole almost completely automatically–with some you simply turn a dial through five numbers to complete each stage of the buttonhole–and for a straight-stitch machine you can buy a special buttonholer attachment.

Whatever method you use it is essential to mark out the fabric with meticulous care, so that every buttonhole is neat and even.

Making a machine-worked buttonhole is different from making a bound buttonhole in one important respect: you mark out the fabric in exactly the same way as for a bound buttonhole but you do it *after* the garment is completed so that the buttonhole can be stitched through the fabric, interfacing and facing.

If the garment you are making has no interfacing (you may, for example, be making a thin cotton dress), it is advisable to slip squares of self fabric or Vilene between the garment and the facing, to strengthen each buttonhole, in the same way as for a bound buttonhole.

After the buttonholes have been made, press the fabric and then carefully cut through each buttonhole centre, using small, very sharp, pointed scissors. Some people like to use the little unpicking tool for this job, but it needs skilful handling to avoid cutting too far.

Hand-worked buttonholes

Like machine-made buttonholes, these are worked on the finished garment. Again, you must not neglect the preliminary marking out with tacking thread previously described, which makes all the difference between a professional finish and an unprofessional one. Buttonholes which are uneven in length, or do not run with the grain, or are unevenly stitched, become the most noticeable feature of a home-made garment.

After marking out the buttonhole positions, press the work using a damp cloth, and then stitch round the buttonhole line with the sewing machine, stitching only $\frac{1}{16}$ in. from the line (**155**). This holds the layers of fabric together and also serves as a guide for the buttonhole stitching.

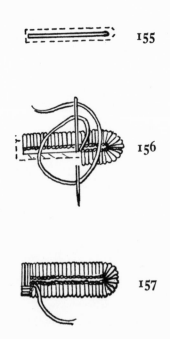

155

156

157

Cut along the buttonhole line, then follow the diagrams (156 and 157) for the method and direction of stitching. Use strong thread or silk twist, depending on the fabric you are making up.

Normally, horizontal buttonholes have fan-shaped stitches (156) at the end which take the strain of the button shank, and a bar tack at the other end (157).

Vertical buttonholes (as a rule only specified for front closings not subjected to strain) usually have both ends finished with a bar tack.

Tailored buttonholes

If you mean to become a specialist in hand-worked buttonholes you could try a tailored buttonhole–a corded buttonhole with an eyelet at one end. For this you will need fine silk cord or waxed thread, a stiletto, and perhaps a little extra patience.

After the buttonhole is marked and before it is cut, punch a hole in the outer end with the stiletto. Cut along the buttonhole line and overcast the edges of the buttonhole and eyelet. Now work the buttonhole stitches over a length of the cord, looping it neatly round the curve of the eyelet and winding the ends round a pin at the opposite end to keep the cord taut until the buttonhole is worked. Snip the ends of the cord when you have finished the buttonhole stitches. Finally finish the ends with a neat bar tack.

POCKETS

There are good reasons why you should know how to make pockets expertly. Every once in a while they come into fashion, and also, if you are making children's clothes, it is wise to add a pocket, whether or not the pattern calls for one.

The main types of pocket are the patch pocket, the bound pocket, the welt pocket and the simple skirt pocket set in a side seam.

Patch pocket

Patch pockets may be rectangular or have a rounded shape, as shown in 158, 159 and 160.

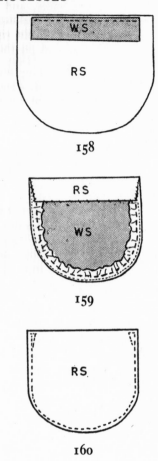

158

159

160

The rounded type is illustrated, as it is the one which needs a little more explaining.

I find it helpful in making up a pocket to have a 'template'–a piece of firm cardboard cut to the actual shape of the pocket minus turnings, i.e. to the size the pocket will be when finished.

The pocket and facing are cut out and the facing is stitched on to the top of the pocket as shown (158), right sides together. Press the facing, folding it over to the wrong side of the pocket piece along the seam line.

Then run a line of gathering stitches round the outside of the pocket piece, $\frac{1}{4}$ in. from the raw edge, place the cardboard template on the wrong side of the pocket and draw up the gathering thread. Press carefully to secure this shape, then slip out the cardboard template and tack round the edge of the pocket.

Turn under the three edges of the facing piece next, pressing carefully, and then hem down neatly by hand (159), making sure that the stitches are not obvious on the right side.

Pin the pocket in position on the garment, then tack and finally stitch (160). Notice in the diagram the way the stitching doubles back on itself at the corners, to ensure a strong pocket which is unlikely to be pulled away from the garment.

Bound pocket

This is made in a very similar way to a bound buttonhole, and is the type of pocket one would find in a classic suit or a child's tailored coat.

Where it is specified in a paper pattern, the exact sizes of the pieces will be set out for you to follow, but you may perhaps not find it easy to follow the method of making up, which can be a little confusing. Here, step-by-step, is the way you can produce a neat bound pocket.

Using tailor's chalk and a ruler, mark on the garment piece the precise position of the pocket opening, and mark each end of the pocket opening with a line exactly at right angles to it. Be very meticulous–this is the most important stage of all. Make the marks more permanent with very straight lines of hand-stitching or loose machine-stitching.

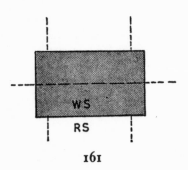

161

161. Cut a patch of fabric 3 in. deep, and 2 in. wider than the pocket opening. This patch may be cut straight with the grain of the fabric or on the cross–experiment on oddments of fabric to find out which way you prefer to work. Place the patch centrally over the pocket opening line on the right side of the fabric, right side

downwards, wrong side uppermost, and tack along the pocket opening line.

162. Machine-stitch all round the pocket opening line, keeping $\frac{1}{4}$ in. from the line on each side. Be sure your stitching makes an exact rectangle.

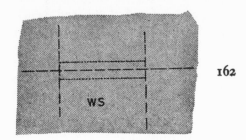

162

163. Cut along pocket opening line as shown, cutting out v-shapes at each end so that the cuts reach right to (but not through) the stitching. Draw the patch through to the wrong side of the garment and pull gently so that a neat rectangular hole is left. Press lightly to preserve this rectangular shape.

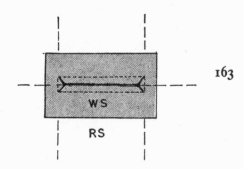

163

164. Make neat folds in the patch fabric (see buttonhole section, 151 and 152 – the method is the same). Press and secure with a few stitches.

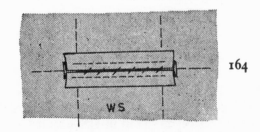

164

165. Take the smaller of the two inside pocket pieces and place as shown; for the moment the piece is upside down and the right side of the pocket piece is facing the wrong side of the garment. Tack along pocket edge in the position as shown. Now turn to the right side of the garment and stitch evenly through the various thicknesses of fabric, alongside the seam where the pocket binding is joined to the garment (see 168 which shows how the finished pocket will look from the right side).

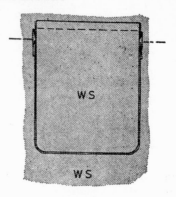

167

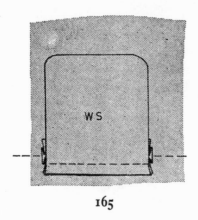

165

166. Turn the pocket piece downwards and press.

168. Turn to the right side of the garment and again stitch evenly close to the seam line between garment and pocket binding. This time complete the full rectangle of stitching, so that the finished effect is as shown in 168.

168

169. Now tack and then stitch together the two pocket pieces, which until now have

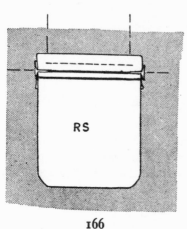

166

167. Take the other, larger, pocket piece and place over the first, right side against right side, as in the diagram. Tack as before.

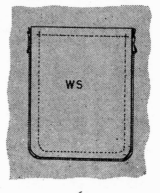

169

been separate. The pocket should be left free—be careful you do not inadvertently stitch in part of the garment when you are sewing the two pieces together.

This type of pocket is normally put in a

garment which is lined, and the raw edges will therefore be concealed. If, however, the garment is unlined, you may wish to bind all inside seam edges using a matching bias binding, to give a neater effect. Again, be sure that none of the stitches come through to the right side of the garment.

Welt pocket (like the pocket in a man's jacket) **170.** Mark out the position of the pocket first with a ruler and tailor's chalk, then with neat running stitches or large machine stitches.

171. Make up the welt: cut a piece of fabric $1\frac{1}{2}$ in. longer than the width of the pocket opening and 3 in. deep. If the fabric is light it is a good idea to use a piece of iron-on interfacing to give the welt body—this is the only part of the pocket which will actually show so it is important to get it right. Fold the welt piece in half, right sides together, press, tack and stitch across the ends, leaving $\frac{5}{8}$ in. turnings.

172. Trim the seam allowances close to the stitching line, turn the welt right side out and press. Tack flat, all the way round the welt.

173. Pin the welt piece to the right side of the garment, raw edges of the welt aligned with the pocket opening line. Tack in position.

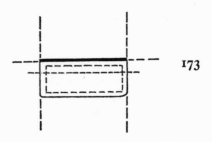

174. Place the two pocket pieces as shown, right side of pocket pieces against the right side of the garment, top edges just touching. Tack in position.

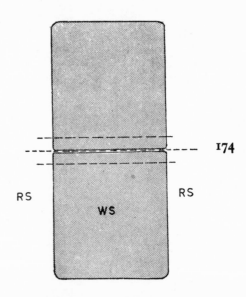

175. On the wrong side of the garment, stitch along the guide lines on either side of the pocket opening. Do not stitch across the ends.

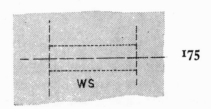

For extra strength at the ends of these two important sewing lines, use the reverse stitch on your sewing machine, or sew twice along the same line. Tie the ends if necessary, trim off loose threads.

176. Cut along the pocket opening line to about ⅜ in. from the ends, then cut out to the corners as when cutting for a bound buttonhole (170).

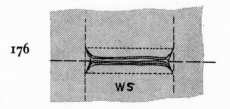

176

177. Draw the two pocket pieces through to the wrong side of the garment, at the same time turning the welt to cover the pocket opening, and ensuring that the ends of the opening are neat and concealed. Press again lightly, pressing all seam edges away from the opening. Snip the top of the pocket piece as shown so that it lies flat. Pin together the two pocket pieces and stitch. As with the bound pocket, be careful you do not catch the main part of the garment in with this stitching.

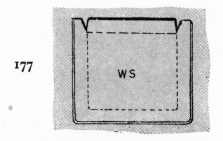

177

178. Catch the welt into position, concealing the stitches behind the welt.

178

Skirt pocket

When making a child's dress it is a good idea to add a pocket to one of the side seams—normally the right side of the dress is the one for the pocket.

179. Cut two pocket shapes as shown, from two rectangles of fabric each measuring approximately 6 in. by 4 in.

Before joining the skirt pieces, pin one pocket piece to the right-hand side of the skirt front just below the waist, and the other to the corresponding skirt back.

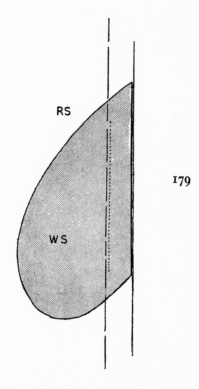

179

Note the way the pocket pieces are laid on the skirt pieces, right side of pocket piece against right side of skirt. Stitch as shown, leaving ⅝ in. unstitched both top and bottom. This stitching line should be ⅛ in. from the seam line, as shown, i.e. about ½ in. from the edge of the fabric.

Repeat with the other pocket piece, tacking it in position first (especially important here because it is so easy to put in the other pocket piece upside down or facing the wrong way).

180. Press both pocket pieces away from skirt pieces.

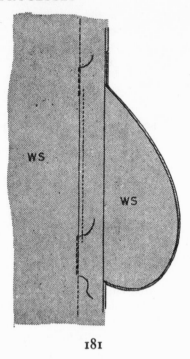

181

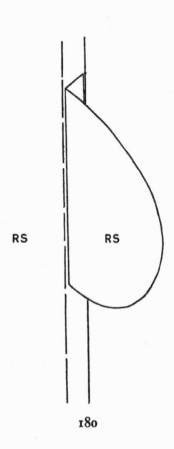

180

181. Pin the skirt pieces together, right sides facing; and first tack, then stitch along the seam allowance, omitting the pocket opening. If possible, machine-stitch in reverse at the seam ends nearest the pocket opening, to strengthen an area which will probably soon pull apart if it is not properly finished.

182. Press all seam allowances around the pocket away from the skirt sections. Stitch the two pocket pieces together as shown, ensuring a strong seam by using a small machine-stitch. Bind the seam allowances of the pocket if necessary. Turn to the right side and press. The finished seam should be smooth, and the pocket opening almost unnoticeable.

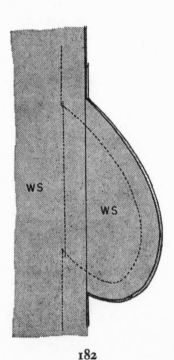

182

NECKLINES AND COLLARS

The neckline of a garment is usually finished in one of several ways:

(i) It may be **faced** with matching fabric to give a plain edge, in one of a variety of styles (for example round neckline, v-neckline or square neckline).

(ii) It may be fitted with a **plain collar** (for example a Peter Pan collar or a pointed collar).

(iii) It may be finished with a **revere collar**.

(iv) It may be finished with a **soft collar**.

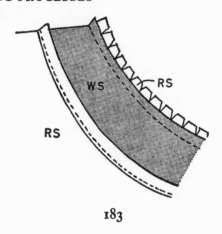

183

Necklines

A faced neckline should be interfaced with a suitable type of interfacing such as Vilene or Pellon bonded interlining or iron-on interlining. The interfacing should be cut from the same pattern as the facing unless the pattern gives other instructions, and the interfacing pieces should be tacked in position on the wrong side of the garment pieces before stitching (or ironed on if you are using iron-on interlining) so that the two are made up together.

ROUND NECKLINE

Shoulder seams, if any, should be sewn first, on the main garment and, if necessary, on the facing pieces. Press these seams out flat, then trim the seam allowances to a minimum to avoid bulk.

Next pin and tack the facing into position on the right side of the garment, carefully matching notches, seam turnings and shoulder seams. Machine-stitch round the neck edge, following the seam line and using a fairly small stitch on curves. Be careful that the facing and interfacing lie smoothly and easily in position, and that neither drags on the garment.

Before the facing can be turned to the wrong side of the garment, the seams must be graded and clipped, to prevent pulling and to ensure that the faced neckline is smooth and flat (183).

Next, turn the facing to the wrong side of the garment and tack it into position, rolling the seam towards the inside between finger and thumb, so that no facing fabric is visible from the outside. Press from the inside with a steam iron, or use a damp pressing cloth.

Neaten the *outside* edge of the facing by overcasting by hand or machine, or by turning under the edge about ⅛ in. and machine-stitching. Press again if necessary. Very carefully stitch the facing edge in position, using only very tiny stitches and spacing them well apart.

With garments made of light or slippery fabrics it is often a good idea to secure the facing invisibly so that it does not at any point

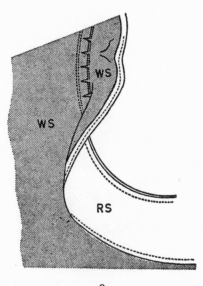

184

start showing above the neck edge. To do this, make up the facing and attach as previously described, but before the facing is finally stitched down, turn to the wrong side of the garment and machine-stitch through the facing and all turnings (184), keeping as close to the original seam line as possible. Finish the facing as before, with a few tiny stitches to secure the edge to the garment.

An experienced sewing instructor gave me this tip, and said that she treats ready-made garments with a neck-facing in the same way, to prevent the facing 'riding up'.

V-NECKLINE

V-shaped necklines need reinforcement at the point to ensure a sound seam between garment and facing. A pattern will normally give you exact instructions for cutting out the facing and interfacing, but it may not necessarily remind you to reinforce the work. So here's how to do it.

Take a small length of fabric or ribbon binding about ¾ in. wide, fold as indicated (185), and tack it in position over the facing piece at the point of the v.

Stitch facing to garment, stitching through reinforcement piece as well at the point. When the facing is turned through to the wrong side and pressed firmly, the reinforcement will be hidden.

SQUARE NECKLINE

A square neckline also benefits from reinforcement. Cut the facing as recommended in the pattern you are following (alternatively a neat way of facing a square collar with mitred corners is shown in 186). Then cut an extra piece of self

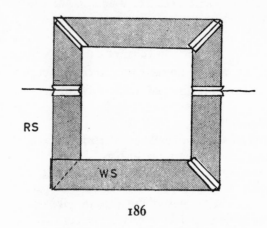

186

fabric for each corner, measuring about 1½ in. square (187). Place one of these small squares of fabric in position at each corner, right sides facing, and secure with a line of tacking stitches. Stitch the reinforcement, facing and main garment piece together, then slash the corner to the point of the seam line. Turn the facing to the wrong side.

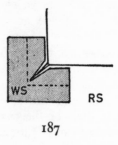

187

Collars

PLAIN COLLAR

A paper pattern will normally provide for a collar to be faced with self fabric and interfaced with suitable fabric for the garment. Cut

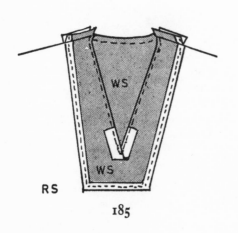

185

all three pattern pieces carefully, ensuring that the notches are cut accurately, and then pin the collar and its facing together, right sides facing. Pin the interfacing on to the facing (or press in position if using an iron-on interlining).

Tack the three pieces of fabric together along the seam line, snipping off the corners of the interfacing as shown in 188. Press on the interfacing side if the work is at all crumpled.

Next machine-stitch the three layers together. In order to produce a smooth collar without pushing or distorting the layers of fabric, it is a good idea to stitch in two stages: begin at the centre of the collar and work to one end, then remove your work from the machine, turn it, and begin stitching from the centre to the other end.

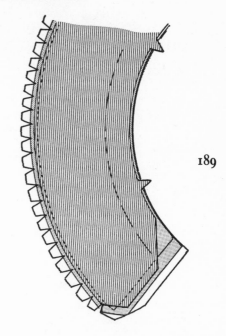

189

to the point of the stitching (see note below) and grade, i.e. trim, the seam allowances as in 188. The interfacing material should be cut as close to the stitching line as possible.

Next, clip the seam allowances at intervals to make the collar lie smoothly when turned (189).

Turn the collar to the right side, rolling the seam line between your finger and thumb until it lies on the underside. Tack carefully with small

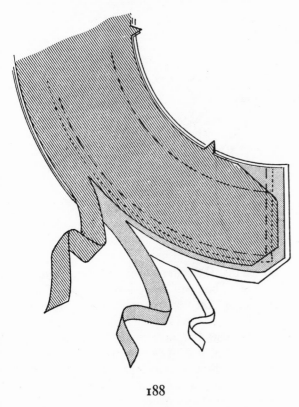

188

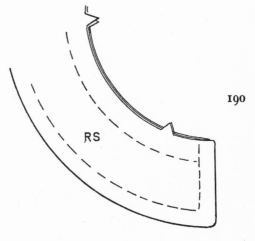

RS

190

Now trim away as much as possible of the surplus fabric on seam turnings: trim the points of the collar diagonally, as near as possible

tacking stitches round the outer edge of the collar (190) and then press.

In a rounded collar very special attention must be paid to the stitching and the clipping of the seam allowance so as not to spoil the curve of the collar. If you find you cannot always stitch accurately, it is worth marking the seam line with a pencil or chalk as a guide when you machine-stitch.

Note: Whatever shape the collar, when trimming the seam turnings the points of the collar need special attention. 191, 192 and 193 show ways of trimming back the corners of a rounded, a square and a very pointed collar.

It is essential to position the collar on the garment correctly. Match notches exactly (194)

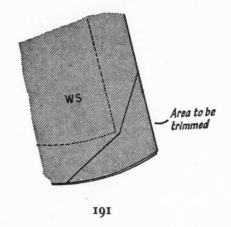

Area to be trimmed

191

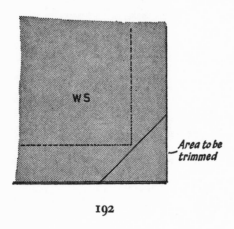

Area to be trimmed

192

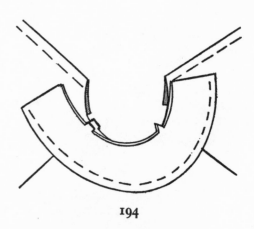

194

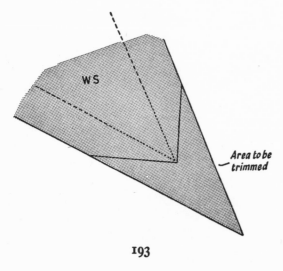

Area to be trimmed

193

and see that the collar sits centrally and without twisting. This will be perfectly easy if you have done the preliminary work carefully. When you have tacked the collar in place and are sure that the positioning is correct, pin, tack and then machine-stitch the collar, following the stitching line with particular care when you reach the front facings. It is here that it is most possible to go wrong.

Turn the garment to the right side and press.

Now the raw edges must be dealt with. Trim ('grade') the seam allowance, then bind the raw edges by pinning one side of a strip of matching fabric (cut on the bias) all round the collar seam, with the right side of the bias strip touching the right side of the collar. Tack carefully (195) and then stitch. See page 84 for cutting bias strips.

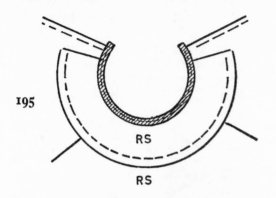

195

Press the garment, pressing the raw edges and the bias strip away from the collar. Turn the free edge of the bias strip on to the wrong side of the garment, turn a small hem under and stitch in position with neat hand stitches (196).

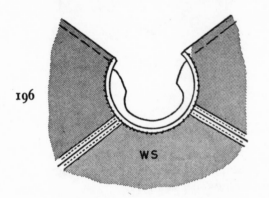

196

If the collar is designed to come right to the edge of the front facing, there is a neater way to conceal the turnings; see the directions for attaching a rever collar.

REVER COLLAR
After the collar has been made and the facings have been stitched to the fronts of the garment, you are ready to attach the collar. First run a line of machine-stitching along the seam line to prevent distortion. This is called stay-stitching. Then notch the neckline at $\frac{1}{2}$ in. intervals,

taking each v-notch $\frac{1}{2}$ in. into the fabric where the seam allowance is the normal $\frac{5}{8}$ in. (197).

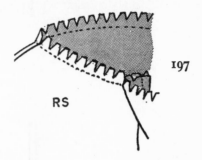

197

198. Pin the collar to the neckline, carefully matching the notches and shoulder seams. This is vital, because if you position the collar wrongly at this stage, it will be one-sided when you have finished.

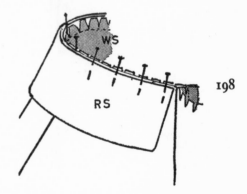

198

199. The front facing, already attached down the front seam, can now be pinned in position over the collar. Again, match the notches carefully.

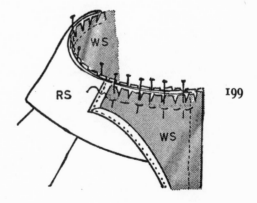

199

200. Tack by hand through the four thicknesses of fabric from the front edge of the bodice to the shoulder seam of the garment.

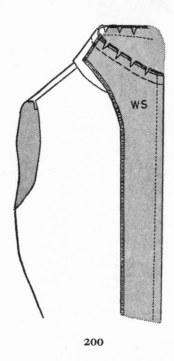

200

Now stitch along the line you have tacked, using a fairly small stitch on your sewing machine. Pay particular attention to the corner of the facing, where the facing joins the main part of the garment at the neck edge (**201**). Make a ½ in. cut into the top layer of the collar at exactly the point where the facing ends.

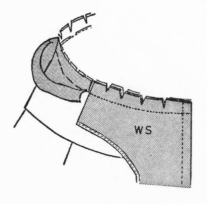

201

Repeat the preceding steps with the other front facing.

Now tack along the collar edge between the two ½ in. cuts (until now it has still been pinned). Machine-stitch along this line with precision, to meet the machine-stitching holding down the facings.

202. Trim the seam allowance as shown, grading the different layers of fabric to ensure a smooth finished effect.

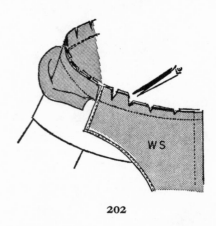

202

203. Press the collar and bodice flat in readiness for finishing off. Turn the raw seam edges back towards the collar and press.

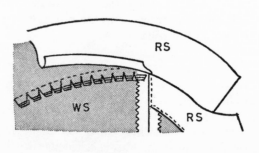

203

204. Turn under the collar seam allowance, press and hand-stitch as shown. Neaten the front facings.

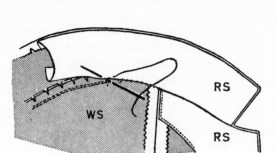

204

SOFT COLLAR
The collar just described is for a tailored garment normally, and I would recommend that the beginner tries several sample collars before she embarks on an actual garment. There is, however, a rather simpler collar–the sort which is put on shirtwaist blouses and light garments. It is usually referred to simply as a soft collar. Here is the way to do it.

205. Join the facing pieces, normally two front facings and a back neck facing, and press open the joining seams. Join the front bodice to the back bodice at the shoulder seams. Press open the seams.

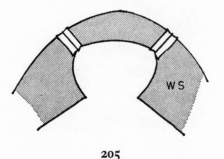

205

206. Join one piece of the collar to the facing, sewing in a light interfacing too, if wished. Join the other piece of the collar to the main part of the garment. Press open the seams, trim and notch.

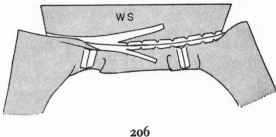

206

207. Pin the facing piece to the main bodice piece, right sides facing, ensuring that the collar pieces meet exactly, and facing pieces are square to the edges of the front bodice. Tack from one front facing to the other, going right round the edge of the front facing and the collar. Stitch and press, and stitch edge of facing too. Notch any seams which will have to curve.

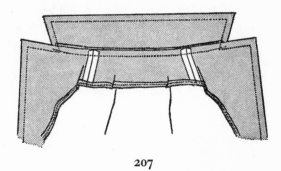

207

208. Turn the garment right side out, pin the collar to hold it in position while you try the garment on. Press, rolling the edge of the collar underneath the collar where it will not show. If the fit is right, secure the facing in position, and continue with the rest of the garment.

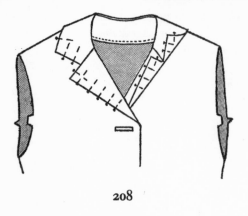

208

SLEEVES

Although in my opinion, one of the most satis-fying tasks in dressmaking is setting in sleeves it is one aspect of home sewing that seems to daunt many beginners. There is, however, no need to be worried by it. If you go about it the right way you will have a perfectly-set sleeve with not a pucker or a twist to be seen.

Most patterns obviously include in their instruction sheets some detailed guidance on making up the sleeve. The hints that follow are not intended to conflict with any advice you are given by the manufacturer of the pattern, but rather to supplement that advice, and amplify any points which you do not quite understand.

Main types of sleeve

Plain sleeve
Puff sleeve
Raglan sleeve
Dolman sleeve
Cap sleeve
Kimono sleeve

The plain one- or two-piece sleeve and puff sleeve are set-in sleeves, and are cut with a sleeve cap that is larger than the armhole into which it must fit—the extra fullness is necessary for the sleeve to fit over the arm and hang

correctly. This fullness must be distributed evenly across the sleeve cap, and on good patterns there will be special markings and v-notches to help to make the easing more straightforward.

The raglan sleeve is set in, but easing is seldom necessary as the armhole is very much deeper and often the sleeve piece is taken up as far as the neckline.

Dolman sleeves, cap sleeves and kimono sleeves are cut in one piece with the garment, in ways I shall describe individually further on in this section.

Plain sleeve

If you follow each of these stages carefully you should have no difficulty in producing a very smooth and professional result.

The sleeve can either be a one-piece sleeve, with only one underarm seam, or a two-piece sleeve, sometimes known as a tailored sleeve, which has two shaped seams instead of one.
209. Make two lines of gathering stitches round the head of the sleeve between the v-markings. One line should be fractionally outside the seam line, the other $\frac{1}{8}$ in. further out, so that once the sleeve is in position these lines of stitching will not show and will not need to be removed unless you prefer it.

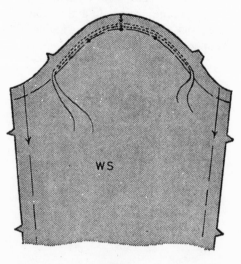

WS

209

210. Now make up the sleeve, joining the seams as directed in the pattern. If the sleeve is three-quarter-length or full-length, there will probably be darts to make up first, or a section of seam near the elbow to be eased. If darts are called for, complete these first in the same way as for an ordinary dart (see page 73).

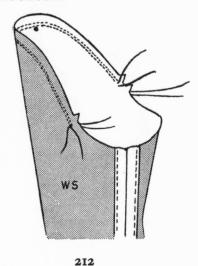

212

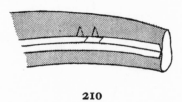

210

211. If the seam is to be eased do this as shown on page 81, making sure that the fabric is eased smoothly and not puckered. If the fabric is suitable—a fine wool for example—the slight fullness can be shrunk out by ironing over the eased area with a very damp pressing cloth, before you finally machine-stitch the seam, and while it is still just tacked.

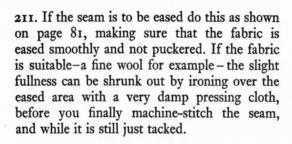

211

inside out, or set the right-hand sleeve into the left-hand armhole. The v-notches will guide you here: match single v to single v, double v to double v. Pins should be placed at right angles to the seam line.

Turn the garment right way out once the armhole seam is pinned, just to check that all is well.

212. Having completed the darts or the easing, stitch the seam, press, and finish off the seam edges as necessary, using one of the seam finishes described in the seam section. Choose a finish which is as flat and unbulky as possible.

213. Now pin the sleeve into the armhole, matching the underarm seams and notches exactly. If you have transferred the pattern markings correctly, there should be a tailor's tack or a marking to indicate the point where the top of the sleeve should match up with the shoulder seam.

Take care that you do not set in the sleeve

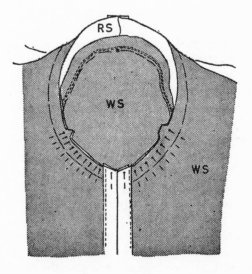

213

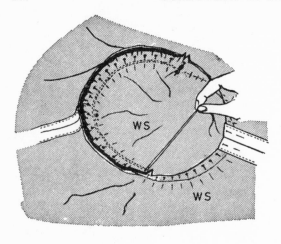

214

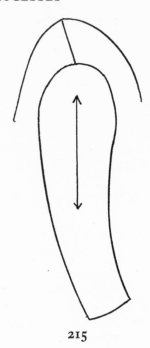

215

214. Turn back to the wrong side. Draw up the parallel gathering threads and make sure that the two layers of fabric between the notches are now equal in length, pinning carefully and using plenty of pins to secure the gathered fabric to the armhole edge. Wind the ends of the threads round a pin at each end of the easing, to secure.

Tack along the seamline, using a small tacking stitch so that every gather is neatly taken in, and making sure that the shoulder seam and underarm seams are opened flat.

If the fabric is woollen, shrink-press the easing, i.e. press over a very damp pressing cloth to shrink out as much of the fullness in the sleeve cap as possible.

215. Before stitching, turn the sleeve right side out and hold it up (or place the garment on a dress form if you have one) to see that it hangs correctly, with the straight grain of the fabric running down from the shoulder seam without any twisting.

216. Finally, stitch sleeve into the armhole with the sleeve part uppermost on the machine. Begin stitching at the underarm seam and finish by overlapping the stitching for a couple of inches to add strength to the seam. Take care that there are no tucks stitched into the sleeve head, and that seam turnings at intersections

lie flat. As you remove the two pins which held the gathering threads, tie the two threads together on each side to secure, and cut off the loose ends.

To neaten the inside of the armhole seams, trim back the spare corners of fabric at intersecting seams.

Seams joining sleeves to bodice, i.e. armhole seams, are pressed downwards towards the wrist except where otherwise advised in the

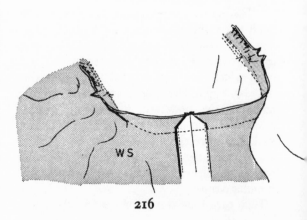

216

pattern instruction sheet. It gives an extra-professional finish if you lightly press the shoulder seams from the right side too, over a press mitt, using a damp cloth. Do not over-press and thus cause shine.

Then machine-stitch the two layers of seam allowance together, $\frac{3}{8}$ in. from the seam line, and cut back turnings almost to this line.

Cut back seam turnings to reduce bulkiness, and clip and notch where necessary. If wished overcast by machine (217) using zigzag stitch, or by hand (218). If necessary (i.e. if the fabric is very sheer or inclined to fray) bind the seam allowance with bias binding.

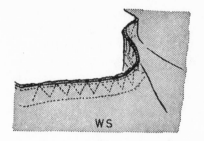

217

Some fabrics are far easier to deal with than others when you are setting in sleeves. Loosely-woven woollens are the easiest, for they can usually be press-shrunk and moulded without difficulty so that any hint of fullness or gathering can be smoothed out.

Some cotton fabrics, on the other hand, particularly glazed and specially-finished cottons, have great stability of weave, and it is extremely difficult to shrink or ease-in any fullness. Here you will have to use a little cunning if you are to avoid puckering.

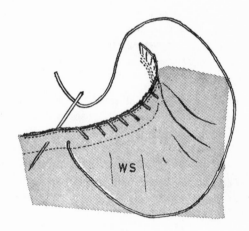

218

Test a piece of the fabric first if you are in any doubt, making two lines of stitching on the bias and seeing how they react to easing.

If the fabric is not too harsh, you may find you can soften it sufficiently for taking in ease, by rubbing the seam line together between your fingers before drawing it up, to break down any surface finish. It must, however, be said that some of the most modern easy-care fabrics are made drip-dry and non-iron not by a surface finish but by a chemical change (see the section on fabrics and fibres), and in this case no amount of rubbing will soften down the finish.

If the fabric is obviously very stable indeed, try this trick which should reduce the amount of easing necessary without changing the length of the armhole. It is better explained by illustration (219) than by words.

Mark the $\frac{5}{8}$ in. seam allowance line round the top of the sleeve with white pencil, tailor's chalk or dressmaker's carbon. Next, mark a line $\frac{1}{8}$ in.

219

inside the seam line, tapering from the original seam line at the notches and back to the original seam line at the centre of the sleeve cap.

Using a large machine-stitch, sew between the notches along this new line. Then make another line of stitches parallel to it but $\frac{1}{8}$ in. in towards the seam allowance, exactly as with a normal sleeve – see page 102 or 209. There should now be less drawing of fabric necessary, and the gathering should therefore be less noticeable.

A *short sleeve* will, of course, be set in in exactly the same way as a three-quarter or full-length sleeve, the only difference being that there will probably be no shaping in the sleeve seam.

Puff sleeve

This is made up in a similar fashion to plain sleeves, but it is a good idea to make the gathering stitches along the armhole edge of the sleeve at the same time as you gather the top of the sleeve. As the intention is that the gathering should form a decorative feature of the sleeve, there is of course no need for shrink pressing.

If I am making a puff-sleeved dress for a baby or very small child, I prefer to attach the puff sleeves to the bodice of the garment *before* the underarm seams of the bodice and sleeves are joined.

220. Put the double line of gathering threads across the top of the sleeve (as 209), and another

line at the bottom of the sleeve. Draw up the gathering in the top of the sleeve.

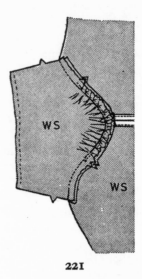

221

221. Pin the sleeve piece to the bodice, which you have already completed along the shoulder seam. Match v-notches carefully, and adjust the gathering evenly between notches. Tack and then stitch. Finally press all turnings towards the sleeve. Repeat with the other sleeve.

222. Turn the garment inside out, pin the underarm seams of bodice and sleeves, ensuring that the intersecting seams meet exactly and that the v-notches correspond. Tack and

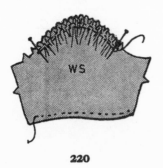

220

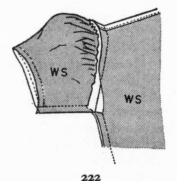

222

stitch. Finish the seam edges with a finish suitable to the fabric– hand-oversewing or a bias binding is often used in fine garments for small children.

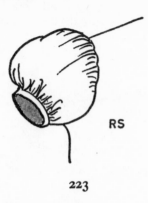

223

223. Now draw up the ends of the sleeves, using the gathering thread you have already stitched in. Finish the sleeve ends by applying a bias-cut strip of self fabric or a cuff, according to the finish called for in the pattern.

Raglan sleeve

A raglan sleeve is set in, but easing is seldom necessary as the armhole is very much deeper than the conventional type, and often the sleeve is taken up as far as the neckline, with a diagonal seam running from underarm to neck.

The sleeve itself may be cut in one piece (as in 224) or in two pieces. If it is cut in one piece, there will probably be a dart to make and press before you proceed further, the dart running from the neckline to just over the shoulderline to give shaping to the garment. If the sleeve is cut in two pieces the seam that will run down the top of the arm should be completed first.

Next, join the sleeve to the bodice, matching the seams carefully and ensuring that the v-notches correspond. Pin, tack and stitch these seams, and then press them open. If the seam is a curved one, rather than a straight raglan, you will need to snip along the seam edges to allow the seam to curve smoothly (225). Press again.

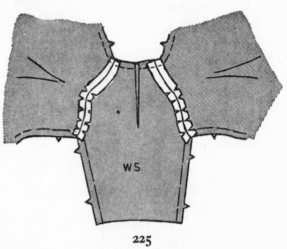

225

With the garment turned inside out, pin the underarm seams of the sleeve and bodice together in one continuous seam, matching v-notches and the intersecting seams (226). Tack,

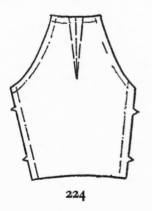

224

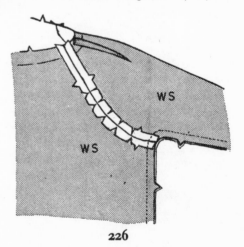

226

stitch and press the seam open, and finally finish the seam edges in a suitable way.

Dolman sleeve

A dolman sleeve is cut in one with the bodice. Dolman sleeves are not recommended for women with a heavier figure or for sports garments. The design does not allow for completely free movement of the arms, and any undue activity may over-strain the fabric and cause it to split, particularly as the underarm area is vulnerable to the fabric-weakening properties of perspiration.

After the seam has been stitched it should be clipped along the curve (227), taking the cuts as close to the seam line as possible without weakening the seam. Press the seam open (228)

then pin a line of ribbon or bias tape right down the seam line on the inside of the garment. Tack in place, and stitch from the right side to secure the tape to the garment. If your machine has a three-step zigzag stitch (229) or a serpentine stitch, use this to secure the tape to the garment.

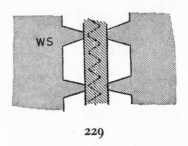

229

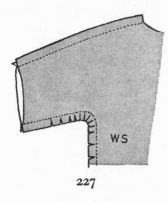

227

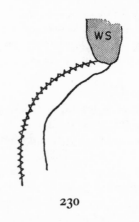

230

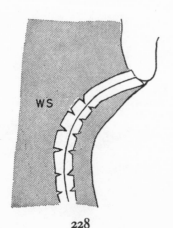

228

The result will be a neat, strong seam (230) which will not burst open at the least movement. If you have only a straight-stitch machine, two lines of stitching, about ⅛ in. each side of the seam line, will give similar results.

If you have made up a dolman sleeve and find it too restricting, you can probably remedy the problem provided you have some spare scraps of the fabric.

Try on the garment and make a mark with a piece of tailor's chalk roughly at the centre of the underarm. Take off the garment and mark the other sleeve at the same point along the seam line. Now cut two squares of fabric 3 in. by 3 in., exactly on the straight of the grain (i.e. following very precisely the warp and weft of the fabric). Press a $\frac{1}{2}$ in. turning on all four sides of each square of fabric.

Take one square of material and place it on the right side of the underarm seam, centering the square exactly over the mark you have made. Pin. Tack the square in position, then stitch, using a small zigzag stitch if your machine is a swing-needle type, or two lines of straight stitching.

Turn to the wrong side of the garment, make a cut across the underarm seam and cut away the fabric behind the fabric square, leaving $\frac{3}{8}$ in. turnings. These should be oversewn together with the turnings from the fabric square to produce a neatly finished effect.

Cap sleeve

This is a very small sleeve, and like the dolman sleeve forms part of the bodice pieces. However as it is usually very short, it produces very little strain on the underarm area. Normally the inside of the bodice and cap sleeve will be faced.

It is a good idea to stitch in a length of ribbon or bias tape with the underarm seam to give extra strength where the fabric is light or inclined to stretch (see under Dolman sleeve).

Kimono sleeve

Kimono sleeves are cut in one with the main part of the garment, and traditionally the front and back of the garment are cut in one piece so that there is no seam along the top of the sleeve. Like the dolman sleeve, the kimono sleeve is subject to a good deal of strain, so that a fitted waistline is out of the question–normally a loose tie belt is provided so that when the arms are lifted the garment can adjust accordingly.

The underarm seam may be strengthened with a strip of bias ribbon. You can choose narrow ribbon and stitch it in with the seam, or alternatively choose a wider ribbon and pin it in place after the seam has been stitched, snipped at intervals and pressed open. Tack down the seam line to secure the ribbon, then stitch down from the right side of the garment, with

two lines of machine stitching, one each side of the original seam line. This will give a good strong seam that will finish the raw edges of the seam turnings at the same time.

WAISTLINES

A good paper pattern will give explicit instructions for joining the bodice and skirt of a garment, varying according to the style. Generally speaking, if you have done your preliminary work with care, the waist should be very straightforward, and it will merely be a matter of pinning the two halves of the garment together, matching all seams and notches (231), then

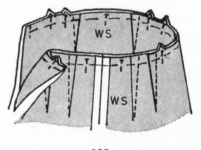

231

tacking and stitching. The turnings are normally pressed upwards towards the bodice (232a) and

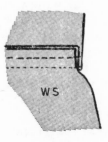

232a

if wished the seam may be top-stitched (232b) to hold the seam turnings in position.

Skirts and slacks will need some form of stiffening at the waistline – either buckram, petersham or a heavy-quality bonded interlining. The pattern will advise on the method of inserting this.

If you put on weight easily and your waistline tends to fluctuate, you may like this alternative method of finishing a skirt waistband: it is ideal for the skirt of a two-piece suit made from a jersey or similarly stretchy fabric. Sew the darts and side seams as usual, but make the waistband slightly more slack than you would normally. Instead of backing the waistband with stiffening, thread it with wide flat elastic, drawing up

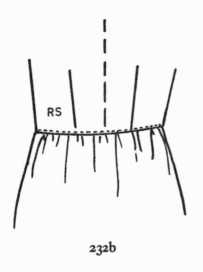

232b

the elastic to fit the waist comfortably before sewing. The jersey will give slightly with the elastic, so that there will be a minimum of restriction even after a heavy meal. Even if the waistband is a little less smooth than the traditional stiffened waistband, it will be concealed by the jacket, and certainly very comfortable to wear.

If the waistline has no seam at all, as in a one-piece dress with a back zip, it may be

preferable to strengthen the area with a petersham or buckram band to take the strain off the zip. Cut it to fit the waist plus an overlap of 3 in. for turning back the raw edges, then stitch two hooks and eyes to hold band in place round your waist. The hooks and eyes are positioned behind the zip. Stitch the band to the dress at the side seams only, making sure that the securing stitches do not show on the right side. After the garment is put on, the hook and eye are fastened before the zip is closed.

BELTS

If you are making a garment with a belt, it is advisable to have this made up professionally—most large stores offer a belt-making service. Or you can buy a buckle-covering kit, which enables you to cover buckles yourself.

ZIP FASTENERS

Sewing in a zip fastener often bewilders the beginner, even when there is an instruction sheet with the pattern, and in spite of the fact that most zips are sold with instructions for fitting. It is certainly well worth the beginner's while to sew a few practice pieces beforehand to try out the different ways of inserting a zip. You can unpick the practice piece when it is complete, and try again a different way, until you are thoroughly familar with a few simple methods. It may prove a little hard on the zip fastener, but its cost will be money well spent in terms of the garments you make.

First, what sort of zips can you buy? They usually fall into one of the categories on the facing page, and be sure, when you buy a zip, that it is suitable for the article you are making. Both trouser and upholstery zippers are very unlikely to commend themselves to you if you are a beginner to dressmaking – trouser zips, especially, are best left to a tailor until you have reached a certain level of sewing proficiency. Other zips, however, are perfectly simple if you work carefully and follow the simple rules set out here.

	Type	Usual lengths	Available
SKIRT ZIPPER	Open at the top	7 in. and 9 in.	Medium to heavy weight, metal or plastic
NECKLINE ZIPPER (also used for sleeves, narrow trousers, under-arm blouse closures, etc.)	Open at the top	4 in. up to 36 in. length	Light, medium and heavy weight, metal or plastic
DRESS ZIPPER	Closed top and bottom, with a top bridge stop	10, 12 and 14 in. lengths	Light, medium and heavy weight, metal or plastic
JACKET ZIPPER (used for coats and jackets, housecoats and sports jackets)	Open top and bottom	10 in. up to 24 in. lengths	Medium to heavy weights in metal
TROUSER ZIPPER (less readily available)	Open at the top, extra-wide tape for specialised treatment	11 in. but is cut to fit front opening	Medium weight, metal
UPHOLSTERY ZIPPER (for loose-covers)	Closed top and bottom or open at the top	24 in. to 36 in. lengths	Heavy weight, metal

Inserting an open-top zip fastener

You will now have reached the stage where your garment—skirt or dress—is seamed together, and the place where the zip is to go will have been left open and unfinished. If it is a skirt the waistband will be fitted after the zip fastener is completed. If it is the neckline of a dress, the facings will be completed after the zip is happily settled.

I shall describe three ways of putting in this sort of zip. In all cases it is necessary to use zipper foot.

METHOD I. ZIP COMPLETELY CONCEALED BEHIND LAPPED SEAM

The first stage is to close the zip opening in the garment, using a very large machine-stitch and loosening the top tension slightly so that the

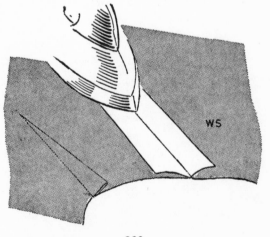

233

stitches can be removed easily when you are ready. Be sure you allow at least ⅝ in. seam turnings, and be sure you make an accurate and straight stitching line by pinning and tacking first.

Press open the seam you have made (233), using a steam iron or a dry iron with damp pressing cloth.

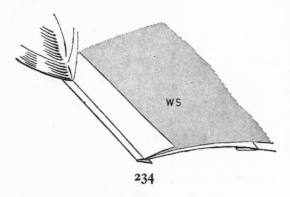

234

Fold back the garment pieces as shown (234), right sides touching, and make a fold along the lower seam allowance just ⅛ in. from the stitched seam line. Press this fold firmly with an iron. In a *skirt* the back seam is the one which should be folded and pressed.

Lay the folded seam allowance over one edge of the zip and pin, then tack as indicated (235), taking the fold almost up to, but not touching, the teeth of the zip. Stitch. With the garment positioned as shown in 235, bring over the

garment piece so that the zip is positioned behind the seam allowance. It will now be to one side of the seam line, and not centred on it.

Pin, tack and stitch the other side of the garment to the other side of the zip, ensuring that the fabric lies smoothly without twisting. The zip slider may, if it is fairly bulky, make straight stitching difficult when you reach the top end of the zip. In this case, cut open the top 2 in. of the securing stitches (the large machine-stitches you made down the seam line at the beginning), and move the slider out of the way until you have stitched the rest of the seam.

Finally unpick the large securing machine-stitches (236) and remove all loose thread ends. Finish the skirt or neckline as appropriate, making sure that the fabric ends of the zip are neatly folded away and concealed – do not under any circumstances cut the ends off (only a special trouser zip may be cut to fit).

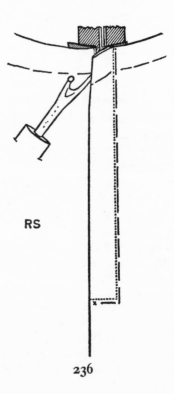

RS

236

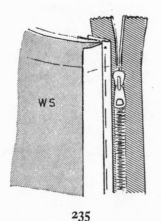

WS

235

METHOD 2. ZIP CENTRED ON SEAM LINE

This method can be used when setting a zip on a neckline (centre front or centre back seam), or for sleeves, legs of narrow trousers, etc. It makes a neat, strong seam and virtually conceals the zip.

First complete the seam as far as the point indicated for the end of the zip. Then pin and tack together the part of the seam that contains the zip opening, and machine-stitch, using a very large stitch and a slightly looser top tension (237). Press the seam open.

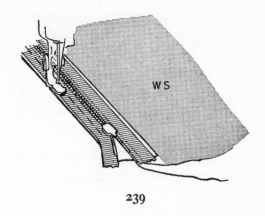

239

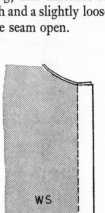

237

allowance. The teeth of the zip should just come level with the seam line. Stitch close to the teeth (the instructions on the zipper packet will tell you how close you can stitch – it depends on the type you have chosen). Stitch from one end of the zip to the other, then remove the work from the sewing machine. Close the zip and place the tab on the slider upwards, towards the top end of the zip. This means that it is not locked.

Next re-fold the fabric so that you can tack and then stitch the other side of the zip to the other seam allowance (239). When you are stitching near the slider you will need to move it out of the way temporarily if it interferes with

Now place the zip fastener face down on the wrong side of the seam, folding the layers of fabric to one side as shown (238) so that you tack and stitch the zip only to the one seam

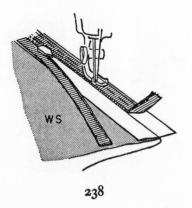

238

240

the stitching line. Be sure, when you tack before stitching, that the zip lies face down to the seam allowances, and that there is no pulling or puckering.

Turn to the right side of the garment and tack, then stitch through the garment, seam turning and zipper tape on each side of the zip, ensuring that the stitching line is neat and square (240)

Finally remove the tacking stitches down the centre of the seam line, so that the zip is exposed.

METHOD 3. RING ZIP

This is the kind of zip that is meant to show. The fabric fold is pinned, tacked and then stitched as close to the teeth of the zip as possible, barely $\frac{1}{16}$ in. from the edge of the fabric fold.

With the garment facings already stitched in position, turn back the seam allowances to exactly the width provided for in the pattern, and press along the seam lines to make the fold unmistakable. Pin the zip to the fabric, keeping it closed and taking care not to pull it to one side as you pin. If you do not keep the zip taut while you pin, it may buckle once you have stitched it in place. At the lower end of the zip hold the fabric with your thumb while you pin in such a way that the edge curves round and leaves the zip teeth clear of fabric (241).

Stitch along the fabric fold, very close to the zip teeth, using a small machine-stitch and, of course, the zipper foot, and taking the stitching line in a curve round the bottom of the zip (242).

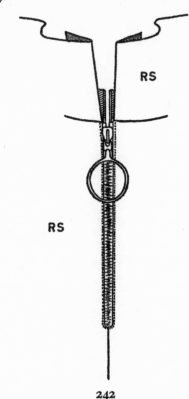

242

Fold back the tops of the zip so that the tapes are at a slight angle, clear of the zipper teeth. Tack in these positions (243). Hem the facing edges.

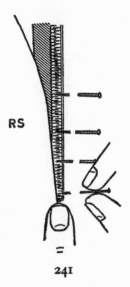

241

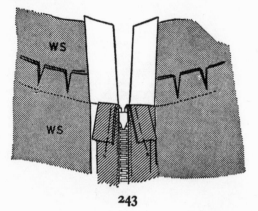

243

Press the facing down on to the wrong side of the garment and tack round the neck edge, rolling the facing slightly to the inside of the garment so that the seam round the neck is not visible from the right side. Hand-stitch the facing to the garment, concealing the turned-down ends of the zipper tapes and all raw edges (244).

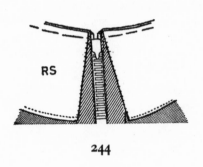

244

The finished effect should be neat and even (245). This is an ideal method for a child's playsuit or a caftan type dress or coat. You can, of course, choose an open-ended zip for a coat, in which case the stitching method is very similar except that it is of course not necessary to shape the fabric round the bottom of the zip as described above.

Inserting a zip closed at both ends

METHOD 1. LAPPED SEAM

This is the method to use for the zip in the side seam of a dress, for it gives a secure, concealed zip fastening. It can also be used on a centre front or centre back seam. You should however practise this method with spare pieces of fabric until you have mastered it.

246. When the bodice has been joined to the skirt, stitch together the side opening using a large machine stitch and loose top tension, stitching between the points marked for the ends of the zip. Be sure to stitch exactly along the seam allowance line, which should be at least $\frac{5}{8}$ in. Trim off the spare corners of fabric at the seam intersections as shown, to reduce bulk, and press the waist seam turnings upwards.

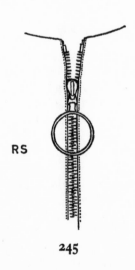

245

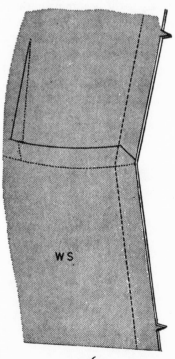

246

247. Press open the seam where the zip is to be fitted.

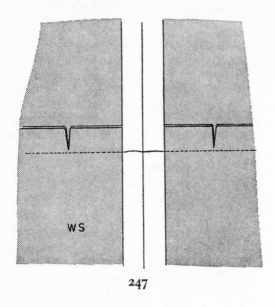

247

248. Open the zip and place it face down on the seam allowance of the back of the garment (back seam allowance). Match the bottom stop of the zip to the beginning of the temporary machine-stitching, with the centre edges of the zipper teeth just level with the seam line. Tack and then machine-stitch the tape of the zip to the back seam allowance only, using the zipper foot on your sewing machine to sew very close to the zip teeth.

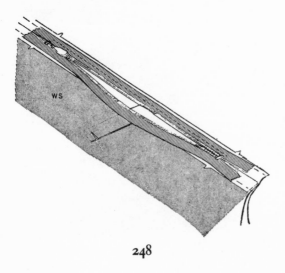

248

249. Keeping the garment in the same position, lift the free side of the zip and turn it over, so that the right side of the zip is uppermost. Close the slider of the zip. Press the fabric away from the zip, forming a fold in the back seam allowance, along the zip tape. Stitch close to the zip teeth, from the bottom of the zip, through the folded back seam allowance and the zip tape.

Spread the garment flat and turn the zip face down over the front seam allowance. Pin and tack the zip flat in this position. There will be a small pleat in the back seam allowance at the top and bottom of the zip.

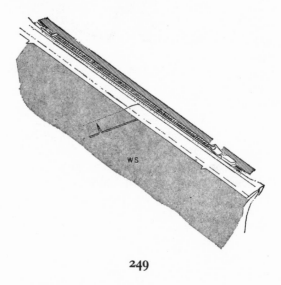

249

250. Starting at the seam line, stitch across the bottom of the zip at right angles to the seam line. Stitch up the front side and across the top of the zip. Keep an even distance from the teeth, sewing through the front of the garment the seam allowance and the zip tape. You must, obviously, stitch straight – otherwise the stitching is liable to run into the zip teeth or off the edge of the seam allowance. When you reach the slider, unpick the temporary machine stitches and pull the tab down slightly so that it does not interfere with your stitching.

Finally remove all the temporary large machine stitching. The placket will, if properly made, conceal the zip most satisfactorily.

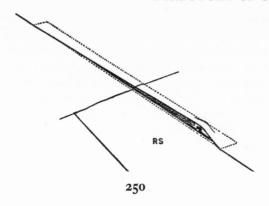

250

think the lapped seam is preferable because once you have mastered the technique you will, in fact, find it easier to produce a satisfactory result. However, if the fabric you are working is fairly thin, you may be quite content with a centred zip. This is how you do it.

251. Close the zip seam with large machine stitches and a loose top tension. Press open this seam and also the waist seam. Trim away the corners of fabric at the intersections of the seams to reduce bulk.

METHOD 2. CENTRED ZIP

Although it makes the fastening rather more noticeable, you can simply place the zip centrally over a side seam, or the centre front or centre back seam. The method is simpler than the lapped seam just described, but I personally

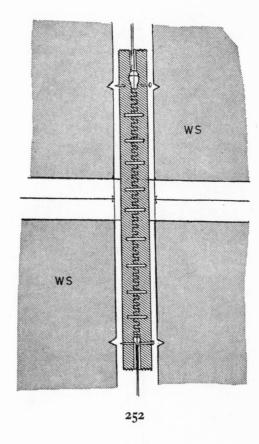

252

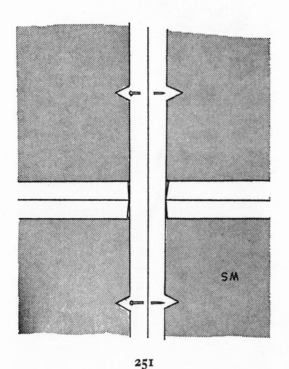

251

252. Place the zip centrally over the temporary seam line, face down, and pin in position from the right side, placing the pins in alternate directions. Keep the zip pulled taut as you pin.

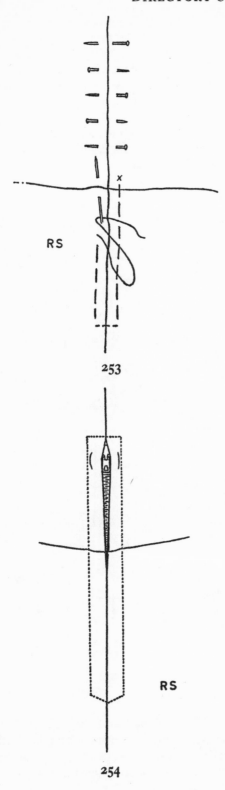

253

254

RS

RS

253. Tack round the zip, removing the pins as you go.

254. Stitch the zip in position, either by machine or, if preferred, by hand. The finished zip should be as neatly stitched as possible. The stitches at the bottom of the zip may either go straight across at right angles to the seam line, or the stitches may be taken to a point as shown in the illustration.

METHOD 3. BLIND STITCHED ZIP

Zips may also be set in with the blind stitch which is possible with many of the more modern swing-needle sewing machines (**255a**). The sewing machine instruction book will tell you the method to use with your own machine. The result will be a neat, inconspicuous zip (**225b**).

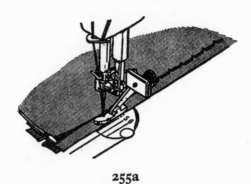

255a

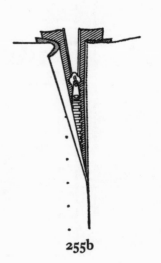

255b

HEMS

Never make the mistake of thinking that once you have decided the length of a garment, you can simply measure it off from the waist seam with a tape measure. People in general–even children–are *not* shaped straight up and down like a pillarbox, and hems should therefore always be measured from the floor up to hem level, with a yardstick or a hem marker (256).

256

If you are making a garment for yourself it is always preferable to have a helper. A yardstick would be impossible to manage on your own. However, if you have a hem marker and a long mirror, it is possible to mark out the hem yourself unless the skirt is very full.

Let us assume that you have a helper and a yardstick or a hem marker and are about to complete the hem of a garment for yourself. You are wearing the same sort of undergarments and shoes that you will wear with the garment when finished.

You decide on the hem length by pinning up

a section at the front, and a section at the back as well, to make sure.

The person being fitted–in this case you–should stand still (on the floor, not on a chair), while the helper measures round the skirt, from floor to hem level, and places a line of pins right round the skirt. She should work round you while you stand still, in your normal posture. A hem marker is used in the same way, except that a chalk line is puffed on to the skirt at the correct level, and then marked with pins.

When the length has been clearly marked, with pins an inch or so apart along the hem line, take off the garment carefully so that pins are not dislodged. Turn the hem to the inside along the markings and press along the hem line fold (257). Tack round the hem ½ in. from

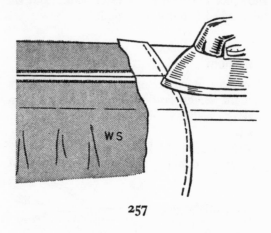

257

the fold, removing pins as you tack and ensuring that the vertical seam lines fold back on themselves exactly.

Now measure the hem allowance–this will probably be indicated in the pattern, and is usually 2 in. to 3 in. for a straight skirt and ½ in. to 2 in. for a full skirt on the bias. Use a ruler for this measurement, or better still a hem gauge (shown in 258), cutting away the surplus fabric as you measure.

How you finish the hem will depend partly on whether the skirt is straight or full. It will also depend on the fabric you are using.

Various hem finishes are described below; in each case the directions assume that the

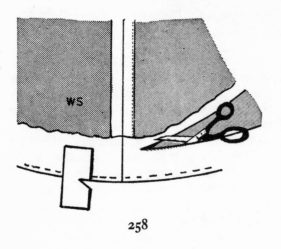

258

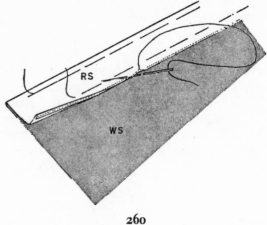

260

hemline has already been pressed, the hem allowance trimmed to an even width, and the hem tacked ½ in. from the fold.

STRAIGHT SKIRTS
Plain hem

This hem finish is suitable only for light or medium-weight fabrics. Heavy coating materials or suitings would be too bulky to finish in this fashion.

Make a ¼ in. turning all round the edge of the hem allowance, pressing it neatly (259).

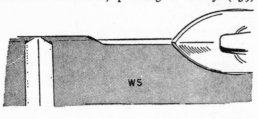

259

Pin, tack and machine-stitch this turning, close to the fold. Pin the finished edge of the hem allowance into position on the wrong side of the skirt, check that there is no twisting or pulling, and then tack. Press again. Finally slip-stitch the hem into position (260). Do not make the mistake of putting in too many stitches. Even if they are as small and neat as can be, the hem will look clumsy and overstitched. Make the stitches neat, certainly, and conceal them as

much as possible, but space them well apart. Close, minute, painstaking stitches are not called for here. Obviously, though, you must finish off firmly when you reach the end of the thread, or the hem will soon drop and need restitching.

Tailor's hem

This hem, particularly useful for fairly heavy fabrics that will not fray, is simple to do and makes the most inconspicuous seam finish of all. It is not suitable for garments which will be machine-washed, because the stitching is quite light.

Firstly, machine-stitch round the hem allowance, ¼ in. from the raw edge, with the top tension fairly loose. This helps to strengthen the edge. Draw up the thread a little if necessary, to ease out unwanted fullness. Pressing with a very damp cloth will also help to smooth away unwanted fullness.

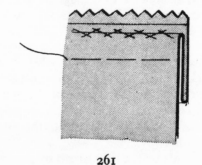

261

Fold the hem into position as tacked, and press. Tack again about ¾ in. from the raw edge of the hem allowance, to keep the hem firmly in position. Now fold the hem upwards on to the right side of the garment, so that the edge of the hem allowance protrudes by about ⅜ in. beyond the fold (261). Pin and tack the additional fold temporarily in this position, while you catch-stitch the hem allowance to the garment as shown. I must stress again that this stitching must be firm yet very light–not only must the stitches not show on the right side of the fabric, but their outline must not show. Space the stitches well apart; a mass of impeccable stitches may show what a splendid needlewoman you are, but they will not prove you to be a good *dressmaker*.

Once the temporary tacking stitches have been removed the hem can be unfolded and the stitching will be entirely invisible both from the outside and the inside of the garment (262).

Blind-stitched hem

This is similar to the tailor's hem described above: the fabric is folded in the same way, but instead of hand-stitching, the fabric edge is secured by machine blind-stitch. The sewing

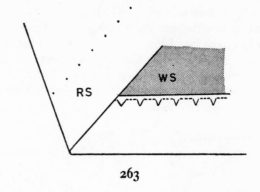

263

the fabric, the more inconspicuous the stitching will be. Blind stitch is only possible, of course with a swing-needle machine.

It is an advantage if your machine has a slow speed, as this stitch requires great care and precision. It is advisable to practise on sample pieces of fabric before you tackle an actual garment, otherwise you may very easily become discouraged.

Bias-bound hem

This is a good hem finish for a fabric of any weight, but particularly for the medium-to-heavier materials where bulk must be kept to a minimum. Bias binding, in a colour which matches the garment, is pinned, tacked and then stitched to the raw edge of the hem allowance (264).

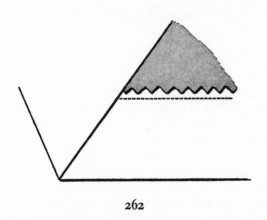

262

machine instruction book will give you guidance on the actual method of stitching. If done skilfully, stitches will barely be noticeable on the right side (263) and the thicker

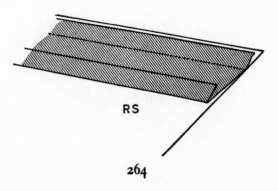

264

Press the bias binding away from the garment, taking care that you do not press away the other fold in the bias binding. Pin the other edge of the bias binding to the garment (265), tack and finally hand-stitch in position. Again, do not overstitch–avoid at all costs that 'loving-hands-at-home' look.

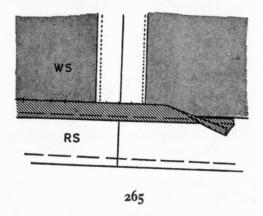

265

Catch-stitched hem

This method is used for a straight skirt made of a heavy coating or suiting material, where bulk could be even more of a problem.

Firstly examine the raw edge of the hem allowance. If it is closely-woven you need do nothing more than catch-stitch the edge to the garment, as shown in 266. Again, do not be over-industrious with the stitches–even fairly large stitches can be used provided the stitching is firm and unlikely to come loose, since in any

case this type of garment will probably be lined. Too many stitches, especially tight stitches, will show through to the right side of the garment even if you try hard to make them invisible.

If the skirt is just slightly shaped, you can still use this stitching method provided you first make a line of large machine stitches along the edge of the hem allowance; keep the top tension loose and draw up the stitching very slightly, to accommodate the extra fullness.

Some heavy fabrics–certain tweeds for example–fray very easily, and here the raw edge will have to be well secured before it is catch-stitched to the garment. You can do this by hand-oversewing the edges (267). Alternatively

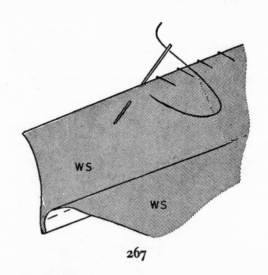

267

the edge can be machine-finished, using, say, a zigzag stitch, a three-step zigzag or a serpentine stitch, depending on the stitch available on your machine. A very skilled Swedish sewing demonstrator I know is particularly pains-taking when making up a tweed coat or suit, and using the three-step zigzag stitch on her automatic machine she finishes every raw edge – side seams, hem edge, etc.–at least once or twice before she makes up the garment, to ensure that no fraying occurs. This is a particularly good idea for the hem edge, because it means that you can lightly catch-stitch the hem in position afterwards, and the hem will be securely stitched yet not lumpy.

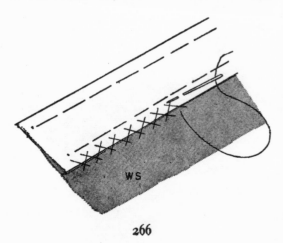

266

Bias-bound catch-stitched hem

The bias binding is attached as described under 'Bias-bound hem'. If there is a slight flare in the skirt, the extra fullness in the hem allowance should be distributed evenly by first stitching a line of fairly large machine-stitches $\frac{1}{4}$ in. from the raw edge, and drawing up the stitching slightly.

When one side of the bias binding has been machined to the hem allowance, press the hem and tack the other side of the bias binding to the garment. Finally catch-stitch the bias binding to the garment as shown in 268.

of approximately $\frac{1}{2}$ to $\frac{5}{8}$ in. Press a $\frac{1}{4}$ in. turning along the other edge of the false hem. You can if you like stitch along this fold with small machine-stitches to secure the edge if the garment is a washable one–with a dry-cleanable type garment it is not normally essential to do this.

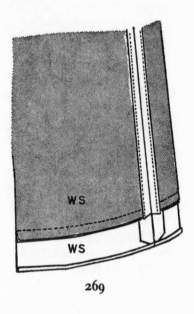

269

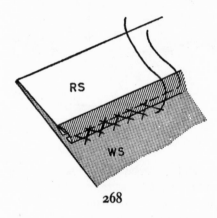

268

False hem

If you are making a garment using very thick, bulky material, or are letting down a skirt with not enough hem turning left, it is very useful to know how to make a false hem.

Cut a piece of fairly fine, closely-woven material the same colour as the garment. It should measure about 2 to $2\frac{1}{2}$ in. in width, and be the length of the hem plus 2 or 3 in. (the surplus fabric will be trimmed off later). The strip should be cut on the straight grain of the fabric for a skirt which is straight or only slightly flared–a bell-shaped or full skirt needs a false hem cut on the bias.

With right sides together, stitch the false hem piece to the hem edge, leaving seam allowances

Join the ends of the false hem as shown in 269. This illustration is, for clarity, cut away on the left to show the positioning of the fabric. Press open the seam and trim off excess seam allowance fabric. If the skirt itself is especially bulky it may be advisable to trim the edges of the hem allowance too, before you proceed further.

Now press the false hem up on to the wrong side of the skirt, pressing both seam allowances towards the waist seam. See 270, which is cut away on both sides to show the positioning of the fabric and false hem. Normally you would not see this view, of course, as the hemline is continuous.

Pin and tack the top of the false hem in position, then slip-stitch or catch-stitch to the main part of the garment, depending on the weight of the fabric. Press lightly.

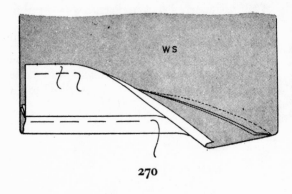

270

¼ in. from the raw edge of the hem allowance, the second just inside that line. Draw up the threads until the hem allowance lies flat on the skirt, and secure the thread ends by twisting them round two pins (272). Check that the front, back and side seams turn back on themselves, as shown in the illustration.

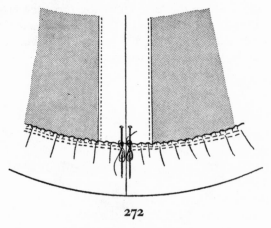

272

SHAPED OR FULLER SKIRT

Curved hem, bias-bound

If the skirt is full and there is a pronounced curve on the hemline, bias binding is an excellent way of finishing the hem. Try to keep the hem depth to a minimum, or the finished effect will be lumpy.

On a child's garment, it is a mistake to allow the customary deep hem 'for growing' if the hem edge is very curved. Instead, keep some of the fabric left over from the dress, and when you need to lengthen the hem you can attach an entirely new hem with strips of fabric cut on the cross. The join can be concealed with a braid or fancy machine-stitch.

To bias-finish a curved hem, first make two lines of gathering stitches (271), the first

Pin and distribute the gathering evenly; each pin should be at right angles to the hem, and spaced about 1 in. from its neighbour.

Press the gathers to neaten and to check that the curve of the hemline is intact, with no 'threepenny-bit' edges. If the fabric is wool, use a very damp pressing cloth so that some of the excess fullness is reduced by slight shrinking. When you press the gathered hem allowance you can protect the main fabric by slipping in curved shapes of cardboard or strong paper between the two layers of fabric. This is an especially wise idea if you are shrink-pressing or if the fabric is sensitive to heat, as in the case of some types of rayon.

Now attach the binding: unpin the hem, then pin and tack one side of a length of bias binding all round the gathered line, pulling the binding taut and checking that the gathers are even. Machine-stitch along this line.

Next, pin and tack the other edge to the garment. Finally slip-stitch or catch-stitch (see 273).

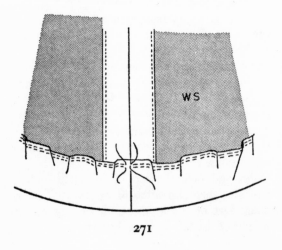

271

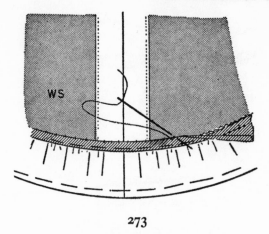

273

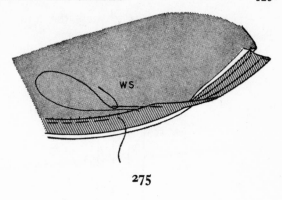

275

Circular skirt–bias-bound hem

Circular hems are perhaps the most difficult of all, both to make level and to sew neatly. A circular skirt should be allowed several days to drop before hemming. When you have measured the correct hem length all round, cut the hem allowance to only ⅜ in. Pin and tack the opened-out edge of a strip of bias binding all round the edge of the skirt, pulling the binding as you pin, so that when you turn the binding to the inside of the garment, some of the excess flare will have been taken up. Stitch along the tacked line (274). Press all round the hem, pressing the binding away from the skirt.

Pleated skirt

It is essential to keep the hem allowance to a minimum on a pleated skirt, and a false hem of fine fabric is a good way to finish the hem as it will not interfere with the hang of the pleats. Alternatively you can finish the hem turning with ribbon binding if the hemline is on the straight grain of the fabric, or bias binding if the skirt has sunray pleating. In this case leave only a ½ in. turning at the hemline, and finish with bias binding as indicated for straight skirts or curved hemlines.

Where a pleat is formed on the line of a seam, both turnings should be pressed into the pleat (276). Where the seam line is hidden behind

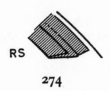

274

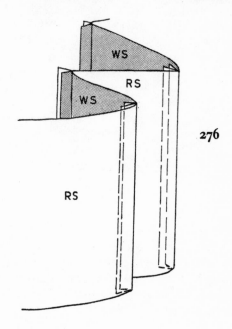

276

Now turn the binding on to the wrong side of the skirt (275), keeping the hemline as originally marked. Pin and tack the free edge of the binding flat in position, making small tucks if necessary to take in excess fullness. Finish with a very neat slip stitch, with the stitches light, fairly well-spaced but secure.

a pleat, it is usually best to press the seam allowance open (277). Where a seam line – whether at the fold or in a pleat–reaches the

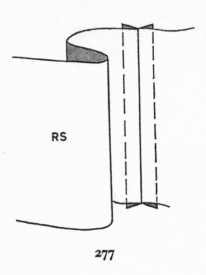

277

pleat, it should be trimmed back as much as possible (278) to reduce bulk.

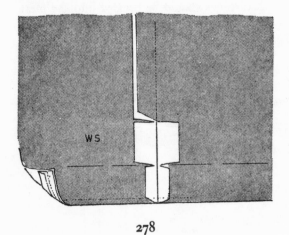

278

If you have to lengthen or shorten a pleated skirt which has been professionally pleated, it is usually best to put the alteration in professional hands. Your local dry-cleaner will usually be able to give advice.

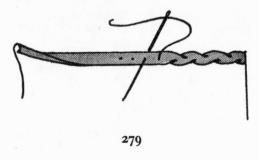

279

HAND–SEWN HEMS

Plait stitch hem edging (279)

This is a very useful edging for underwear or children's clothes, and is very simple since it involves only two stitches. Make as tiny a hem as possible (no more than $\frac{1}{4}$ in.), folding it down twice and pressing it between your fingers. If you have had some practice you will not need to tack: you can simply turn down the edge as you proceed.

Insert the needle as for hemming, but each time bring it through the centre of the hem, taking one stitch right over the top of the hem and the other under it. This stitch can be used on the straight or for curved edges.

Rolled and overcast hem edging

Again this is a hem which is used only for very fine fabrics, where a hand-rolled edge is the only one which will match the fineness of the article.

You roll the edge of the fabric towards you with the left thumb and index finger while overstitching with the right hand (280). Be sure that you keep the stitching line even.

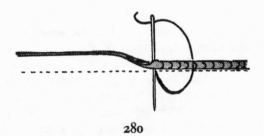

280

CUFFS AND SLEEVE EDGES

Your paper pattern will tell you which particular way the sleeve edge should be finished – there may be a facing to complete, or the sleeve may simply be turned back and hand-stitched in position. Try to practise a few of the methods beforehand, with left-over scraps of fabric. This will give you confidence when you have to do it in earnest.

Below are some typical ways of finishing a sleeve.

Sleeve edge turned and stitched

This is a way of finishing the sleeves of washable garments such as cotton dresses though not a way greatly to be recommended. Turn under a ⅛ to ¼ in. hem and press. Top-stitch with the sewing machine stitch set fairly small. Stitch very close to the fold. Turn under the full sleeve hem allowance and press again, then tack the edge in position. Slip-stitch the hem edge to the sleeve, making small stitches which are very nearly invisible on the right side. If you choose a thread of a suitable thickness, in a colour which matches the fabric, and if you pick up only two strands of fabric with each stitch, and do not make the stitches too close together, the hem should barely show, even on a fine fabric. The stitches should be tiny, firm but well-spaced.

If you are making up a heavier material, say for a coat or suit, the hem allowance should not be edge-stitched; instead, if the fabric is closely woven simply hand-stitch the edge in exactly

the same way as the tailor's hem on page 120. 281 shows how this hem is stitched – notice how the sleeve edge is folded back while you stitch.

If the fabric is inclined to fray, it is best to bind the edge first with bias binding, and then stitch down as in 282.

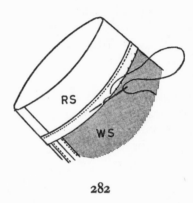

282

Faced sleeve edge

The facing may be cut from a much finer fabric than the main garment, or it may be exactly the same fabric – this depends on the garment.

The facing piece is usually joined at the ends to form a tube; you then finish the free edge of the facing, either by turning up a small hem, pressing it and then top-stitching about 1/16 to ⅛ in. from the fold with small machine stitches (283) or by binding the edge with bias or seam binding.

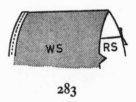

283

Next, stitch the facing piece to the edge of the sleeve, and press the seam allowances between the sleeve and the facing upwards towards the sleeve. Trim off the excess seam allowance fabric (284), and clip or notch the seam if necessary, to allow freedom of movement.

281

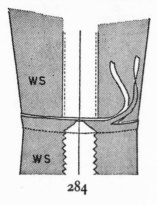

284

285. Pin the exact centre of the facing to the line which marks the placket opening, with right sides together and edges aligned at the bottom of the sleeve. Tack in position, then stitch along each side of the marking line, starting ¼ in. from the line. Take the stitching to a point, but take one stitch across the point before you turn and stitch down the other side of the line. Cut along the marking line between the stitching, right to the point of the stitching.

286. Turn the facing to the inside of the sleeve and press flat.

Position the facing on the inside of the sleeve, rolling the seam line between your finger and thumb to ensure that the seam inclines to the inside of the garment. Slip-stitch the facing into position.

Shirtwaist sleeve with faced lap placket and a cuff

A placket is necessary for the kind of slashed opening you find on a shirt-waister dress or blouse. It is best to put in the placket before you stitch the underarm seam or set in the sleeve.

First cut a placket facing–a rectangle of material, square with the grain of the fabric, measuring 3½ in. wide and ɪ in. longer than the placket opening. Turn in the long edges ¼ in. and press to the wrong side of the facing.

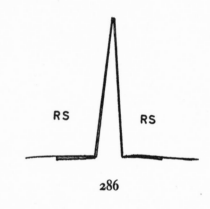

286

287. Turn back to the wrong side. Tack and hem the turned-in edges over each line of stitching.

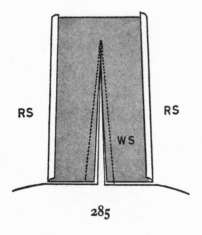

285

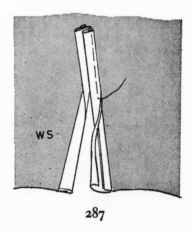

287

288. Now fold in the faced edge nearest to the front of the sleeve. Stitch the upper edges of the facings together (free of the sleeve) and tack the lower edge of the front facing *to* the sleeve.

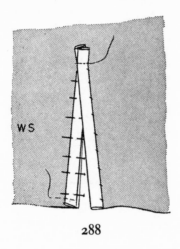

288

When the sleeve seam has been finished and the sleeve set in, you are ready to add the cuff. **289.** Make two rows of large machine stitches at the lower edge of the sleeve. Draw up the stitching slightly and secure the thread ends on a pin at each end of the gathering.

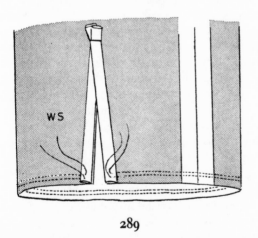

289

290. Now make up the cuff. Even where no interfacing is specified it is well worth using some (the cost is infinitesimal), to give a smooth 'tailored' look. Tack the interfacing to the inside of the cuff pieces, with one edge at the fold line. Secure the edge with tiny hand stitches. If you use an iron-on interlining, you follow the manufacturer's instructions.

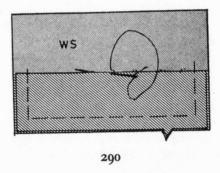

290

291. Fold the cuff in half, right sides meeting, and press. Stitch the ends. Trim the interfacing close to the stitching. Grade (trim back) the seam allowances. Turn the cuff to the **right** side and press.

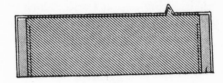

291

292. Adjust the gathering stitches on the sleeve edge to fit the cuff, pinning the notched edge

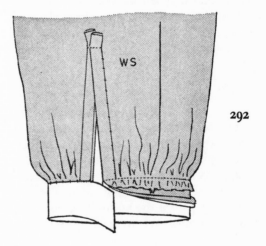

292

of the cuff to the notches on the sleeve edge, right sides together, and adjusting the gathers.

Make sure the front placket is folded back flat. Tack and stitch the seam, trim back the seam allowances, and press the seam towards the cuff.

Turn under the free edge of the cuff and press. Hem this edge over the seam. Finish the cuff with a button and buttonhole.

BUTTONS

To set the seal on your well-made garment you will need to choose buttons of the right style, colour, weight and shape. Take care to avoid a fussy, over-elaborate effect, especially if the garment itself is very complicated. Well-chosen buttons can however transform even a very simple style. Where a more tailored effect is required, buttons covered in the same fabric look best. You can have the buttons covered professionally–your local pattern department can usually arrange this–or you can do it yourself by using button forms, which can be bought in a set from haberdashery departments.

If you make up a garment which you intend to have dry-cleaned, it is obviously not especially necessary to pick a button which appears to be robust, since you will probably remove the buttons for cleaning anyway. A washable garment, of course, *must* have washable buttons–if this sounds like stating the obvious remember that buttons are still sold which dissolve like jelly in the washing solution. Some buttons are sold as boilable, which is obviously an advantage with those items which will go into the very hot wash.

Positioning the buttons

First close the garment in the way that it will be when worn. The centre front tack-markings should still be in position to guide you.

With the two layers of fabric pinned together, place a pin through each buttonhole (which of course has already been worked–see page 85), as shown in 293. Do not allow the pin to secure any part of the buttonhole, but only the fabric beneath. When each buttonhole has

been marked in this way, separate the two layers of fabric as if unbuttoning the garment, but taking care to leave the pins undisturbed. Using

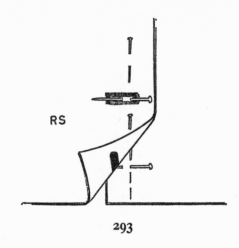

293

tailor's chalk, make a mark at the point where the pin enters the fabric. Place the centre of the button on the mark and sew it in position.

Sewing on the buttons

Use either heavy-duty thread or buttonhole twist. The thread should be double only if it seems necessary or you are in a great hurry because strong thread when double is too clumsy to work easily.

Most buttons which will actually be used (i.e. that are paired with buttonholes) should be sewn with a shank. The length of the shank depends on the thickness of the material you are sewing–a fine fabric needs a short shank, a heavy suiting or coating material needs quite a long shank. Only when the button is strictly for decoration should the shank be dispensed with.

To stitch a button with shank, first take several very small stitches on the right side of the garment to secure the thread at the point where the button is to be stitched. Then bring the thread through the button and place a heavy pin or a matchstick or an orange stick on top of the button (294). Take the thread back through the button and fabric, always including the pin or stick, until the button is securely

294

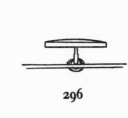

296

stitched. Bring the thread to the right side of the fabric, just under the button and leave it on the needle. Pull out the pin, or break the matchstick or orange stick to remove it, pull the button up to the top of the threads, and wind the thread –still with needle–around the stitches between the button and the fabric several times, to form a neat, firm shank. Take a stitch through the centre of the shank (295) then take the thread to the wrong side of the fabric and fasten off with small stitches.

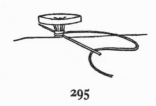

295

Should you knot the thread before you begin sewing? Personally I do not, because often you find the needle gets entangled with the knot and stitching becomes difficult.

METAL SHANK BUTTONS (296)
These can be a problem, because the metal seems to cause extra friction which quickly wears away the thread so that buttons fall off. A very strong thread is essential; if the garment is fine (when a strong thread would be too clumsy) you could use nylon thread, sewn double or even treble.

The point where the shank is stitched down may be bulky, and it is therefore preferable to have the stitches running at the same angle as the direction of the buttonhole–in other words

you should place the loop of the metal shank at right angles to the buttonhole.

Reinforced buttons

With coat buttons–and especially the top coat button–it is even more important to make sure that the button is securely fastened. I would therefore suggest that when you are making a coat you use two buttons for each fastening– the normal sized coat button chosen to suit the garment, and a small button of, say, $\frac{3}{8}$ in. in diameter. You also need a piece of fabric for each fastening, measuring about $\frac{5}{8}$ in. square; a matchstick, orange stick or very thick pin; some strong thread and a fairly long sewing needle.

Begin as for a shank button, placing the matchstick on top of the larger button (297).

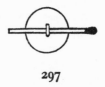

297

Take the needle through the button, fabric, small fabric square and the small button (298).

298

Stitch up again through the same layers. Continue stitching as before, and make the shank after you have removed the matchstick or pin. If you wish you can make a smaller shank on the wrong side too, between the small button and the fabric square. 299 shows the reverse side of the fabric, with the small button backed by the fabric square. If wished, a square of bonded interlining may be used instead, if you have some to spare.

299

One point should, perhaps, be stressed again. Just as it is essential to align the buttonholes exactly, it is imperative that buttons be stitched at the right intervals. If you are a little uncertain as to whether your positioning is exactly right, it is a good idea to stitch on each button with a few simple stitches, and try on the garment before proceeding further. Few things can be more irritating than sewing on a button firmly and with infinite care, only to find that it is just a fraction too high, or too far to the left or right.

HOOKS AND EYES

Hooks and eyes give a secure and unobtrusive fastening, and can be used in conjunction with buttons and buttonholes, or press fasteners, or at the top of a zip.

Many ready-made garments have hooks and eyes stitched on mechanically, and they are unfortunately very liable to detach themselves from the garment far more speedily than hand-stitched hooks and eyes. It is a good idea, therefore, to check a new garment to see whether there are any that should be re-sewn; and if so, you should remove each hook and eye in turn, marking its position carefully and pulling out all loose threads before re-stitching.

Choosing and positioning

Obviously the colour of the hooks and eyes (they can be either black or silver) will depend on the garment, and so will the weight which ranges from that of a fine lingerie fastener to a heavy-duty fastener suitable for bulky jackets and coats. If you are fastening the top or bottom of a garment where the edges overlap, you should use a straight metal eye (300), though of course you can make a hand-stitched eye if you prefer.

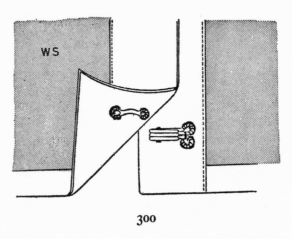

300

If you are making a garment where the edges just meet—for example an edge to edge jacket, or a zip-fastened dress—you should choose the round type eye (301), and allow the curve of the eye to overlap the edge very slightly. The hook should be set in from the other edge very slightly to correspond with the eye so that when the garment is fastened, its edges will just meet.

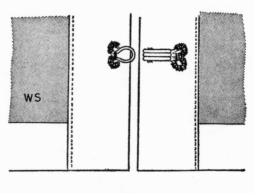

301

Correct stitching

Use a strong sewing thread or a buttonhole twist, depending on the weight of the fabric. Fine lingerie or baby garments may be best sewn with a synthetic thread, which is strong but light.

Once you learn to sew hooks and eyes correctly you will never be content with careless stitching methods. This is the way I learned to do it—it is not the only right way I am sure, but it works well for me.

The main stitch used to secure metal hooks and eyes is buttonhole stitch. In 302 you can

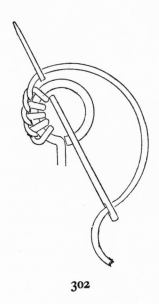

302

see an enlarged diagram showing how buttonhole stitching is taken round the metal ring, in a clockwise direction. When you have completed the circle, take two stitches over the end of the bar, then take the needle through to the other side of the bar, concealing the stitch between the top fabric and the facing material. Take two stitches over the other end of the metal bar, then buttonhole-stitch round the metal ring as before. Secure the thread on the wrong side of the fabric with a few neat stitches.

The metal hook is sewn on in a similar fashion. When you have determined the position of the hook, thread the needle and take a few tiny stitches at that point. Bring the needle out just beside the little hump in the centre of the hook. If the needle is fine enough I take it through this hump (303) and back through the fabric, just to fix the position of the hook before starting on the permanent stitching.

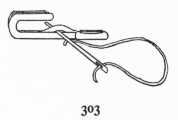

303

Now stitch the hook as shown in 304: Bring the needle out near the tip of the hook, past the hump and take three or four stitches to secure the hook end. Next, slide the needle between the two thicknesses of fabric, and bring it out in one of the rings of the hook, so that you can take a couple of stitches between the rings to secure the other end of the hook.

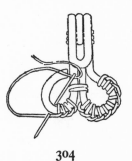

304

Now stitch the two rings as described for the metal eye (302), using a neat and careful buttonhole stitch and working steadily round each metal ring in turn.

Finally fasten off neatly on the wrong side of the fabric.

If you decide to make a hand-stitched eye, it

can slightly overlap the garment edge as in 305, in which case the hook would be inset slightly to give an invisible fastening. Alternatively the eye can be positioned as previously described in 300, and in this case you will not make such a pronounced loop – the strands of thread on which the buttonhole stitching is based should be drawn taut.

305

SNAP FASTENERS

Once you have determined the correct position for the fastener, it is a simple matter to

306

stitch it in place. First make a small knot in the end of the thread – one of the few occasions when a knot is permissible – and insert the needle through the hole in the lower half of the press fastener, then through the fabric at exactly the position you have marked (306). Now stitch it in place, with neat oversewing stitches at each hole position (307). Fasten off the thread on the wrong side of the fabric.

307

Take the top half of the fastener, press it into the lower half, and position the other side of the garment as it will be when stitched. Push the needle through the fabric to come out in the centre of the top half of the fastener (308); hold it in this position while you pull the two halves apart. Oversew each hole as before, checking that neither half has moved out of position.

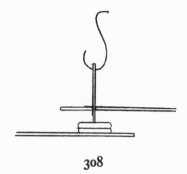

308

6

FABRICS, FIBRES AND FINISHES

It would be impossible to list all the names of dress fabrics now available, for the many families of man-made fibres have brought with them an Aladdin's cave of textiles, which grows more richly stocked with every month that passes by.

You can however get to know a little of what this vast subject of textile fibres is all about if you know the basic fibres from which all textiles are made. A textile may contain one, two or more different fibres, but as long as you know what they are, you can at least have an inkling of the performance of the fabric in question.

Even so, you will probably not be able to identify a fabric at a glance, every time. Often it is impossible even for highly expert textile technologists to do this without making several tests. However, on pages 142 to 173, I have taken each of the main types of fibre in turn, and also the main finishes, and tried to describe in a simplified way something of their properties, behaviour and requirements in home laundering, so that you can go to a fabrics department forearmed with at least a little knowledge of what is to be expected from the different types of fabric.

To a textile technologist these next pages will seem an almost sacrilegious over-simplification of an extremely complex subject. Whole books can be devoted to one fibre alone, or to one group of fibres. Each family of fibres can include a vast range of variations, so that two members of the same family may have very different characteristics and performances.

On the other hand to the home dressmaker who has no knowledge of, or interest in, chemistry, some of the details may seem over-technical, but nevertheless I thought it worth including them. In the sections headed 'Background', for instance, there is information on the derivation of fibres. I hope you will share my fascination at the strange beginnings of some fibres–beginnings which if you have never studied the subject before sound highly unlikely. Would you have thought, for instance, that nylon is derived from air and water and oil (petroleum), and Terylene from what we know as motorists' 'anti-freeze', together with other chemicals derived from the petroleum industry?

I hope that knowing a little about a fibre's origins will help you to differentiate one fibre from another and perhaps delve a little deeper into the subject's ramifications. If the basic facts given here encourage students to take the book to the science laboratory for further technical knowledge, then this chapter will have done its work.

HOME LAUNDERING

Because the subject of textiles is now so vast and confusing, it is more important than ever before that the home dressmaker should know how to treat the fabrics with which she is working.

Women in pre-war days had no difficulty in knowing how to deal with the fabrics they could buy–everyone knew how to wash and care for cotton, wool and linen, and even about the deference due to silk. A housewife could pride herself on her expertise in washing and starching and ironing, although when 'artificial silk' came along, it did cause a few problems.

However with the advent of man-made fibres, and in their wake, specially-finished fabrics, the situation changed so completely that even the professional launderer or dry-cleaner could not always select the right treatment by instinct alone. In fact, even the industries most closely concerned with textiles and their making up into garments were far from agreed on correct washing methods, ironing temperatures and dry-cleaning processes. Most garment manufacturers, faced with a host of new man-made fibres, played safe whenever they did label a garment, by marking it, say, 'Dry-clean only' (even when the fibre was an eminently washable one) or 'Wash by hand in lukewarm suds'. A legacy of this attitude remains today, especially in the less forward-thinking companies and stores. And of course many housewives, because of the early 'consumer education' they were given, much of it misguided as we have since seen, still stick to their 'Wash-by-hand' mentality, and find it extremely difficult to accept a newer, more closely researched point of view.

At the beginning of the 1960's, when it became obvious how much confusion and mis-information existed, attempts were made to rationalise the problem. A significant stage was reached when a document called the Washing Temperature Agreement was published by a newly-formed British organisation called the Home Laundering Consultative Committee—significant because the agreement was drawn up not by just one group of industries but four different groups, all with a deep interest in the home-washing of textile articles.

The Molony Report brought more thought to bear on the subject, and then the British Standards Institution published in 1964 the BS: 2747 Care Labelling Code, which set down many of the agreed findings of HLCC on water temperatures, ironing temperatures and general washing and dry-cleaning terminology.

Nowadays there is an impressive amount of agreement and co-operation among all leading British companies concerned with the production of fibres, making-up and retail-selling of gar-

ments, manufacturing of washing machines and marketing of washing powders. The HLCC in Britain (now retitled Home Laundering Consultative Council instead of Committee) have gone on from strength to strength; and while in future years they may announce many more advances in the field of care labelling, their achievements even up to the time of writing are considerable. They have now agreed on a set of eight washing processes, each process distinguished by its own symbol: a large number set in a stylised washtub. These processes are printed on millions of garment labels, on washing machine instructions, and on almost all washing product packs. They tell housewives the correct method of hand- or machine-washing the labelled article; what the water temperature should be, where she should wring or spin dry or neither, and whether any special factors are involved, such as drying the garment flat or not using bleach. The eight processes are given on the facing page.

Three types of machine wash are referred to: maximum, medium and minimum. They apply to the duration of the wash which will depend on the type of washing machine you use.

A pulsator machine is likely to have a more vigorous washing action, so a maximum wash may take 5 minutes (as normally recommended for white cottons); a medium wash 2 minutes and a minimum wash 1 minute (as normally specified for wool).

An agitator machine, on the other hand, may take longer to complete a wash, so that a maximum wash may take 12 minutes (the usual recommended time for cottons in such a machine); a medium wash 6 minutes and a minimum wash 3 minutes (again, as normally allowed for wool in such a machine).

Most washing machine literature now gives an interpretation of these 'washtub' labels, and existing owners need only write to the manufacturer of their own machine for a full explanation of the HLCC washing processes as they apply to the machine in question.

Even launderette users need not be excluded from the labelling scheme, as instruction literature has been produced for them too.

White cotton and linen articles without special finishes

	MACHINE	HAND WASH
1	Very hot maximum wash (85°C) to boil	Hand-hot (48°C) or boil
	spin or wring	

Cotton, linens or rayons without special finishes where colours are fast at 60°C, 140°F (this is what we normally call the colour-fast wash)

	MACHINE	HAND WASH
2	Hot maximum wash (60°C)	Hand-hot (48°C)
	spin or wring	

White nylon

	MACHINE	HAND WASH
3	Hot medium wash (60°C)	Hand-hot (48°C)
	Cold rinse. Short spin or drip-dry	

Coloured nylon; Terylene; Terlenka; cottons and rayons with special finishes (the latter are the materials often labelled 'drip-dry' or 'minimum iron' or 'non-iron' or 'easy-care'); acrylic/cotton mixtures

	MACHINE	HAND WASH
4	Hand-hot medium wash (48°C)	Hand-hot (48°C)
	Cold rinse. Short spin or drip-dry	

Cotton, linen or rayon where colours are fast at 40°C, 104°F but not at 60°C, 140°F (you should be able to establish this when you buy the fabric)

	MACHINE	HAND WASH
5	Warm medium wash (40°C)	Warm (40°C)
	spin or wring	

Acrilan, Courtelle and Orlon; acetate and Tricel, including mixtures with wool; Terylene / wool blends

	MACHINE	HAND WASH
6	Warm minimum wash (40°C)	Warm (40°C)
	Cold rinse. Short spin. Do not wring	

Wool, including blankets, and wool mixtures with cotton or rayon

	MACHINE	HAND WASH
7	Warm minimum wash (40°C)	Warm water (40°C) Do not rub
	Spin. Do not hand wring	

Washable pleated garments containing Acrilan, Courtelle, Orlon, nylon, Terylene, Terlenka or Tricel; glass fibre

	HAND WASH ONLY
8	WARM (40°C)
	Warm rinse, Hand-hot final rinse, Drip dry

Note: For temperature conversion see page 141.

Labelling and the home dressmaker

There are a few stores where a care label is supplied with every fabric length sold. There are also a few fabrics which are always supplied with a care label. At the moment, however, such pioneers are unfortunately in the minority.

However, any fabric which you buy *should* be labelled with the fibre content, at least. It may be on a swing label attached to the bolt of fabric, or lettered along the selvedge edges. The store should, of course, know the appropriate care advice for the fabrics they sell and should have it available. If this is not so, and the assistant is unhelpful, ask to see the buyer. Be persistent, and if you meet with indifference or opposition take your custom elsewhere. Choose the right moment however–such requests on a Saturday morning or at sales time will not make you popular.

Once you have the care advice, you can in some cases make your own care label, as long as you bear certain points in mind. I have just set out the eight washing processes, and given examples of how they apply. Look down the list and establish which category you think your fabric falls into, and make a note of the appropriate process number. You can then make your own care label in this way. Pencil on to a piece of tape, or on to an inside seam in the actual garment, the appropriate process number, quite small. Pencil round it the simple little washtub symbol. Now, using a length of bright cotton thread or embroidery silk, sew along the pencil lines with a neat backstitch (see page 177) or fine chain stitch (see page 178). It need not be elaborate—just clear and firm. After that you need never worry about which washing method to use, for almost all detergent packs will also carry the little number-in-a-washtub for reference.

There is one point about making your own wash care label that you must bear in mind—and that is that the process number only tells you what is *normally* suitable for the fibre: it may not be suitable for the actual made-up garment. Trimmings, linings, interlinings, sewing thread and method of making-up could well convert a washable fabric into a 'dry-clean only' garment.

Therefore whenever you make up an easy-care fabric into what you want to be an easy-care garment, be sure you choose equally washable trimmings, linings and interlinings, suitable sewing thread, and that you finish seams strongly enough to withstand regular tubbing.

Let me give two examples. Tricel is a wonderfully washable fabric which when made up will normally ensure a superbly washable garment. But suppose you want to make an evening dress which is heavily boned, lined and interlined, and has a great deal of intricate decoration—sequins perhaps, or tiny pearls. It is obvious that you would then have to have the dress dry-cleaned. Similarly if you make a plain white cotton pillowcase, you would wash it as if it were labelled with a process 1 symbol. But should you decide to trim the pillowcase with, say, a decorative ribbon-insertion, it would

clearly be foolish to give it a process 1 wash, more especially if the ribbon were coloured.

However if you buy a fully-washable fabric, and use only fully-washable extra materials, and make up the garment with strong, well-finished seams, there is no reason why you should not include it in with the machine load.

A NOTE ABOUT MAN-MADE FIBRES

The production of a man-made fibre is extremely complex and millions of pounds' worth of machinery and factory space are involved, However, the manufacturing processes for all man-made fibres have much in common, whether the fibre is a purely synthetic one derived from mineral sources, or one which is chemically regenerated from natural raw materials, or produced by chemical treatment of cellulose.

The raw materials are treated chemically, and in some cases melted by heating to form a viscous liquid, which is then extruded, or thrust out, through very fine holes in a nozzle called a spinnaret. (There are three methods of extrusion, wet, dry and melt.) The threads, or filaments, which emerge are then solidified in various ways.

The colour may be added to the yarn either by dyeing the spinning solution, so that the fine filaments which are extruded are already the required colour (this is called spun-dyed yarn) or the yarn may emerge as pure white filaments and be dyed after extrusion. The spun-dyed fibre normally has a greater degree of colour fastness.

The extrusion process can be compared with the production of silk filament by the silkworm, but behind the fine filaments which emerge there is not a simple silkworm producing the fine filaments, but a complex and vastly expensive production plant.

Once the filament has been produced it must be made into yarn and then into fabric. Just as the silkworm provides the raw material for silk, the flax plant the raw material for linen, and the cotton boll the raw material for cotton, so the various man-made fibres are at this stage merely raw materials for the textile industry, and

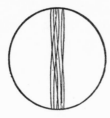

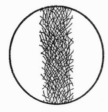

Top: Continuous filament yarn.
Bottom: Staple fibre.

they require just the same sort of machinery as the natural fibres for making them into yarns and fabrics.

First the filaments are drawn and twisted together lightly to form what is called *continuous filament* yarn. Such yarns are used for weaving or knitting into smooth-surfaced fabrics. Some filament yarns may undergo additional processes such as crimping or bulking.

Many man-made fibres are also produced in *spun* or *staple* form. This means that continuous filament yarns are collected together into a rope or tow and cut into short 'staple' lengths, and the result is a soft fibrous mass known as 'staple fibre'. These fibres are then combed, drawn and spun into yarn, known as staple yarn. In this sense they are similar to natural fibres, which are also a collection of short staple lengths spun together.

Staple fibres are generally used in fabrics which are warm to the touch and have fullness

of handle, such as those used for knitted garments, sports shirts, blankets and soft furnishings.

Tow may have industrial uses but is of no consequence at consumer level.

Filament and staple yarns can be controlled at certain stages of manufacture to meet various requirements of the textile industry. They can, for example, be manufactured in any degree of fineness, in any length of staple, and be either lustrous or dull. They can also be spun-dyed, i.e. manufactured as a coloured filament or staple by the dyeing of the spinning solution. This gives a fibre with a very high degree of colour fastness.

Mixtures and blends

The tables on the following pages give details of the individual fibres, both natural and man-made. Remember, however, that these fibres can appear in varying proportions in mixtures or blends with other natural or man-made fibres, and the final properties of the fabric may well be affected by the marriage.

When you are washing a fabric which is a blend or a mixture (and where no care label is provided), always wash according to the fibre requiring the milder treatment, unless I indicate otherwise under 'Home Laundering'.

Mixtures and blends—in case you are wondering what the difference is—are defined by the British Man-Made Fibres Federation as follows:

MIXTURE indicates that a fabric is constructed of two or more different yarns during weaving or knitting, for example a woven fabric with a nylon warp and a rayon or cotton weft.

BLEND means that a fabric is woven or knitted from blended *yarn*, for example a yarn that is spun from a blend of rayon staple fibre and wool.

Mixtures and blends are important developments in the man-made fibre industry. They open up a vast new field of fabric design and weave—particularly in fashion fabrics—and enable the manufacturers to produce a far greater variety of textures and colour effects than has ever been possible before.

Moreover, it has now been established that

this mixing and blending can *improve* the properties of fabrics–such as their strength, handle, drape, durability and stability, particularly in washing–and can also produce fabrics with a far wider *range* of properties than similar fabrics made from one fibre, natural or man-made. Man-made fibres cannot make a poorly constructed fabric good but they can, without doubt, make a good fabric better when used properly.

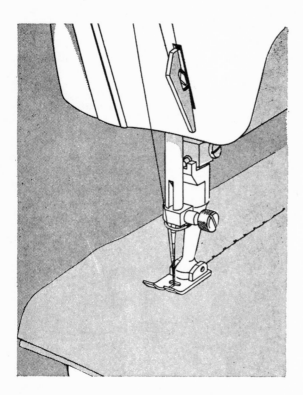

THE MODERN STRETCH FABRICS

The modern stretch fabrics such as Helanca and Crimplene as used for ski-pants and sportswear need a true stretch stitch if seams are to be perfect. A true stretch stitch is normally only available on fully-automatic machines.

Left: The seam is stitched using the setting for stretch stitch advised by the machine manufacturer.

Below: The result is a neat seam combining elasticity with extreme strength.

PICTURES BY COURTESY OF BERNINA SEWING MACHINES

A NOTE ABOUT THE TABLES
TO FOLLOW

When studying the tables of fibres and finishes, the following points should be borne in mind throughout:

1. The home laundering advice applies to British-produced man-made fibres only, as fibres deriving from other countries will not necessarily have identical characteristics. 'Chief properties' and 'Uses' may also differ somewhat for fibres manufactured elsewhere.

2. For a fuller explanation of the washing-process symbols, see the list on page 137.

3. The iron settings mentioned under 'Home laundering–ironing' are those recommended by the Home Laundering Consultative Council, and appear only on the newer irons. If you have an iron without these numbered settings, follow the temperature *descriptions* (cool, warm, medium hot or hot) which are given.

4. Fabrics containing man-made fibres are especially easy to wash and dry, and they should be washed frequently. With any fibre, once dirt or stains become ingrained the marks will be extremely difficult to remove.

5. Fabrics containing man-made fibres should always be washed in clean suds, and white articles should be washed separately from coloured. If this is not done, white fabrics may be permanently discoloured by the transfer of dye or soiling from the other articles. It is particularly important not to wash coloured cottons and white nylon in the same load.

	85° C = 185° F
TEMPERATURE	60° C = 140° F
CONVERSIONS	48° C = 118° F
	40° C = 104° F

BACKGROUND

The cotton plant grows in countries where the climate is humid and sub-tropical: in parts of the USA, Russia, China, India, Egypt and the Sudan, South America, and Turkey for instance. The type of cotton varies with the area in which it grows. The cotton flower is white-to-yellow, and after it has fallen, the green seed pod or boll which is left swells in size as the fibres on the seeds develop. Finally the boll bursts to reveal a mass of fluffy fibres, rather like a thick powder-puff. Then the cotton is picked and the fibres are carefully separated from the seeds by a process called ginning. (The seeds are processed to yield cotton-seed oil, used in the manufacture of certain fats and soaps.)

The cotton is imported into Britain in bales, and cleaned, carded and sometimes combed. Then it is drawn out, twisted and spun into yarn. The yarn is wound on to bobbins ready for weaving or knitting into fabric. Bleaching and dyeing (if not already done at the yarn stage) then follow. Many cottons are given special finishes (see page 172), but the first and most widely used process is mercerisation.

FABRICS

Fabrics which may be made from cotton include: batiste, calico, cambric, chintz, corduroy, denim, dimity, drill, flannelette, gaberdine, gingham, lace, lawn, muslin, nun's veiling, organdie, pique, plisse, poplin, repp, sailcloth, sateen, satin, seersucker, sheeting, terry towelling, tulle, velvet, velveteen, voile, winceyette.

USES

Cotton fabrics, both in knitted and in woven form, are used for virtually all types of clothing for men, women and children. It is also used extensively for household purposes, including towelling, curtaining, upholstery, bedding, tablecloths and glass cloths.

CHIEF PROPERTIES

Appearance: Cotton fabrics can take on a vast range of forms, depending on the processing of the yarn and the type of weave. Cotton can be as sheer as gossamer or thick and chunky; it can be smooth as satin or distinctively rough-textured; it may be glazed or matt, and any degree of stiffness or softness is obtained.

Wearing qualities: Strong even when in a fine fabric, and even stronger when wet.

Reaction to chemicals: Strong acids applied hot in a dilute form, or acids in a concentrated cold form, cause disintegration of the fibre. Weak acids have no effect if cold, but they do cause some weakening of the fibres when heated. Weak alkalis have little or no effect on the fibre, although the controlled use of alkalis in strong solution is used as a means of swelling and adding lustre to cotton, thus enhancing its natural properties. This process is known as mercerising.

Resilience: Fair to good, depending of course on the fabric, weave and finish.

Reaction to moisture: An outstanding property of cotton is its excellent absorbency in many of its forms, which makes it ideal for terry towelling, sheeting and clothing.

Other points: Unsuitable conditions, such as a warm and humid atmosphere, may encourage attack by mildew, to which cotton is susceptible. Rot-proofing treatments may be applied where fabrics will be subjected to these conditions. Cotton fabrics do not deteriorate to any great extent with age, but if subjected to prolonged exposure to sunlight or excessive heat, there is a tendency for white fabrics to acquire a yellowish tinge, and the tensile strength will be affected.

ELECTROSTATIC PROPERTIES
Virtually non-static.

INSULATION VALUE
Varies from low to quite good, depending on the weave and weight of cloth. Usually an excellent hot-weather fibre.

IDENTIFICATION
See pages 174–5 for burning test and chemical test.

MICROSCOPIC VIEW
The usual cross-section is a collapsed circular shape with a central void or canal. The longitudinal appearance is similar to a ribbon with frequent twists along its length.

SEWING NOTES
Many types of cotton fabric have great firmness of weave and are very easy to sew, non-fraying and not subject to slipping while being cut out and made up. Some specially-finished cottons have, indeed, such dimensional stability that it is difficult to ease or mould them satisfactorily (see comments under Special Finishes, page 172). Cotton lace, on the other hand, may need to be backed with another fabric—say nylon net—to hold the shape of the garment.

Use mercerised cotton thread for sewing.

HOME LAUNDERING
Washing: Unless otherwise stated on the care label, wash as follows:

WHITE COTTONS WITHOUT SPECIAL FINISHES:

FAST-COLOURED COTTONS WITHOUT SPECIAL FINISHES:

COLOURED COTTONS WITHOUT SPECIAL FINISHES WHERE COLOURS ARE FAST AT 40°C, 104°F, BUT NOT AT 60°C, 140°F (this should be indicated by the manufacturer):

SPECIALLY-FINISHED COTTONS:
See page 172.

Ironing: Iron when slightly damp. Steam-iron, or if dry-ironing use a HOT iron, setting 4, with a damp pressing cloth if necessary. A VERY HOT iron, setting 5, is sometimes used for very thick cottons.
Home dyeing: Takes home dyes extremely well. Follow dye instructions to the letter.

BACKGROUND

The flax plant, from which linen is produced, grows in most temperate climates. The flax used for the familiar Irish and Scottish linen comes mainly from Belgium, France and Holland, and some from Russia. The flax fibre comes from the stem of the plant after the bark and pith have been removed. When growing, the flax looks like a cornfield, but it has blue or white flowers. When the flowers fade and the seeds are fully ripe, the flax is harvested. The stalks are processed (dried, cleaned, soaked and fermented) until the fibres are freed. The fibres are then prepared and spun into yarn. The seeds yield linseed oil, which has many industrial uses.

Flax is a generic name given to the straw which grows in the field. It also defines the grey fibre extracted from the straw, and normally describes all stages of manufacture up to yarn. When the yarn is woven into cloth it is described as linen. When the grey flax yarn is chemically processed, as in bleaching or mercerising, it is often referred to as linen yarn. When converted to a thread it is known as linen thread.

Under a new process, the Kirkpatrick process, the purification, bleaching and dyeing are carried out at the fibre stage, and the resultant sliver, top or staple is best described as linen fibre. This purified and bleached linen fibre has been given the name Linron.

The Linron concept resulted directly from research and development carried out by Kirkpatrick of Ballyclare in a much wider context, involving the chemical modification of cellulosic fibres to impart easy-care properties.

FABRICS

By variations in the manner of weaving, it is possible to produce many different types of linen. Each has its own qualities which make it best suited to certain types of goods. There are plain weaves (in all weights), huckaback weaves, twill weaves, drills and jacquard weaves for example. For suits and dresses heavier linens are used—they are fully shrunk and given a crease-resist finish.

Some linen fabrics may contain a proportion of resilient man-made fibres or be given special easy-care treatments (see page 172).

USES

Plain weaves are used for bed-linen, table-linen, tea towels and glass cloths, dress linens, suitings, heavy curtaining and embroidery fabrics. Huckaback weaves are used for hand towels and guest towels. Twill weaves are used for kitchen cloths. Linen drill is a weave used in some types of suiting, particularly men's suitings. Jacquard weave is used for damask tablecloths and napkins.

Linron has opened up a new field of uses – it is used alone and in blends, such as Linron and cotton for bedlinen, and Linron and Courtelle in knitwear.

CHIEF PROPERTIES

Appearance: Linen is easily recognised by its characteristic slightly uneven texture, giving surface interest. It is naturally crisp and lustrous, and feels cool and smooth to the touch. Linron enables softer, bulkier yarns to be produced in greater variety than hitherto possible.

Wearing qualities: Hardwearing–the strongest of all natural fibres, and in fact one which is 20 per cent stronger still when wet.

Reaction to chemicals: Strong acids cause the fibre to disintegrate when in hot dilute solutions or in cold concentrated form. Strong alkalis cause swelling and add lustre to the fibre, so that certain linen finishes are produced by the controlled use of strong alkalis. Weak alkalis have little or no effect on the flax fibre.

Resilience: Fair, or very good when specially-finished.

Reaction to moisture: Fairly absorbent.

ELECTROSTATIC PROPERTIES
No static problem.

INSULATION VALUE
Low, therefore ideal as a hot-weather fabric.

IDENTIFICATION
See pages 174–5 for burning test and chemical test.

MICROSCOPIC VIEW
In cross-section flax fibres have a thick-walled, many-sided structure with a minute central canal. In longitudinal section the fibre is slightly distended at irregular intervals, with faint transverse markings at these points.

SEWING NOTES
Linen fabrics are inclined to fray during sewing, and therefore the finishing of raw edges becomes especially important. See the section of seam finishes on page 77.

Because of the high tear strength of the flax fibre, do not attempt to tear across the width to straighten the fabric–always cut it.

Use mercerised sewing cotton. Remember to buy the right thread thickness–a No. 40 mercerised thread is the one most generally used, being suitable for sewing fine to heavy fabrics.

If using one of the bonded interlinings, the iron-on grade is very suitable for interfacing pocket flaps, cuffs and so on. In ordinary bonded interlinings, the choice of grade depends on the weight of the linen you are making up.

HOME LAUNDERING
Washing: Unless the printed label advises differently, wash as follows:

WHITE LINENS WITHOUT SPECIAL FINISHES (e.g. white bed-linen and table-linen):

FAST-COLOURED LINENS WITHOUT SPECIAL FINISHES (e.g. fast-coloured bed-linen and table-linen):

COLOURED LINENS WITHOUT SPECIAL FINISHES WHERE COLOURS ARE FAST AT 40°C, 104°F, BUT NOT AT 60°C, 140°F (the label on the garment or length of cloth should indicate this):

Ironing: Iron when damp. Steam-iron, or if dry-ironing use a HOT iron, setting 4, with a damp pressing cloth if necessary. A VERY HOT iron, setting 5, is sometimes used for very thick linens.

Home dyeing: Takes home dyes well, though linen needs a stronger dye solution than cotton.

BACKGROUND

Silkworms are cultivated in China (where they have been used for silk for over four thousand years), in India, Japan and the USSR, and to a much smaller extent in France and Italy. The cultivated silkworm feeds on the leaves of the white mulberry tree, and the wild silkworm off mountain oak.

The silkworm, after it has hatched from the egg, eats and grows steadily until it is about three inches long, when it spins itself a cocoon. It does this by excreting a fluid from holes each side of its head. The two silk filaments pass out as a double thread cemented together with a gum-like substance, known as sericin, which the silkworm also produces. There may be over $2\frac{1}{4}$ miles of double thread in one cocoon. The cocoon hardens, and the silkworm becomes a chrysalis and then emerges as a moth. But before it can emerge (which it does by moistening the cocoon to soften the silk) the silk is wound off the cocoon after the chrysalis has been destroyed by steam or other heat treatment.

FABRICS

Particular types of silk are indicated by such names as antung, barathea, brocade, chiffon, douppion, crêpe, faille, foulard, georgette, jersey, lace, marquisette, moire, net, organza, pongee, satin, shantung, surah, taffeta, tulle, tussore, velvet.

Pure dye silk indicates a fabric with no weighting or dressing except for any metallic weighting used in the dye.

All silk indicates that although there is a certain amount of weighting added to give the material fullness, the fabric is made from pure silk.

Nett silk is the continuous filament yarn made from the best part of the cocoon.

Spun silk is made from the slightly less high-grade short fibres which are re-spun.

Tussah is wild silk (i.e. produced from wild silkworms). From this come tussore, shantung and douppion, which have a rough, uneven surface.

Fabric finishes

Some silks are sized for stiffness (the finish can be replaced during dry-cleaning); some silks are durably finished to give spot-, stain- and perspiration-resistance, and/or crease resistance.

USES

Day and evening dresses, suits, scarves, pyjamas and summer dressing gowns, lingerie, baby gowns, and ties. Also fabrics for curtaining and upholstery.

CHIEF PROPERTIES

Appearance: A lustrous sheer fibre with natural sheen and excellent draping qualities. A silk fabric can vary from lightweight chiffon or organza to heavy brocade or tweed.

Wearing qualities: Great strength in relation to fibre fineness.

Reaction to chemicals: Cold concentrated acids will cause silk fibres to dissolve, and hot concentrated solutions of alkalis will cause decomposition. Weak acids and weak alkalis have little or no effect. Silk is degraded by chlorine bleach.

Resilience: Outstandingly resilient in most weaves, with natural crease-shedding properties and elasticity. Some silk fabrics also have a property known as 'scroop'–a distinctive crisp, crunching sound when the fabric is crushed in the hand.

Reaction to moisture: Fairly absorbent.

ELECTROSTATIC PROPERTIES
Slight tendency to static.

INSULATION VALUE
Excellent. Silk is cool in summer and warm in winter.

IDENTIFICATION
See pages 174–5 for burning test and chemical test.

MICROSCOPIC VIEW
In cross-section silk fibres appear as triangles with rounded corners, with the exception of wild silk, where the cross-section view is much more wedge-shaped. In longitudinal view the fibre appears as a continuous filament–in wild silk the filament is flatter and has twists at intervals along its length.

SEWING NOTES
Some silks–for example silk chiffon–can be so slippery that keeping the length on the table can be quite a problem. Covering the table with an old sheet or tablecloth sometimes provides the answer, but if the table is not really large enough try to cut out on the floor. Before positioning the pattern pieces, press the silk (WARM iron, setting 2), then pin the selvedges together (at right angles to the selvedge) to prevent slipping. Tack the pinned edges together.

Use very fine steel pins for silk, and try to keep all pinning within the seam allowances, so that the pin marks will not show. Change the sewing machine needle for a fine one. If the silk is very sheer, tack tissue paper strips along the seamlines, before machine-stitching. Or the fabric may need mounting on tissue paper for sewing–the paper is left there until the garment is complete, and then removed.

Adjust the pressure of the sewing machine if necessary, and check the tension. Sew silk always with silk thread. Practise sewing oddments of the material before starting on the garment. Tack and try the garment on before you machine-stitch, because if you unpick a line of stitching the needle marks may show.

For silks which have a nap or sheen, all the pattern pieces must be placed in the same direction.

Obviously you should handle the fabric as little as possible when making up, especially the pile fabrics like silk velvet.

HOME LAUNDERING
Washing: Though many silks must be dry-cleaned because of the special treatments given to them, some silk garments are washable by hand. Do not, however, wash silk fabrics in a washing machine. It is important to test silks for colour fastness before washing. If the manufacturer's label states that the garment is washable, treat as below:

| Do not machine-wash | Hand wash only Warm wash (40°C, 104°F) Do not rub |

When washing, never use household bleach (chlorine bleach), as it destroys silk. In wear, protect silks from perspiration, which will harm the fabric unless it has been specially-finished.

Ironing: Fabrics with 'slubs' in the weave (shantung, douppion, tussore), and crêpes, should be ironed when they are quite dry; other silks should be ironed when they are slightly and evenly damp. Press first on the wrong side, then finish lightly on the right side. Use a WARM iron, setting 2. Silk velvets should be pressed on a velvet board, using a steam iron.

Home dyeing: Silk may be dyed with certain types of home dye, but read the instructions carefully before going ahead. Usually only pastel shades may be obtained.

BACKGROUND

All over the world, in countries including Britain, Australia, New Zealand, Canada, South Africa, the continent of Europe, Japan, Argentina, Uruguay, Chile and Peru, sheep are bred to provide wool. The three main types of wool fibre produced are merino, crossbred and carpet. Some types are best for knitwear, some are best for woollen cloths, and some for carpet-making.

After the sheep have been sheared, the wool is sorted and then washed or scoured (imported wools are often not scoured until they reach this country). Certain scouring processes produce important by-products, such as lanolin. Many further processes follow before the fibres are actually spun into yarn, and bleaching and dyeing of the wool may take place before or after spinning.

Wool yarns are spun on either the woollen or worsted system, and wool yarns may be classified as 'woollen' or 'worsted' according to the methods used in the making of the yarn.

In the worsted yarns the long staple fibres are combed by special processes so that they lie in only one direction, and short fibres are removed. In woollen yarns, however, short fibres lie in all directions and produce a fluffier effect. Worsted yarns, which generally go into making smooth, sleek, tightly-woven cloths, are always made from combed pure new wool (new and unused wool). Woollen yarns may be made from pure new wool only, or from mixtures of pure new wool and waste wool (either processed wool rags or else spinning waste and noil – the short fibres left after the yarns have been combed in the worsted process).

Special finishes

Some special finishes are obtained by the different weaving or processing – for example by fulling, felting, napping or shearing. Some treatments are chemical, such as those for shrink-resistance, moth-proofing, durable pleating (the latter process includes heat treatment as well as chemical treatment). There are now wool cloths, knitted garments, blankets and also some knitting wools which are sold as machine-washable.

FABRICS

Many types of wool fabrics are available, including: barathea, bedford cord, bouclé, broadcloth, cavalry twill, crêpe, flannel, wool gaberdine, wool georgette, jersey, serge, tweed, velour and whipcord.

USES

Virtually all types of clothing for men, women and children, particularly where warmth and comfort are needed in a garment.

CHIEF PROPERTIES

Appearance: Wool has an unmistakable softness of handle and feel.

Wearing qualities: Fairly strong.

Reaction to chemicals: Sensitive to alkaline solutions and household bleach. Never bleach woollens.

Domestic (sodium hypochlorite) bleach decomposes all animal fibres and sets up a yellow discoloration. (This, paradoxically, is in spite of the fact that the textile industry sometimes uses hypochlorite bleach under controlled conditions to modify the 'scales' during one of the processes to create shrink-resist wools.)

Resilience: Outstanding – sheds wrinkles easily in most cases and possesses great elasticity.

Reaction to moisture: Wool fibre is capable of absorbing up to approximately 30 per cent of its own weight of water without appearing damp, and for this reason it is said to be hygroscopic.

Other points: Non-flammable – does not ignite and does not support combustion. Wool shows very little deterioration when stored properly, but exposure to sunlight causes it to develop a harsh feel and to lose tensile strength. It has good resistance to mildew, but is attacked by moth grubs, especially where food has been splashed on garments and allowed to dry in. Unless it has been effectively treated during manufacture, wool may felt or shrink if carelessly laundered. Felting is, of course, a valuable characteristic of wool in some forms of manufacture – in milled cloths and in the making of felts and hat-felts for example.

ELECTROSTATIC PROPERTIES
Good electrostatic 'bleed-off' due to moisture-absorption properties.

INSULATION VALUE
Extremely good, in fact unparalleled by any other fibre.

IDENTIFICATION
See pages 174-5 for burning test and chemical test.

MICROSCOPIC VIEW
In cross-section the fibres are irregular rounds or ovals of slightly differing thicknesses. In longitudinal view the external cells appear as thin horny plates of irregular shape; the 'scales' are side by side and overlapping each other, rather like roof tiles.

SEWING NOTES
Wool fabrics are usually very pleasant to work with, very malleable and they can be eased and moulded by shrink-pressing to give an outstandingly smooth line and fit. When pressing, use a tailor's mitt or tailor's ham for curves, and make use of a seam roll or strips of cardboard when pressing seam allowances open, to avoid marking the garment.

Most wool fabrics are pre-shrunk, but if in doubt, test as described on page 59.

Lining improves any garment, and loose weaves of wool benefit particularly if they are lined.

For heavier or very open weaves of wool, a bonded fibre interlining, in addition, is recommended–the iron-on variety will give stability to a loosely woven cloth. Or you can interline with unbleached calico.

Loosely-woven wools are inclined to fray, and the edges may need finishing with a zigzag stitch or hand oversewing. All curves and bias seams should be reinforced with a line of stitching, or in some cases tape stitched in with the seams may be preferable. Jersey is particularly prone to pulling out of shape.

If, while making up a wool fabric, it is necessary to press the work frequently, it may develop a flat, overpressed look. To freshen the appearance, hang the garment in a humid atmosphere, for example in the bathroom.

HOME LAUNDERING
Washing: Some wool cloths and many wool garments are now labelled as machine-washable and may bear the following label:

WOOL/RAYON AND WOOL/COTTON MIXTURES: PROCESS 7 as above.

Some wool fabrics are washable but not machine-washable.

Some wool fabrics cannot be laundered at home, and must be dry-cleaned only. NEVER BLEACH WOOL. **Note:** The International Wool Secretariat recommend that where domestic water is hard, a mild detergent is probably preferable to a soap product, for woollens.

Use of a fabric softener in the final rinse is beneficial.

Ironing: Press when very slightly damp. Steam-press, or with a dry-iron use a WARM iron, setting 2, with a damp pressing cloth. Always *press* wool, do not slide the iron along but lift and replace.

Home dyeing: Wool may be home-dyed in certain circumstances. Read the directions carefully, and ensure that you have the right type of dye.

BACKGROUND

Acetate, a regenerated fibre, was the second man-made fibre to be produced in this country on a commercial scale. Cellulose, obtained from wood pulp, is the main source of the basic material used. By a process of reacting the purified cellulose with acetic anhydride in the presence of acetic acid, and using a catalyst such as sulphuric acid, the spinning gel is prepared. Slight variations in formulae give different chemical properties to the fibre.

FIBRE TYPES

Celafibre (British Celanese Ltd.–Courtaulds)
Dicel British Celanese Ltd.–Courtaulds)
Lansil (Lansil Ltd.)

ALSO PROCESSED YARNS SUCH AS:
Dicel KN; Lancola.

SOME OVERSEAS TRADEMARKS

Albene	Italy
Estron	USA
Minalon	Japan
Rhodia	Brazil, France, Germany and Italy
Silene	Italy

USES

Acetates are used for a wide range of fabrics for men's, women's and children's wear. Used particularly for woven dress fabrics such as satins, taffetas, brocades and moires, also in knitted dresses and underwear. Widely used for furnishing fabrics and ribbons.

The most important textile outlet is for women's wear linings; most important non-textile outlet – for cigarette filter tips.

Also used widely in blends for a variety of fabrics, and for hand-knitting yarn and wadding.

CHIEF PROPERTIES

Appearance: Rich, attractive appearance, in dull or bright forms; drapes well; resembles silk more closely than any other fibre.

Wearing qualities: Gives good wear if properly cared for.

Reaction to chemicals: Dissolves readily in acetone, concentrated formic acid and glacial acetic acid.

Resilience: Good natural recovery from creasing.

Reaction to moisture: Absorbent.

ELECTROSTATIC PROPERTIES
Inherently non-static, therefore ideal as a lining fabric, especially for man-made fibres which have a tendency to cling.

INSULATION VALUE
Good—acetate is used in certain forms for heat and sound insulation.

IDENTIFICATION
See pages 174–5 for burning test and chemical test.

MICROSCOPIC VIEW
When viewed under the microscope, acetate fibres in cross-section look something like a clover-leaf. The dull types of fibre show small dark particles of de-lustrant, while the lustrous kinds appear transparent. In longitudinal view the fibres appear ridged along their length.

SEWING NOTES
As with any man-made fibre, if you intend the garment to be washable, choose trimmings which are equally washable. Fully-shrunk or non-shrink trimmings must be used. This applies to bindings, tapes and ribbons as well as contrast fabrics, linings and interlinings. Every material used must be compatible with the fabric, and sufficiently colour-fast to withstand process 6 washing (see Home Laundering opposite).

If you intend to machine-wash the garment, washable trimmings and very careful seam-finishing become even more important.

Cut the fabric with very sharp dressmaking shears; use fine steel pins, and pin into the seam allowances as much as possible to avoid marking the main part of the article. Curved and bias seams may be stay-stitched if the weave is loose.

When you sew, use nylon or Terylene sewing thread, check the machine tension and pressure.

If using a bonded interlining, choose the correct grade for lightweight fabric. An iron-on interlining may be used (in small areas) unless the fabric is pure white.

During pressing, be careful to avoid pressure marks from the iron; slip strips of paper under seams; if possible use a seam roll and tailor's ham (see page 31); do not sprinkle the fabric with water to dampen; do not over-press during making up.

As the fibre is non-static, it is particularly valuable as a lining fabric, to minimise the clinging tendency of some man-made fibres.

HOME LAUNDERING
Washing: Unless printed washing instructions advise to the contrary, acetates and mixtures of acetate with wool may be washed as follows:

Ironing: Iron slightly damp. Steam-iron, or if dry-ironing use a WARM iron, setting 2, with a damp pressing cloth. Do not sprinkle with water to damp down for ironing. Instead, re-wet the whole article and roll it in a towel before pressing.

Home dyeing: Some types of home dye may be used, but normally the cold-water type is not recommended as it will not 'take' readily. Consult dye manufacturers' directions.

Stain removal: Warning – never use acetone or nail-polish remover to treat stains on acetates, or the fabric may be seriously damaged.

BACKGROUND

Rayon, sometimes known as viscose rayon, was one of the first non-natural fibres to be produced.

It is a cellulose fibre and is chemically regenerated from a natural raw material – wood pulp. The manufacturing process is somewhat similar to that of a totally synthetic fibre. Rayon accounts for over 50 per cent of all the man-made fibres produced throughout the world. Two of the reasons for this are its enormous versatility and its not-excessive production costs.

Basically rayon divides into two categories, filament rayon and the staple fibres, which include a whole new range of modified rayons, with fundamental differences in their properties. These include Evlan and Evlan M (crimped rayon fibres designed for carpets and also now going into upholstery cloths), Sarille (a fine denier crimped rayon which gives a warm, full handle to woven and knitted dress fabrics), Durafil (a strong staple fibre with high resistance to abrasion), and Vincel (a polynosic fibre with characteristics similar to those of cotton).

There is another type of rayon, cuprammonium or cupioni, but this is not produced in this country and is unlikely to be met with in fabrics by the yard.

FABRICS

Within the Courtaulds rayon family there are many trademarks, but these are used mainly in the trade and are of little significance to the retail customer. But as already described, the modified rayons include: Durafil, Evlan, Sarille and Vincel.

SOME OVERSEAS TRADEMARKS

Alastra	Belgium
Avisco	USA
Coloray	USA and Canada
Colva	West Germany
Danufil	West Germany
Enka rayon	USA
Fibrenka	Holland
Flisca	Switzerland
Floccal	France
Nyma	Netherlands
Phrix	West Germany
Topel	USA
Zehla	East Germany

Cuprammonium and Cupioni

Bemberg, Cupioni,	
Cuprama, Cupresa	West Germany
Cupioni	USA

USES

Standard rayon is used alone and in blends for a wide range of men's, women's and children's wear including many knitted and woven cloths with easy-care finishes. Also used in soft furnishings, upholstery and carpets, and for many industrial uses.

Filament rayon is the main yarn used for men's wear linings. It is also used in velvets and toy pile fabrics, and also in elastic webb and braided materials – corset cloths, braces etc.

Modified rayons have a range of specialised uses. Evlan, for example, is used for knitwear, men's suitings, upholstery and carpets, Sarille is extensively blended with polyester fibres for trousers and also for dress fabrics and soft furnishings, Durafil for uniforms and school wear and Vincel for knitted wear and in woven fabrics, particularly for underwear. Among the most recently-introduced fibres is Raycelon, a filament blend yarn which combines rayon and Celon (Courtaulds nylon) by a secret process.

CHIEF PROPERTIES

The range of modified rayons have properties so different from standard rayon that it is not possible to list each individually. The chief properties listed below cover standard rayon only:

Appearance: An inherently white fibre which takes dyes well and is found in a wide range of brilliant as well as soft colours. Excellent blending qualities, drapes well, pleasant handle. Can be resin-finished for easy-care properties.

Wearing qualities: Reasonably strong but considerably weaker when wet. This is significant only in lightweight dress fabrics, such as chiffon or net.

Reaction to chemicals: Unlike acetate, rayon is not affected by acetone.

Resilience: Fair to good.

Reaction to moisture: Good moisture absorption.

ELECTROSTATIC PROPERTIES
Inherently non-static.

INSULATION VALUE
Good.

IDENTIFICATION
See pages 174–5 for burning test and chemical test.

MICROSCOPIC VIEW (Standard rayon)
In cross-section the fibres are circular or irregular ovals, with an indented outline. When viewed longitudinally it is possible to see deep grooves running the length of the fibre.

SEWING NOTES
Press all double or treble thicknesses of fabric with extreme care, and if possible use a seam roll, press mitt or tailor's ham (see page 31). Use strips of tissue paper under seam edges when pressing seam allowances open.

Use sharp dressmaker's shears, sharp fine steel pins and fine sewing needles and machine needle. If you require the garment to be machine-washable, very great care must be taken with seam finishing and buttonholes (the fabric may be inclined to fray at the raw edges). Fully washable, non-shrink, non-run trimmings and linings must be chosen.

HOME LAUNDERING
Washing: Unless printed washing instructions advise to the contrary, wash rayons as follows:

COLOURFAST RAYONS:

SPECIALLY-FINISHED RAYONS:

RAYONS WHERE COLOURS ARE FAST AT 40°C, 104°F BUT NOT AT 60°C, 140°F: Manufacturer makes this decision and labels garment accordingly:

See page 149 for wool/rayon mixtures.

Ironing: Iron when slightly damp. Steam-iron or if dry-ironing use a MEDIUM HOT iron, setting 3, with a damp pressing cloth if necessary. If over-dry, never sprinkle rayon with water or spotting may permanently damage the fabric. Instead, rewet the whole garment in clear water and roll it in a towel until damp-dry.
Home dyeing: Home dyes may be used. Follow directions to the letter.

BACKGROUND

Tricel is the most recently introduced of the cellulosic fibres. It was developed by British Celanese Ltd. (Courtaulds group) and is produced by them exclusively in Britain. It is derived from chemicals obtained from oil, and wood pulp. First produced in 1955 on a commercial scale, its market has expanded extremely rapidly.

USES

Dresses, blouses, ribbons, ties and scarves, lightweight dressing gowns for men. Also blended with natural or other man-made fibres for men's and women's washable slacks, lightweight suits, rainwear and children's wear. It is also used as a washable filling for quilts and quilted clothing. A new 'marriage' of fibres—Tricelon—is a combination of Tricel and Celon (Courtaulds nylon) in a filament blend yarn.

CHIEF PROPERTIES

Appearance: Rich, attractive appearance with soft feel and silk-like sheen. Somewhat similar in appearance to acetate.

Wearing qualities: Moderately strong, similar to acetate.

Reaction to chemicals: Avoid the use of trichlorethylene or acetone, which may damage the fibre.

Resilience: High degree of resilience and crease-shedding, but after laundering a light touching-up with a WARM iron may be necessary.

Reaction to moisture: Low absorbency; the fabric is very quick-drying.

Other points: Resistant to mildew; moth-proof.

FABRICS

Tricel (British Celanese Ltd.)

AND MIXTURES SUCH AS:

Tricel/Sarille, Fergolin (Tricel-and-rayon)

SOME OVERSEAS TRADEMARKS

Arnel	USA
Rhonel	France
Trilan	Canada

ELECTROSTATIC PROPERTIES
Subject to static, and although precautions are taken to minimise the effect, it may be considered wise to use lining fabric which is non-static, such as cotton, acetate or rayon. Use of a fabric softener in the final rinse may be found beneficial.

INSULATION VALUE
Good to excellent.

IDENTIFICATION
See pages 174–5 for burning test and chemical test.

MICROSCOPIC VIEW
This is not a satisfactory means of identifying triacetate, as this fibre closely resembles acetate in cross-section. To obtain any definite conclusions by this method it is advisable to use the chemical test (page 175). Whereas acetate fibres will dissolve in an acetone solution, triacetate fibres will not.

SEWING NOTES
See note above with regard to the use of non-static lining fabrics.

Before laying on pattern pieces and cutting out, press the length of Tricel (WARM iron, setting 2), then pin the selvedges together to prevent slipping, and tack the pinned edges together. Use fine steel pins for pinning out the pattern, and cut fabric with very sharp dressmaker's shears.

While pressing, be careful to avoid pressure marks from the iron, by slipping strips of paper under seam allowances.

Use synthetic thread for sewing. Check tension and pressure before machine-stitching.

If you require the garment to be machine-washable, pay particular attention to seam finishing and ensure that trimmings and linings are fully washable.

HOME LAUNDERING
Washing: Unless printed washing instructions advise to the contrary, wash as follows:

TRICEL:

PLEATED TRICEL:

Ironing: Usually little or no ironing is needed. If necessary, however, use a steam iron, or if dry-ironing use a WARM iron, setting 2, with a damp pressing cloth if necessary.

Home dyeing: Not recommended for this fibre.

BACKGROUND

Acrylic fibres are pure synthetics with a high percentage of a substance called acrylonitrile in their formulation. This is, of course, an over-simplification and a more technical definition of acrylic fibres might be: those fibres in which the fibre-forming substance is any long-chain synthetic polymer composed of a substantial proportion of acrylonitrile units. Acrylonitrile is a liquid derivative of petroleum.

Acrylonitrile was discovered by Moureu in 1893, but it was only during the last war that its value became fully apparent. At that time a good deal of research was conducted on the production of synthetic rubber, and in the process many new chemicals were examined. One was acrylonitrile which was found to have fibre-forming properties. Once a suitable solvent was found for it, it eventually became possible to manufacture the acrylic fibre. The three main acrylic fibres we know best, Acrilan, Courtelle and Orlon, have distinctive differences in performance and appearance, even though they come from the same chemical family.

FIBRE TYPES

Acrilan (Monsanto Textiles Ltd.)
Courtelle (Courtaulds Ltd.)
Orlon (Du Pont (UK) Ltd.)

SOME OVERSEAS TRADEMARKS

Creslan	USA
Crilenka	Spain
Crylor	France
Dolan	West Germany
Dralon	West Germany
Kanekalon	Japan
Nymcrylon	Holland
Orlon	USA, Holland
Prelana	East Germany
Redon	West Germany
Tacryl	Sweden
Wolcrylon	East Germany
Zefran	USA

USES

Women's and children's woven and knitted dresses and suits; infants' wear; men's knitted shirts; underwear; blankets; fur-type (pile) fabrics; fleecy linings for rainwear, ski-jackets, slippers, gloves and shoes; fillings for quilted garments and bedspreads. Also in blends with wool for suits, trousers, skirts and dress fabrics. Also blended with cotton and with rayon. Also used, of course, for curtain fabrics, upholstery and carpets.

CHIEF PROPERTIES

Appearance: Warm to the touch, soft, lightweight.
Wearing qualities: Extremely strong and hard-wearing, with no appreciable loss of strength when wet.
Reaction to chemicals: Unusually high resistance to corrosive chemicals, yet has excellent processing properties (acrylics will take specialised finishes such as water-proofing).
Resilience: Good-to-excellent natural recovery from creasing during washing and wear.
Reaction to moisture: Low absorbency, quick-drying.
Other points: Acrylics are sensitive to heat, and in fact acrylic fibre has heat setting properties, so that fabrics made from 100 per cent acrylic fibre, or blends of 50 per cent or more, can be durably pleated.

Resistant to weathering and attack by mildew. Naturally moth-proof. Many people who cannot wear wool next to their skin find that a bulked acrylic fibre makes an excellent and non-irritant alternative.

ELECTROSTATIC PROPERTIES

Tendency to static build-up. You can minimise this by lining the garment with non-static fabric (cotton, rayon or acetate). Use of a fabric finisher in the final rinse may also prove beneficial. So will wearing a cotton slip under a dress made from acrylic fibre, instead of a nylon slip.

INSULATION VALUE

Fleece fabrics and knitted goods have a high insulation value, some woven acrylics have much less.

IDENTIFICATION

See pages 174–5 for burning test and chemical test.

MICROSCOPIC VIEW

Acrilan fibres vary from round to kidney-bean shape; Orlon fibres are dog-bone shaped and Courtelle fibres are round. Acrylic fibres are transparent unless pigment-dulled.

SEWING NOTES

As with any man-made fibre, if you intend the garment to be washable, choose trimmings which are equally washable. Fully-shrunk or non-shrink trimmings must be used. This applies to bindings, tapes and ribbons as well as contrast fabrics, linings and interlinings.

Where the fabric is of a jersey construction, be sure when you begin cutting out that the whole weight of the fabric is supported on the cutting table (or cut on the floor). Do not allow the fabric to hang off the cutting surface.

Cut the fabric with very sharp dressmaking shears; use fine steel pins and needles, and pin into the seam allowances as much as possible to avoid marking the main part of the article. Curved edges, necklines and armholes may need to be stay-stitched after cutting out.

Lining is sometimes advisable for acrylics.

Pay careful attention to seam finishing, especially if you intend to machine-wash the garment. Use nylon or Terylene sewing thread; check machine tension and pressure. Try to avoid the need for unpicking especially after pressing: pin, tack and try on the garment before machine-stitching, otherwise the stitch marks may show even after it has been unpicked. Press sparingly and with care.

For marking it is recommended that white limestone or clay chalk be used – a white school chalk will be fine if you have one. Wax or resin-based chalks and coloured chalks are liable to leave white marks which could become permanent. When finishing a facing or hem by hand, do it with a loose stitch so that there is sufficient 'give'. If your machine is a swing-needle type and offers utility stitches, seams and seam finishing will be far easier.

HOME LAUNDERING

Washing: Unless printed washing instructions advise to the contrary, wash as follows:

ACRYLICS AND MIXTURES OF ACRYLIC FIBRE WITH WOOL:

ACRYLIC/COTTON MIXTURES:

PLEATED ACRYLICS AND PLEATED ACRYLIC/WOOL MIXTURES: hand-wash only, as below:

Ironing: Many acrylic fabrics (especially such things as knitted jumpers and cardigans) never need ironing. There are some acrylic fabrics, however, which may benefit from light ironing. *Do not use the steam setting.* Use a COOL iron, setting 1, when the fabric is dry. *Do not use a damp cloth.* Press sparingly and with extreme care, avoiding heavy pressure, especially over double thicknesses.

Home dyeing: Acrylics cannot normally be home-dyed successfully.

Dry cleaning: May be dry-cleaned by all normal processes: not affected by white spirit, carbon tetrachloride, trichlorethylene or perchlorethylene.

BACKGROUND

Polyurethane synthetic elastomer fibres, more usually referred to as elastomerics or synthetic elastomer yarns and more recently as elastofibres–are textile fibres with elastic properties. They are used in conjunction with other fibres to produce fabrics with high stretch recovery. Synthetic elastomers are said to have all the advantages of rubber with none of its disadvantages.

Fabrics which incorporate synthetic elastomers are not to be confused with stretch fabrics where the fibre–say nylon or Terylene–is processed to give the fibre elasticity.

Elastomer fibres are made from polymers consisting of segmented polyurethane, a product of the petrochemical industry.

In America synthetic elastomerics are often known as 'Spandex' yarns.

FIBRE TYPES

Lycra (Du Pont (UK) Ltd.)
Spanzelle (Courtaulds Ltd.)

SOME OVERSEAS TRADEMARKS

Enkaswing   Holland
Glospan   USA
Lycra   USA, Holland, Canada
Vyrene   USA

USES

Used in foundation garments, swimwear, socks and lightweight support hose. For these end-uses elastomerics are generally to be found as a covered or wrapped yarn, and are used in conjunction with wool, rayon or nylon. Elastofibres are also used for stockings.

CHIEF PROPERTIES

Appearance: A very light, highly-elastic yarn, used in conjunction with other fibres to produce fabrics with high stretch recovery.

Wearing qualities: Very durable even after repeated washing.

Reaction to chemicals: Unaffected by most household chemicals.

Resilience: Naturally supple and extremely resilient.

Reaction to moisture: Porous and therefore comfortable to wear.

Other points: The fibre is sensitive to heat and the fabric must not be ironed.

ELECTROSTATIC PROPERTIES
Subject to a small degree of static but in view of the way it is incorporated into a fabric this is of no importance.

INSULATION VALUE
Average but of no importance in view of its applications.

IDENTIFICATION
See pages 174–5 for burning test and chemical test.

MICROSCOPIC VIEW
Spanzelle in cross-section is seen to have an irregular indented outline, while Lycra has a peanut or dog-bone shape.

SEWING NOTES
Elastomerics are not widely found in fabrics sold by the yard in retail stores. But if you should have to sew or alter a garment containing such a fibre, there are no special problems as long as the fabric is kept flat and is not extended when cutting and sewing.

Sewing with any stretch fabric is a technique which should be practised on sample scraps of the fabric: a swing-needle is almost essential for stitching seams, and a special utility 'stretch' stitch is ideal for the job as it gives elasticity to match that of the fabric.

HOME LAUNDERING
Washing: Wash the garment or article by hand at 40°C, 104°F. Rinse thoroughly. Do not wring. If the garment is labelled as machine-washable, follow directions with care.
Ironing: Ironing not normally necessary or desirable.

BACKGROUND

Glass fibre is made by extruding glass in molten form into filaments, and the filaments then undergo a finishing process which uses an emulsified oil or an acetate emulsion, to prevent subsequent breakage of fibres.

Glass fibre is usually known to us under the British trade name Fibreglass, and is seen chiefly in curtain materials, for which it is ideal because of its easy-to-wash, totally non-iron properties, its non-flammability and its ability to resist weathering. Certain rules must be followed with Fibreglass: it should not be compressed while in a folded state, or the folds may 'crack' the fibre. Though Fibreglass is an ideal fabric for shower curtains, care should be taken that the curtains are not so placed that they are drawn along the edge of the bath repeatedly. This is because abrasion will wear away the fabric. (Vitreous enamel being a form of glass fused on metal, the abrasion occurs because of a glass on glass action.)

FIBRE TYPES

Deeglas (Deeglas Fibres Ltd.)
Duraglas (Turner Bros. Asbestos Co. Ltd.)
Fiberglas (Owens-Corning Fiberglas Ltd.)
Fibreglass (Fibreglass Ltd.)
Marglass (Marglass Ltd.)

SOME OVERSEAS TRADEMARKS
Fiberglas	USA and Canada
Gevetex	West Germany
Silenka	Holland
Veranne	France and Belgium

USES

Unsuitable for clothing, but excellent as a curtain material. In the USA, glass fibre is used in bed-covers, which match curtaining. Glass fibre also has a wide range of non-textile uses.

CHIEF PROPERTIES

Appearance: Smooth fabric with a fairly hard 'feel'.

Wearing qualities: Very low resistance to abrasion but otherwise reasonably hardwearing.

Reaction to chemicals: Resistant to most household chemicals, but dissolved by hydrofluoric acid.

Resilience: Low resilience – creasing under pressure may break the fibres.

Reaction to moisture: Entirely non-absorbent, and therefore very quick-drying.

Other points: Non-flammable but is melted by extreme heat and therefore must not be ironed.

Resistant to sunlight; fire-resistant, mildew-resistant; free from insect attack; resistant to shrinkage or stretch; rot-proof; moth-proof; resistant to mildew.

ELECTROSTATIC PROPERTIES
Subject to static, but this has little significance in its applications.

INSULATION VALUE
Low to very high, depending on application.

IDENTIFICATION
See pages 174–5 for burning test and chemical test.

MICROSCOPIC VIEW
In cross-section the fibres are perfectly round and smooth. Longitudinally the fibres are regular in width, and smooth, with no indentations.

SEWING NOTES
If at all possible test a scrap of the fabric for the correct stitch, tension and pressure. Normally rather larger stitches than average will be needed, and a looser tension. Ensure that the needle is sharp. If you line glass fibre curtains you should use glass fibre fabric for the linings too. Take care that raw edges are firmly finished to prevent fraying.

HOME LAUNDERING
Washing: Unless printed washing instructions advise to the contrary, wash as follows:
Hand wash only. Warm water (40°C; 104°F).
Do not rub or twist–simply swish in a large container, with a mild washing product.
DO NOT MACHINE WASH.
Ironing: DO NOT IRON.
Home dyeing: Cannot be home-dyed.

BACKGROUND

In the past metallic fabrics had a tinselly smell, they quickly tarnished, and one dared not attempt to wash them at home. However modern metallic fabrics are a revelation to anyone who still thinks in those terms. They are non-tarnishing, and the metallic yarn may be used with most fibres for a wide variety of fabrics, both for fashion and furnishing. Many such fabrics may be washed, depending on the basic fibre. Be sure to obtain explicit care instructions when you buy the fabric.

FIBRE TYPES

Lurex (Lurex Co. Ltd.)
Lurex 500 (Lurex Co. Ltd.)
Rexor (Porth Textiles Ltd.)

OVERSEAS TRADEMARK
Metlon   USA

USES

Mainly women's fashion wear including cocktail dresses, blouses, suits and evening dresses.

CHIEF PROPERTIES

Appearance: The sheen and glitter of metallic yarns adds a distinctive touch to special-occasion garments.
Wearing qualities: Dependent on basic fibre used in the fabric; the metallic yarn has low abrasion-resistance.
Reaction to chemicals: Avoid bleaches.
Resilience: Dependent upon basic fibre.
Reaction to moisture: Not absorbent.
Other points: Modern metallic yarns are non-allergic and non-irritant, and are normally washable, though this is dependent upon the basic fibre.

ELECTROSTATIC PROPERTIES
Not applicable.

INSULATION VALUE
Not applicable.

IDENTIFICATION
Not applicable.

MICROSCOPIC VIEW
In cross-section the fibres appear flat and ribbon-shaped.

SEWING NOTES
Establish whether the fabric has a one-way sheen, before cutting out. Try to avoid the need to unpick seams, by carefully pinning and tacking before stitching. Stitch normally but check tension and pressure. Press with care, using a cool iron on the wrong side of the fabric only, and using a damp cloth.

HOME LAUNDERING
This depends on the fabric. Try to obtain printed washing instructions. Some fabrics may need to be dry-cleaned.

BACKGROUND

Teklan, the modacrylic fibre which is best known in Great Britain, is based on acrylonitrile and vinylidene chloride – derivatives of oil refining and coal carbonisation processes. It is strong, hard-wearing and easy to wash, but its most important asset is its flame resistance which is even better than nylon, as it does not drop molten fibres when it is subjected to flame. Textiles made from Teklan retain their flame resistance even after repeated washing or dry-cleaning. Other modacrylics may be based on polyvinylchloride rather than polyvinyl-idenechloride.

FIBRE TYPES

Teklan (Courtaulds Ltd.)

SOME OVERSEAS TRADEMARKS

Clevyl T	France
Dynel	USA
Verel	USA (staple fibre for carpets, described as a modacrylic)

USES

As Teklan satisfies the requirements of British Standard 3120: 1964, it is particularly valuable for permanently flame-resistant nightwear and children's garments; it also has various industrial applications, including overalls. It is also valuable in net curtaining and furnishing materials as it is resistant to weakening by sunlight.

CHIEF PROPERTIES

Appearance: May be in woven or knitted form, including brushed fleecy form.

Wearing qualities: Strong and hard wearing.

Reaction to chemicals: Good resistance to most chemicals.

Resilience: Good.

Reaction to moisture: Fairly absorbent.

Other points: The major benefit of Teklan is its flame resistance, even after repeated washing or dry-cleaning. It has good resistance to sunlight and bacteria.

ELECTROSTATIC PROPERTIES
No problem.

INSULATION VALUE
Good.

IDENTIFICATION
See pages 174–5 for burning test and chemical test.

MICROSCOPIC VIEW
In cross-section Teklan and Dynel are almost circular, while Verel is peanut or bone-shaped.

SEWING NOTES
Treat generally as an acrylic fibre (see page 157).

HOME LAUNDERING
Washing: Teklan fabrics are permanently flame resistant, even after repeated launderings. Unless printed washing instructions advise to the contrary, treat as follows:

Use of a fabric finisher in the final rinse may be found beneficial.
Ironing: Needs little, if any, ironing. When necessary use a COOL iron, setting 1.
Home dyeing: Cannot be home-dyed successfully.

BACKGROUND

Nylon was one of the first truly synthetic fibres. The first type for textile purposes in Britain was nylon 6·6 (variously referred to as nylon 6 point 6, or nylon six-six). Its raw materials are phenol or benzene from coal, oxygen and nitrogen from the air and hydrogen from water.

There is another type of nylon, nylon 6, derived from caprolactam, which now forms a very important part of British nylon manufacture.

USES

Virtually all types of clothing for men, women and children: sheets and pillowcases, umbrella covers, stockings. Bulked nylon yarn is used for knitwear, knitted dresses, blankets, baby garments, etc. Also used for carpets; and has many industrial uses.

FIBRE TYPES

Blue 'C' nylon (Monsanto Textiles Ltd.) – type 6·6.
BRI-NYLON (ICI Fibres Ltd.)–type 6·6.
Celon (Courtaulds Ltd.)–type 6.
Enkalon (British Enkalon Ltd.)–type 6.

ALSO PROCESSED YARNS SUCH AS:
Agilon, Antron, Cantrece, Cheslon, Crimped Celon, Depalon, Depanyl, Enkasheer, Fluflon, Helanca, Shawflex, Textrallized (for Ban-Lon garments).

SOME OVERSEAS TRADEMARKS

Amilan	Japan
Antron	USA
Cantrece	USA
Chemstrand nylon	USA
Danulon	Hungary
Delfion	Italy
Ducilo	Italy
Du Pont nylon	USA and Canada
Efylon	Hungary
Enant	USSR
Enka-nylon	USA
Grilon	Switzerland and Japan
Grillon	Brazil
Helion	Italy
Kapron	USSR
Lamonyl	Switzerland
Lilion	Italy and Spain
Misr nylon	Egypt
Nailon	Italy
Nipolon	Japan
Ortalion	Italy
Perlofil	Spain
Perlon	West Germany
Rhodiaceta	France
Silon	Czechoslovakia
Stilon	Poland
Trilon	East Germany

CHIEF PROPERTIES

Appearance: Nylon fabrics may be knitted or woven, straight or crimped, bright or matt, sheer or bulked.
Wearing qualities: Outstanding resistance to abrasion, even in the sheerest fabrics, so that nylon fabrics are normally extremely strong and hard-wearing, and remain strong when wet. Extra high-tenacity nylon is produced for industrial use.
Reaction to chemicals: Unaffected by normal dry-cleaning fluids, though concentrated formic acid has a solvent effect on the fibre, and bleaches of the chlorine type should not be used as they degrade nylon.
Resilience: Highly-resilient with excellent recovery from creasing, and natural elasticity.
Reaction to moisture: Low moisture absorption, quick-drying.

There have been dramatic changes in textile thinking, resulting from the development of nylon. Low absorption was thought to be a disadvantage until quick-drying nylon appeared and the technologists developed the bulk-nylon yarns so that the air spaces in the yarns provide absorption lacking in the fibre itself.
Other points: Nylon blends with natural and other man-made fibres to give the best properties of both fibres. It is often added to other fibres to improve the abrasion resistance of a fabric. Nylon has heat-setting properties, i.e. can be set to retain pleats, size and shape after repeated washing. It is sometimes described as self-extinguishing, for when held towards a flame it will not flare up, but the heat melts the supporting threads and the flaring portion drops clear. Warning: should you test nylon for burning, hold the sample with a pair of tweezers as fingers can be seriously burned by the dripping of the fibre during combustion. Nylon is proof against moth and mildew.

ELECTROSTATIC PROPERTIES

Subject to static, but precautions are taken to minimise this. Use of a fabric softener in the final rinse is beneficial.

INSULATION VALUE

Good.

IDENTIFICATION

See pages 174–5 for burning test and chemical test.

MICROSCOPIC VIEW

Fibres in cross-section are usually smooth, round, uniform in diameter, and in longitudinal view smooth and glass-like. Some new yarns, however, such as Enka-nylon, are tri-lobal.

SEWING NOTES

If you intend the garment to be washable, choose trimmings, linings and interlinings which are equally washable. Fully shrunk or non-shrink trimmings must be used. This applies to bindings, tapes and ribbons as well as contrast fabrics, linings and interlinings. Every material used must be compatible with the fabric, and sufficiently colour-fast to withstand process 4 washing (see Home Laundering opposite).

Use very sharp dressmaker's shears for cutting out, and use fine steel pins and needles. Sew with Terylene or nylon thread. Check tension and pressure on the sewing machine extremely carefully on a test piece of the fabric, and if you have a swing-needle machine use a small zigzag stitch or special utility 'stretch stitch' if the fabric has any degree of elasticity. Tape or stay-stitch bias seams. Try to avoid the need for unpicking, which may mark seams (especially seams which have already been pressed), by pinning and tacking the garment and testing for fit before stitching. Press sparingly and with caution (see opposite). Some nylon fabrics cannot be 'eased' during making up, so avoid a style where unobtrusive easing is called for.

See also stretch yarns.

To lessen the cling which nylon may develop, it is a good idea to line the garment with acetate, or to wear a cotton, rayon or acetate slip, all of which are non-static.

HOME LAUNDERING

Washing: Always wash white nylon alone in clean suds. Unless printed washing instructions advise to the contrary, wash as follows:

WHITE NYLON:

COLOURED NYLON:

WASHABLE PLEATED GARMENTS CONTAINING NYLON:

Do not bleach. Do not boil.

Never allow nylon to become too soiled. Shirts should be washed after every wearing, sheets as often as possible. White nylon which has become greyed may be treated with a proprietary nylon whitener.

Ironing: Knitted nylon fabrics do not need ironing. Woven nylon is often improved by light touching up. Read the care label carefully if one is provided. Most nylon fabrics are ironed when nearly dry with a WARM iron, setting 2, or with a steam iron. But some types of nylon may be affected by steam-ironing and may need a dry WARM iron on a dry fabric.

Home dyeing: Can be home-dyed if the dye instructions are carefully followed.

BACKGROUND

Terylene, the world's first polyester fibre, was invented in Britain in 1941, in the research laboratories of the Calico Printers' Association Ltd., and was commercially developed by ICI. It is a truly synthetic fibre, made from ethylene glycol (known to motorists as anti-freeze) and terephthalic acid, both of which are derived from petroleum. Large-scale production of Terylene began in 1955, and polyester fibre is now manufactured in many countries of the world.

Crimplene, the bulked form of Terylene, is now used for more than 50 per cent of the double jersey fabrics made in the UK. It is also used by many Continental fabric knitting firms.

Made in both double jersey and warp-knit constructions, in plain colours, prints and jacquards, Crimplene has become extremely popular because of its hard-wearing, easy-care properties. Fabric weights range from around $3\frac{1}{2}$ oz. (for blouses) through a range of mid-weights for dresses, skirts and suits, to around 16–18 oz. for coats.

Terlenka, the more recently introduced polyester by British Enkalon, has approximately the same uses and applications as Terylene, and bulked Terlenka is approximately equivalent to Crimplene, though of course each manufacturer claims special properties for its own fibres.

FIBRE TYPES

Terlenka (British Enkalon Ltd.)
Terylene (ICI Fibres Ltd.)

ALSO PROCESSED YARNS SUCH AS:
Ban-Lon, Cheslene, Crimplene, Depalene, Fluflene, Helanca, Shawflex, Starlene.

SOME OVERSEAS TRADEMARKS

Dacron	USA
Diolen	West Germany
Encron	USA
Fortrel	USA
Kodel	USA
Tergal	France, Spain, Brazil
Terital	Italy
Tetoron	Japan
Trevira	West Germany
Vycron	USA and Israel

USES

Polyester fibres are used for women's, men's and children's underwear (see first column) and also such uses as curtain nets, pillow, quilt and sleeping-bag fillings, carpets and tablecloths. In blends with wool, it is used for men's suitings, coats and trousers and for women's and children's outerwear. In blends with cotton, polyester is widely used for dress fabrics, shirtings, rainwear, lingerie and sheets. In blends with rayon, it appears for suitings and rainwear.

CHIEF PROPERTIES

Appearance: A naturally transparent, extremely versatile fibre which is dyed during processing and can be used alone or in blends to give fabrics which are easy to care for. May be used in filament form to give smooth fabrics, or as a staple fibre in blends with other fibres. The bulked forms of polyester, Crimplene and bulked Terlenka, make thicker fabrics in a wide variety of textures.

Wearing qualities: Outstanding resistance to abrasion, giving hard-wearing fabrics which do not lose strength in the wet state. Excellent tensile strength.

Reaction to chemicals: Unaffected by normal commercial and domestic stain removers, though phenol will attack Terylene and some strong chemicals may affect the colour. Water-soluble stains respond fairly easily to normal stain removal methods, but some stains, e.g. paint, varnish, marking ink and linseed oil, may leave traces which prove impossible to eradicate.

Resilience: Highly resilient with excellent recovery from creasing; exceptionally low stretch.

Reaction to moisture: Very low moisture absorption; the fibres do not swell in water and the fabric is quick-drying.

Other points: Has heat setting properties, i.e. can be set to retain shape and size after repeated washing, and may also be permanently pleated. Its exceptional resistance to degradation by sunlight renders it ideal for curtaining. It is also moth-proof, and resists mildew.

ELECTROSTATIC PROPERTIES

Subject to static, and although precautions are taken to minimise the effect it may be considered wise to use lining fabrics which are inherently non-static, such as cotton, acetate or rayon. Use of a fabric finisher in the final rinse will help minimise the static.

INSULATION VALUE

From low (making an ideal fair-weather fabric) to excellent, as in waddings and pillow fillings.

IDENTIFICATION

See pages 174–5 for burning test and chemical test.

MICROSCOPIC VIEW

In cross-section the fibres are round, highly transparent and uniform in diameter. The surface of the fibre is smooth and glasslike.

SEWING NOTES

If you intend the garment to be washable, choose trimmings and linings which are equally washable. If you intend to machine-wash the garment, this point is particularly important and so is special care with the finishing of seams. Use lining fabrics of acetate, cotton or rayon to counteract tendency to static. Use sharp dressmaker's shears for cutting out, and use fine steel pins and needles. Sew with synthetic sewing thread. It is used exactly like cotton thread but it is stronger and does not shrink.

Check tension and pressure on the sewing machine, using a test piece of the fabric doubled.

Tape or stay-stitch bias seams.

Try to avoid the need for unpicking, which may leave needle marks, by pinning and tacking the garment and trying it on before stitching.

HOME LAUNDERING

Washing: Unless printed washing instructions advise to the contrary, wash as follows:

TERYLENE AND TERLENKA:

TERYLENE/WOOL BLENDS:

WASHABLE PLEATED GARMENTS CONTAINING TERYLENE OR TERLENKA:

Use of a fabric softener in the final rinse is beneficial.

DO NOT BOIL OR BLEACH.

Ironing: Usually no ironing is neccessary, but if wished touch up with a steam iron or if dry-ironing use a WARM iron, setting 2, with damp pressing cloth.

Home dyeing: Not recommended.

BACKGROUND

Greatly improved absorbency, loft and warmth of handle in a wide range of woven and knitted fabrics and garments made from continuous filament man-made fibre yarns can now be obtained by altering the character and surface of these yarns by a number of special processes. In addition, the fully synthetic yarns can be given varying degrees of stretch and elasticity so that stretch-to-fit garments are a practical proposition.

TRADE MARKS

Agilon: Elasticised nylon yarn with coil spring form.

Cheslon: Bulked, stabilised acetate and nylon yarn.

Crimplene: Modified Terylene filament yarn. Combines high degree of bulk with low stretch.

Fluflene: Modified Terylene yarns with high bulk, low weight, high absorbency, smooth handle and warmth.

Fluflon: Modified nylon yarns (properties as Fluflene).

Helanca: Crimped thermoplastic yarns – nylon, Terylene etc. Various degrees of stretch and bulk.

High Bulk Tricel: Bulked, stabilised Tricel.

Lancola: Solution-dyed bulked, stabilised, acetate filament yarn.

Miralon: Special bulking process for producing crinkle or boucle type yarn in nylon.

Miralene: Similar crinkle or boucle type yarn to Miralon, but based on Terylene.

Taslan: Imparts added bulk without elasticity.

Textralized: Modified filament yarns to give moderate stretch with moderate bulk and softness.

Tycora: Complete range of modified filament yarn. Varying degrees of bulk and stretch according to intended end uses.

USES

Agilon: Stockings, socks, woven and knitted underwear.

Crimplene: Knitwear, woven garments and jersey fabrics.

Fluflene: Socks, stockings, underwear, outerwear.

Fluflon: Fully fashioned outerwear, cut outerwear, shirtings, crepes, warp knits, carpets, furnishings.

Helanca: Hosiery, woven, warp and circular knit fabrics, special qualities for stockings, swimwear, knitted outerwear.

High Bulk 'Tricel': For all types of men's, women's and children's knitwear.

Taslan: Most types of woven and knitted outerwear and underwear, curtain nets, furnishing, filter, overall, proofing and insulation fabrics.

Textralized: Socks, stockings, knitted outerwear and underwear, gloves, dress fabrics. (This yarn used for all 'Ban-Lon' labelled merchandise.)

CHIEF PROPERTIES

The processes which fluff up the surface of the yarn to give extra loft and absorbency and virtually eliminate transparency are usually known as 'texturing' or 'bulking', hence 'textured' and 'bulked' yarns. The processes used to obtain stretch and elasticity are known as 'crimping' or simply 'stretching-twisting', hence 'crimped' or 'stretch' yarns.

Another expression, 'high-bulking', is used to describe methods of obtaining extreme lightness and loft particularly in knitted fabrics made from acrylic spun yarns, hence 'high bulk' yarns.

ELECTROSTATIC PROPERTIES
Similar to the basic yarns in their untreated state

INSULATION VALUE
In many cases there is a greatly improved insulation value, and warmth of handle.

SEWING NOTES
The home dressmaker is most likely to find the warp-stretch fabric in fabrics by the yard. She should, however, always check her pattern to ensure she has the correct stretch fabric.

When laying out pattern pieces, ensure that the fabric is not pulled or extended, for example over the edge of the table. Pin with fine steel pins, cut with sharp dressmaker's shears and stay-stitch all bias edges.

Stretch fabrics are best machine-stitched with a swing-needle type machine, where a small zigzag stitch or special utility stretch stitch will give along seams in wear. Use synthetic thread for sewing. If your machine is of the straight-stitch type, be particularly careful to check pressure and tension on test pieces of the fabric.

Overcasting or finishing of seam edges is important—commercial makers-up normally trim seams to minimum width and machine-finish to a neat, secure, elastic seam. This is possible to reproduce almost exactly with some modern domestic sewing machines, using the special stretch-stitch provided.

For sewing nylon, Terylene and other synthetic fibre fabrics, the old rules of sewing need some modification. In particular their remarkable stability to washing means that sewing threads made from synthetic fibres should be chosen. The two leading suppliers of home sewing threads – J. and P. Coats and English Sewing Ltd. – each market a synthetic fibre sewing thread made from Terylene which can be recommended for nearly all nylon and Terylene fabrics. These are 'Gosamer' and 'Trylko' and the makers of these also provide booklets – on sale in the home sewing departments – which are useful guides about sewing generally and are very helpful to refer to, when tackling the newer types of materials in synthetic fibres. A schappe-spun Terylene sewing thread is marketed by Sewing Silks Ltd. with the brand name 'Perivale Spun Terylene'. For further information about man-made fibre sewing threads apply to the suppliers.

IDENTIFICATION
Similar to the basic yarns in their untreated state.

MICROSCOPIC VIEW
Similar to the basic yarns in their untreated state.

HOME LAUNDERING
Printed washing instructions are almost certain to be provided. If in doubt, wash according to derivative fibre. Ironing is not necessary.

BACKGROUND

Various types of fibres may be specially finished to give extra advantages, but the most widely produced are the specially-finished cottons. Mercerisation is one of the earliest finishes given to cotton, and it remains a popular way of adding a silky sheen and stabilising a fabric to make it non-shrink. Rayon, linen and wool may also undergo special processes to improve their washability and wearability.

Often a fabric may combine a number of advantages—for example it may be non-iron and also shrink-resistant, or it may be showerproof and also minimum-iron and crease resisting.

Fabric finishes may, however, be broadly divided into six main groups:

(a) *Minimum-iron, non-iron, crease-resisting finishes.* Cotton fabric may be treated to give one or more of these finishes. The treatment, usually involving the use of synthetic resins, also makes the garment resistant to shrinkage.

(b) *Water- and stain-repellent finishes.* A fabric is given resistance by the addition of water-repellent and sometimes oil-repellent agents.

(c) *Shrink-resistant finishes.* These may be:

(i) Mechanically pre-shrunk finishes. These include Rigmel, Sanforized and Calpreta Shrunk. All employ essentially the same principle—the fabric passes through a machine which induces sufficient shrinkage in the fabric to ensure that on washing, further shrinkage will be at a minimum.

(ii) Shrink-resistant finishes produced by chemical treatment. These include Calpreta Fixt Finish, and here shrinkage in washing is prevented by chemically setting the cloth dimensions.

(d) *Embossed, glazed, permanently crisp or lustre finishes.* Resins are used in these processes, and the woven cotton cloth is then put through rollers which polish and in some cases emboss the fabric.

(e) *The true non-iron finish*, produced without the use of resins, by treatment of the cotton fabric with suitable chemicals which modify the cotton. These fabrics can be washed by hand or machine, and wrung, hand-wrung or spin-dried. After drying they need no ironing. Generally the process also gives dimensional stability to the fabric. Examples of this type of fabric are BanCare and the Calpreta Carefree Wringable Finish.

(f) *Permanent press finishes.*

USES

Men's shirts and pyjamas; women's dresses and blouses; children's dresses, smocks, aprons, shirts, suits, etc. Men's suits and sportswear.

CHIEF PROPERTIES

Appearance: Similar to ordinary cotton but usually with added smoothness due to finish.

Wearing qualities: Good.

Reaction to chemicals: Affected by household (sodium hypochlorite) bleach in many instances.

Resilience: Good to outstanding.

Reaction to moisture: Usually less absorbent than unfinished cotton.

ELECTROSTATIC PROPERTIES
No static problem.

INSULATION VALUE
Fairly low.

IDENTIFICATION
Means of identification vary slightly, depending on the type of finish, but basically the same results would be obtained as with pure cotton.

MICROSCOPIC VIEW
Similar to the fibre in its pure unfinished form.

SEWING NOTES
While a specially-finished fabric is normally very satisfactory to work with when dressmaking, it is usually very stable, sometimes unyielding, and it may not be possible to 'ease' it satisfactorily. So avoid a style with a set-in sleeve which has a good deal of fullness to adjust, except, of course, with a child's puff sleeve, where the puckers are part of the design. With a set-in shirt sleeve there is less fullness to accommodate. See page 105 for one way to deal with easing of specially-finished fabrics.

HOME LAUNDERING
Washing: These fabrics are often called 'drip-dries', though this may be a misnomer in some cases. With some finishes it is no longer essential to hang a garment to drip-dry; often you will get equally good results if you cool the garment after washing and before spinning with plenty of *cold* rinsing water, then spin briefly and arrange the garment on a hanger. The true non-iron fabrics (category (e) opposite) can be put through a wringer or wrung by hand or spin-dried, and still need no ironing.

Unless the fabric or garment label advises to the contrary, the following washing processes are suitable:

SPECIALLY-FINISHED COTTONS AND RAYONS:

WASHABLE PLEATED GARMENTS CONTAINING MAN-MADE FIBRES:

Ironing: Obviously little ironing is normally needed. If touching up is necessary, however, use a MEDIUM HOT iron, setting 3.
Home dyeing: Specially-finished fabrics will not normally take home dyes.

The tests below, WHICH MUST BE CONDUCTED UNDER STRICTLY CONTROLLED LAB-ORATORY CONDITIONS ONLY, will give an *indication* of the fibre content, but will not be conclusive. A more detailed analysis would be necessary to establish the fibre type beyond reasonable doubt.

For more detailed and technical information, read 'Identification of Textile Materials', published by the Textile Institute, 10 Blackfriars Street, Manchester.

WARNING: As mentioned above, tests by burning and by immersion in an acid should only be made under supervised laboratory conditions. When making the burning test, hold the sample with a pair of tweezers as fingers can be seriously burned by the dripping of the fibre during combustion.

BURNING TEST

Cotton	Ignites and burns readily, with smell of burning paper, leaving a small amount of soft grey ash.
Flax (linen)	Burns readily, with smell of burnt paper. Leaves a small amount of grey ash.
Wool and silk	Burns with difficulty, with smell of burning hair. Leaves a bead of porous carbon.
Acetate	Burns to leave a hard black molten bead. Faint smell of acetic acid.
Acrylic (e.g. Acrilan, Cour-telle or Orlon)	Melts and burns with a smell like burning meat to leave hard black ash.
Polyamide (nylon)	Retracts from flame to form white molten bead. Smell of celery. Nylon 6.6 is said to have a more perfumed odour when burning than nylon 6.
Polyester	Melts and burns with a smoky flame to leave a hard bead.
Rayon	Burns readily with smell of burning paper, leaving white ash.
Triacetate (Tricel)	Burns to leave a hard black molten bead. Faint smell of acetic acid.
Glass	Glass fibre fabrics are non-flammable, but when held in a flame the fibres soften to form a round bead, which glows red, then orange-to-yellow. When it is cooled the bead becomes hard and white. Usually there is a grey smoke during burning and a slight odour of charring paint.
Modacrylic	When slowly advanced towards a flame, Teklan filaments melt and recede from the flame in a manner similar to Courtelle. However, when the fibres are introduced into the flame the filaments show no tendency to ignite but merely melt.

CHEMICAL TESTS

80% acetone/ 20% water by volume	Methylene chloride	Dimethyl formamide 60°C (140° F)	5N Hydro-chloric acid	Concentrated sulphuric acid
Insoluble	Insoluble	Insoluble	Insoluble	Soluble
Insoluble	Insoluble	Insoluble	Insoluble	Soluble
Insoluble	Insoluble	Insoluble	Insoluble	Insoluble
Soluble	Swells but insoluble	Soluble	Insoluble	Soluble
Insoluble	Insoluble	Dissolves slowly	Insoluble	Soluble
Insoluble	Insoluble	Insoluble	Soluble	Soluble
Insoluble	Insoluble	Insoluble	Insoluble	Soluble
Insoluble	Insoluble	Insoluble	Insoluble	Soluble
Swells but insoluble	Soluble	Soluble	Insoluble	Soluble

A drop of hydrofluoric acid will dissolve the fibres after a few seconds' contact.

Teklan may be distinguished from many synthetic fibres by testing for chlorine. This is done by heating a copper wire in a bunsen flame until all green coloration disappears. The wire is then removed from the flame and a small sample of fibre is allowed to melt on the hot end. On re-introducing the wire into the flame, any green coloration indicates the presence of chlorine.

7

EMBROIDERY STITCHES

Hand embroidery is to many people one of the most satisfying of hobbies. It is a complex subject, and you will find on the shelves of your bookshop or public library whole volumes devoted to the many different types of embroidery techniques.

Obviously, in a book of this nature it would be impossible to cover the whole field in detail. So I have chosen just twenty-four embroidery stitches, all of them simple enough for a beginner to tackle, all of them useful to anyone who may need to work some simple decoration without studying the subject in depth.

Simple stitches such as Fly Stitch, French Knot and Bullion Stitch might, at some time, be specified for the decoration of a pram cover, say, or a child's knitted jacket. Arrowhead stitch is very useful for skirts or coats with a kick pleat at the back, where the strain is likely to tear the fabric eventually. Long-and-short stitch is the basis of much of the handiwork in the tablecloth-and-napkin sets for which the needlework magazines offer transfers.

Here, then, is a small collection of embroidery stitches using wool or embroidery silks. If your interest in embroidery is aroused, bookshelves full of further advice await your attention.

NOTE: If you are left-handed the instructions for holding needle and work will not apply to you, and you will have to reverse all left and right directions. It may be found helpful to hold a mirror to the diagram concerned, to see how it looks your way.

Arrowhead stitch (309)

Shown here in four stages, the arrowhead stitch or arrowhead tack is used for strengthening the ends of seams as, for example, at the top of a

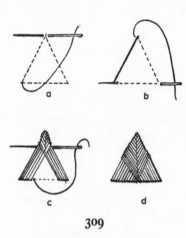

309

kick pleat on a skirt or coat, or for reinforcing the lower edge of a trouser pocket.

1. Mark with tailor's chalk or pencil (depending on the fabric) a neat, symmetrical triangle, at the point to be strengthened. Using embroidery silk and holding the needle in the right hand, make a few tiny securing stitches on the back of the work (left side of triangle) and bring the needle out at the lower left-hand corner, drawing the thread through the work. Then pick up a small stitch horizontally at the top of the triangle.

2. Draw the needle through, and re-insert it at the base of the triangle (lower right-hand corner), then make a long horizontal stitch along the base of the triangle, so that the needle emerges alongside the first thread.

3. Repeat stages one and two, returning to the top and picking up a slightly wider horizontal stitch, just beneath the first one. Take a slightly shorter horizontal stitch along the base of the triangle, emerging just inside the second thread. Continue in this way until you have filled the whole of the triangle with thread.

4. When the arrowhead is complete, finish off the thread neatly at the back of the work, and snip off the end.

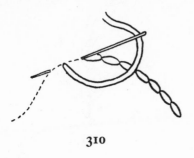

310

Backstitch (310)

If it is very neatly and evenly worked, backstitch can look like machine-stitching, and it is the stitch to use along seam-lines if no sewing machine is available.

Hold the needle in the right hand and work from right to left. Make a few tiny securing stitches on the back of the work (if you are using thick wool it may be neater to tie one small knot and subsequently conceal it under the work).

Bring the needle through to the right side, exactly on the line to be worked, and draw the thread through. Insert the needle a little to the right of this point, making the stitch small and neat if the stitching is meant to be inconspicuous. Bring the needle out a little way to the left of where it first came through, draw the thread through, then re-insert the needle where it first came out of the fabric. Repeat this stitch along the line to be worked.

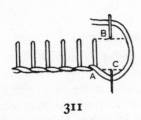

311

Blanket stitch (311)

This stitch is used as an edging for blankets, or as an embroidery stitch. Blanket stitch is similar to buttonhole stitch, but the individual stitches are spaced apart instead of being sewn close together.

Hold the needle in the right hand and work from left to right, stitching towards you. Make a few tiny securing stitches on the back of the work, and bring the needle through at the edge of the fabric (point A). Put the needle into the work where the top of the stitch is to be (point B), holding down the thread with your left thumb, and make a stitch through the fabric to emerge again at point C, keeping the needle over the thread. Continue stitching as before, leaving an even gap between stitches.

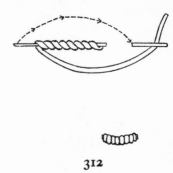

312

Bullion stitch (312)

This is a useful stitch, equally attractive in embroidery silk or wool. It can be used to make up flower shapes with the stitches curving to give the effect of petal edges.

1. Hold the needle in the right hand. Make a few tiny securing stitches on the back of the work, and bring the needle through to the right side. Mark to the right of the point the length the individual Bullion Stitch is to be, and insert the needle into the fabric at that mark. Bring the point of the needle up through the fabric again at the first point, but before drawing the thread through, wind it loosely round the needle as indicated. The number of times it will need to be wound will depend on the length of the Bullion Stitch and the thickness of the sewing thread. (Make a practice stitch on a spare piece of fabric to assess this.) Do not wind tightly.

2. Draw the needle through the twists of thread,

holding them carefully with your thumb and
forefinger while you draw the thread through.
Do not pull too hard or too rapidly: knots may
form which are very difficult to remedy. When
all the slack has been taken up, insert the needle
again at point B and the bullion stitch will be
complete. Bring the needle through the work
again where the next Bullion Stitch is to be.

314

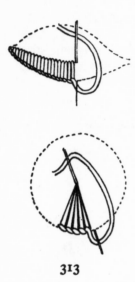

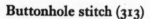

313

Buttonhole stitch (313)

This forms the basis of many embroidery
designs, including cut-out work (Richelieu embroidery). It can be used to outline flower and
leaf shapes, to make scalloped edging, and to
fill in circular shapes (see the diagrams).

Buttonhole stitch is worked in the same way
as blanket stitch, but the strands are sewn close
together. If you wish, you can strengthen the
embroidery by first sewing one or two lines of
small running stitches along the edge to be
worked.

Hold the needle in the right hand and work
from left to right, stitching towards you.

Chain stitch (314)

This is an effective stitch both for single lines
and, with the lines of chains side by side, as a
filling stitch.

Hold the needle in your right hand, the work
in your left, and stitch towards you. Make a
few tiny securing stitches on the back of the
work, and bring the needle and thread through
to the right side. Then insert the needle exactly
at the point where it first emerged, holding
the loop of thread with your thumb. Bring the
needle through the work, a little way along the
stitching line, and draw the thread through to
form a chain. Be sure not to pull up the loop
of thread too tightly. Continue in this way,
always taking care that the point of the needle
enters the fabric at the spot where it emerged,
to ensure a tidy link.

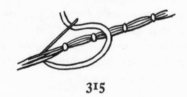

315

Couching stitch (315)

This is a useful decorative stitch, normally
used in wool embroidery. A number of strands
of wool are cut to the same length and then
folded in half so that you have loops one end
and cut ends the other. Using a slightly thinner
wool or thread, first catch-stitch the loops to the
fabric securely. Hold the needle in your right
hand and draw the couching threads to your
left.

Bring the main, finer thread underneath the work and draw it through the fabric a little way along the line. Make a tiny stitch over the thick strands, keeping it at right angles to them for neatness. Take the thread through to the underside of the work again, and again leave a short gap before bringing the thread through to make another stitch. Make sure that the couching threads lie flat.

When you reach the end of the sewing line, take all the strands through to the back of the work and fasten off neatly.

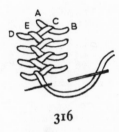

316

Cretan stitch (316)

This is a decorative stitch with an openwork effect, used to form borders and as a filling stitch in embroidery designs. Hold the needle in the right hand, the work in your left and stitch towards you. Make a few tiny securing stitches on the back of the work, and bring the needle and thread through to the right side (point A). Take a long diagonal stitch, putting the needle through the fabric at point B and bringing it out about halfway back, at point C. Now make a diagonal stitch in the other direction, taking the thread from point C to point D, back up through point E and so on. Do not draw the thread tight.

Cross stitch (317)

Cross stitch may either be very fine, if worked in a single strand of cotton thread over linen, or more coarse, if worked in wool over canvas. You can count the threads of the fabric you are working on, to make sure that the stitches are even and orderly.

A line of cross stitch is normally worked from left to right. Hold the needle in the right

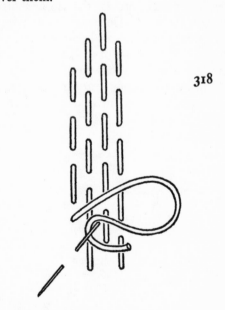

317

hand, the work in your left. Make a few tiny securing stitches on the back of the work, and bring the thread through to the right side (point A). Take the thread down through the fabric again at point B. Bring the thread out at point C, and take it down through the work again at point D. Take a tiny stitch to the next thread or strand (point E) and begin again. It is important that the top stitch should always lie in the same direction.

It is also possible, though perhaps rather less satisfactory, to 'mass-produce' cross stitch, by working all along the row from right to left, taking one stitch across a regular number of threads, and then to work the return stitches over them.

318

Darning stitch (318)

As the diagram indicates, this is a very simple running stitch, with each row alternating the 'ins' and 'outs' of the thread. It is a very useful filling stitch for wool embroidery designs.

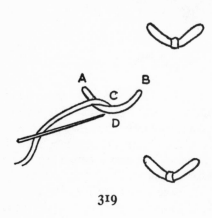

319

Fly stitch (319)

A simple and most effective stitch. The work is held in the left hand, the needle in the right hand. Make a few tiny securing stitches on the back of the work, and bring the thread through to the right side (point A).

Insert the needle through the fabric a little to the right (point B). Do not pull the thread tightly. Bring the needle out between these two points and a little below them (point C), then reinsert the needle to catch down the loop of thread. Bring the needle through the work again at the point where the next fly stitch is to be.

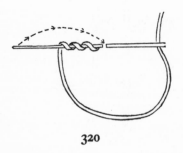

320

French knot (320)

1. Holding the work in the left hand and the needle in the right hand, make a few tiny securing stitches on the back of the work. Bring the needle through to the right side, make a tiny stitch through the fabric, then twist the thread three times round the tip of the needle. Holding the twisted thread carefully with thumb and first finger of the left hand, draw the needle through to form a knot.

2. Take the needle through the work at the point where the thread originally emerged from the fabric.

3. Secure the knot or bring the thread through the work again where the next knot is to be.

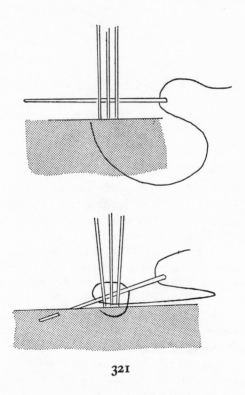

321

Hemstitching (321)

Hemstitching of the type shown is actually part of drawn thread work, where a piece of fine linen is cut to a square, and then three or four threads are drawn out on all four sides, so that when the linen is hemmed, the hemstitching can form part of the decoration. The diagram shows how, once the threads have been drawn, the needle picks up three threads at a time, and the three threads are then worked together in 'bunches', top and bottom, to form an open-work pattern which also secures the hem.

line of running stitches is made in one colour, with the amount of fabric between each stitch equal to the stitch itself. Then the gaps are filled with the other colour, again with simple running stitches.

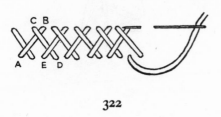

322

Herringbone stitch (322)

For this stitch hold the needle in the right hand, the work in the left, and work from left to right, between two parallel lines. Make a few tiny securing stitches on the back of the work and bring the thread through to the right side (point A) on the lower line. Now make another stitch, inserting the needle at point B and bringing it out at point C. Finally make a diagonal stitch taking the needle in at point D and out at E.

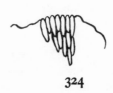

324

Long and short stitch (324)

This is one of the most important stitches in embroidery, the long and the short stitches alternating to produce a smooth effect for petals and leaves. The area can be shaded to give a realistic effect by the use of different tones of embroidery silk.

As can be seen from the diagram, fairly long stitches, alternating with shorter (though never small) stitches, are worked. The needle is held in the right hand, the work in the left. On the second row of stitches, the long and short stitches are interlaced with the first row to leave no gaps. It is rather like building up a brick wall, with the bricks interlocking.

323

Holbein stitch (323)

This simple stitch is normally worked with wool on canvas or linen. Another name for it is double running stitch. Two colours are used. First a

Lazy-daisy stitch (325)

This is one of the simplest of all embroidery stitches. Hold the needle in your right hand, the work in the left, and stitch towards you.

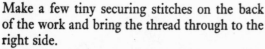

325

327

Make a few tiny securing stitches on the back of the work and bring the thread through to the right side.

(a) Insert the needle at the point where the thread has come through, catching down the loop of thread with the tip of the needle. Draw the needle through but do not pull the loop tightly.

(b) Catch the loop in place by inserting the needle through the work and bringing it out again near the base of the loop.

(c) Make a ring of lazy-daisy stitches to form a flower, and if you wish you can add a cluster of French knots at the centre.

forming part of an embroidery design, especially in wool embroidery. Take care that the stitches are neat and even. Another version of this is Overcast Running Stitch (327)—a popular stitch with young schoolchildren who you may find refer to it as Roly Poly Stitch. It consists of running stitch overcast by another strand of thread or wool, often in contrasting colours.

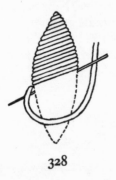

328

Satin stitch (328)

A beginner may not find it easy, at first, to achieve the smooth look which is so important with satin stitch. None of the background must show. As can be seen in the diagram, long stitches are taken from one side of a shape—say, a leaf—to the other. Often the stitches run diagonally across the shape. But they must always remain parallel with each other.

You can give the satin stitch areas a more noticeably raised effect by first padding the background with running stitches in the opposite direction from the lines of satin stitch.

326

Running stitch (326)

There is obviously nothing difficult about running stitch, but it is quite effective when

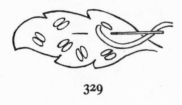

329

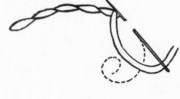

331

Seed stitch (329)

A stitch for decorating outlined areas of pattern, normally using wool. It simply involves two small stitches sewn side by side, and in many different directions. Care should be taken that the wrong side of the work is not puckered or made untidy by the connecting stitch being pulled too tightly.

330

Straight stitch (330)

A stitch of limited decorative value, although for children learning to embroider it can be a good starter stitch. The effect is improved if other stitches are mingled with straight stitch to give variety. As can be seen in the diagram, the stitch simply involves single strands of wool or embroidery silk, here sewn to form a flower-shape.

Stem stitch (331)

An outline stitch used again and again in embroidery for stems and leaf outlines; you hold the needle in your right hand and work from left to right, so that the needle points away from the direction in which you are working. Make a few tiny securing stitches on the back of the work, then bring the needle through to the right side. Take a small stitch back along the line to be worked, making sure that the thread is held away from the stitching line. You may prefer to do this by remembering always to move the thread away, or you may hold it with your thumb. Make another stitch. Notice how the stem stitch lies slightly diagonally across the stitching line.

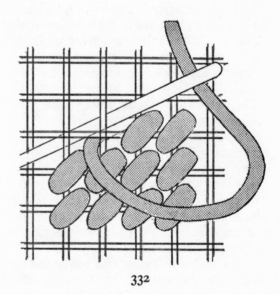

332

Tent stitch (332)

This is the stitch used in Petit Point, where single-thread canvas is covered with a smooth area of stitching. Notice how the needle is taken behind *two* warp threads of canvas to give a thicker, padded effect.

8

CLOTHES CARE

Good grooming is one of the most important aspects of living with comfort and dignity, and the earlier it is learned, the more ingrained the habit becomes. Anybody who is well groomed, no matter whether she is beautiful or plain, can retain that important commodity of self-respect. And self-respect is something a woman can keep all her life, when she no longer has youth or beauty on her side.

Most adult women have established their own standard of grooming, and need no advice or training on the subject. But let us go back to the other end of the scale. What advice would I give to a girl, say in her early teens, about the way to cultivate the habits of good grooming? I think the advice I would give goes along these lines:

The three most basic features of good grooming are

PERSONAL CLEANLINESS

TIDINESS

METICULOUS CLOTHES CARE

The ideal way to be well groomed at all times is to prepare each evening for the following day. This is the sort of idealistic advice which not everyone is able to take, but it is a question of establishing a good routine.

I once had a colleague who followed a set ritual when she arrived home from the office each day. She would not eat a meal or even stop to chat until she had removed her dress or suit, brushed it and removed any stains, and hung it on the back of the bedroom door to air; taken off her blouse and underwear and stockings, changed into clean clothes and washed all the discarded items. Then she would clean her shoes, stuff them with tissue paper and put them to air. Finally she would come downstairs to eat her evening meal.

Now of course there are not many adults who would be able to follow this strict regime; married women who work return home to various responsibilities – preparing a meal, washing up, perhaps catching up with the housework.

But a schoolgirl or young woman at work could try to get into the habit of preparing certain things for the following day before she goes to bed. Here is a checklist she might follow:
Check shoes, clean if necessary.
Put out top clothes for the following day.
Put out clean underwear and stockings.
Have clean gloves ready if summer gloves are being worn.
Put ready a clean handkerchief.

Be ready in time in the morning to give yourself a second glance to ensure you are dressed tidily. If your home has an arrangement of mirrors which enable you to see yourself full length from behind as well as from the front, this is ideal. You will then see yourself without any illusions – the back of your hair (is it too flat or too ruffled?), your posture (are you slouching?), your dress or skirt (is it crumpled or marked?), your stockings (do they have runs?), your shoes (are they scraped and down-at-heel, or dull and unpolished?).

Mirrors like this, well-lighted and uncompromising, can be a girl's best friend, and a chastening experience too, for they enable you to see yourself as others see you.

For many people personal tidiness is part of their nature, but if you are like the young daughter whose father said despairingly: 'She hasn't a tidy thought in her head', it will be a fairly uphill battle to ensure that your grooming is good enough to stand up to the critical glances of those around you. For it is an inescapable fact that you are judged to a great extent by your appearance, and it is not a bit of good wearing a beautifully-made garment which you have created and then spoiling the effect by careless grooming.

Handbag tidiness is important too, though it must be admitted that many of us feel our handbags would hardly bear inspection, with papers, cosmetics, tickets and oddments mixed in together. Try to dust your bag often, tidy it regularly and polish or wipe it (depending on whether it is leather or simulated leather) from time to time. When you tidy it, brush out the inside to remove any dust and loose powder, and wipe it out with a pad of cotton wool dipped in spirit cleaner or carbon tetrachloride. (Note the warnings about the use of carbon tetrachloride on page 187).

Any marks from a ballpoint pen can usually be removed with methylated spirit (denatured alcohol), and lipstick, too, may respond to the same treatment although some red dye may remain which you could treat with diluted hydrogen peroxide.

For plastic handbags there are proprietary liquids which clean and shine the surface at the same time – handbag shops usually stock them.

Care for the clothes you have made

When you have made a garment for yourself, you will want it to last and this means you must take care of it. When you take off a dress or a suit, you should put it on a shaped hanger. A skirt should be neatly folded over the lower rail of a double hanger. A dress or jacket should be fastened properly, the sleeves pulled straight and not tucked in.

Brush the collar to remove any hair or specks of dust which have settled on it. Hang the garment out in the bedroom until morning to allow any body moisture to evaporate, and then put it into the wardrobe. Try to wear clothes in rotation, rather than every day, to give the fabric time to rest and recover its resilience.

Stain removal is dealt with at the end of this chapter.

DRY-CLEANING

Modern dry-cleaning does not, contrary to popular belief, wear out clothes. The only clothes which *do* weaken after cleaning are those that have been left dirty for far too long. In fact, dirt and grit left on the fibres of a fabric can do far more damage than regular drycleaning.

What the cleaning process does, however, is to remove some of the original dressing used to make the fabric appear of a better quality. (This is yet another advantage of home dressmaking – you can choose better quality fabrics from the start.) The re-texturing process which many dry-cleaners offer can restore some of this finish.

You may notice that woollen garments often have a thin, flat look when they return from the dry-cleaner's. This is because the natural moisture always present in wool has been reduced. You can put this to rights quite quickly by hanging the garment in a steamy atmosphere – for example in the bathroom – for a few hours.

Coin-op dry cleaners

Many launderettes have now installed coin-operated dry-cleaning machines, where you can dry-clean a load of garments – usually 8 to 12 lb. – while you wait. Many garments will dry-clean in this way very satisfactorily. Remember, however, that although the cost is much lower, and normally the results are good, they do not provide the advantages of a good dry-cleaning works, where there is a special section to deal with very stubborn marks.

The coin-op machines will normally remove simple grease-based stains, but it is possible that water-based stains will not come out. These should be treated beforehand with water to remove any water-soluble particles, and the article should then be completely dried before being taken to the coin-op machine. Any mark that remains will probably be grease, and the machine will deal with it.

In some coin-ops you may be provided with a

'steam gun' to treat stains before putting the articles in the machine. Always use it with a circular motion and keep it moving at an angle of roughly 45 degrees to the fabric. Do not hold it straight down on to one patch of material—the force could make a hole in the fabric.

HOME LAUNDERING

Whether or not you will be able to launder at home the clothes you have made will depend on the way in which you have made them and the fabrics you have chosen. Provided the main fabric and any lining fabrics are washable, you should be able to launder the article by hand, and if seams are well-finished and trimmings well-chosen, you should be able to machine-wash it too, if you prefer. The charts in a previous chapter describe in detail the washing treatments suitable for all the main fabrics.

It is important to remember that any garment which needs frequent washing, such as a child's dress, a baby's bib, a little boy's pair of trousers or a small girl's overall, will be useless if you have concentrated on its decorative qualities at the expense of its practical potential. A baby's bib such as one often sees for sale, with a bias binding edge and perhaps an appliqué motif in a bright colour, or lined with plastic and edged with flimsy bias binding, and even with bias binding ties, is a poor buy, and a waste of your time to make. Any raw edge finished with bias binding will be completely ruined after a few washes in any normal domestic washing machine—the bias binding is pulled away from the raw edge, which in turn will quickly disintegrate too. Practicality is just as important as prettiness where washable garments are concerned. It you make towelling bibs, turn in and finish off the edges well (the new machines with their stretchy zigzag stitches are an ideal way of finishing turnings on towelling). It is in any case possible to make such articles highly decorative without spoiling their washability. If you add a trimming, see that the colour is not likely to run and that it is stitched down very thoroughly, not just stitched down in one or two places.

DARNING

While preparing this book I have had some interesting comments on darning. A school examiner told me: 'We do not insist on the children learning patching and darning these days, because people have a different attitude to clothes now. If a garment needs repairing they tend to throw it away and buy a new one.'

Another revealing comment came from a demonstrator consultant from a sewing machine manufacturer, who visits schools and colleges: 'Some of the students bring me a darn which they have been working on. Usually it is well sewn, with fine, close stitches, and sometimes it has taken them a whole term of sewing lessons to complete. I show them how the same hole can be darned on a sewing machine in less than five minutes, and the darn is almost invisible.'

From these two statements one could conclude that nowadays no-one darns anything, and if they do, they use a sewing machine. But of course many mothers do still have to darn household linens and their children's clothes, and many families do not have a sewing machine on which they can darn.

Perhaps the wisest course is to learn both ways of darning—by hand and by machine. I do not think it a waste of time for a girl to practise making at least one darn by hand. She may not have to darn her husband's socks when she marries because they will probably contain nylon or some other synthetic fibre. But sheets can develop small holes, a small daughter may put her heel through her skirt, or cut a hole in her best dress with scissors, and the cat may claw at a curtain or furniture-cover. I am sure few families would be in a position to throw such articles away and buy new ones just because of a small tear or hole. If there is no sewing machine, it will be important to know how to hand-darn. So here is the classic method of darning a hole in a piece of cloth or wool:

Thread a needle with thread or wool suitable for the article to be darned. Choose a colour which matches as nearly as possible. Use the thread or wool single unless the article is excessively thick.

If the hole has ragged edges with many frayed threads, press with a damp cloth to neaten. Cut off any threads too frayed to blend in.

Placing the article on a flat surface, run a line of tacking stitches in a round or oval shape around the area to be darned, making sure that the darn will be large enough to cover the thin places round the hole.

Use a darning mushroom, in a colour which will show up against the material being darned.

If you are darning a knitted article where stitches have run, use a fine crochet hook to pick up dropped stitches.

Now with the needle threaded, begin darning with the grain of the fabric (or with the direction of the row in the case of knitting). Start at least ¼ in. beyond the edge of the hole–or further away if the thin area is extensive. Make the first line you darn equal to the length of the hole at its widest point.

Weave the needle in and out with small stitches, crossing the 'gap', and when you reach the end of the row, turn round and start to darn back down the fabric again, making sure that the second line of stitches is parallel to the first but very slightly longer. Leave a loop of thread or wool at the end of the first and subsequent rows–this will allow for shrinkage in the wash and elasticity in wear. Continue to darn, increasing the length of each row so that the final shape of the darn is round or oval. If you do it in this way, the edge of the darn will not pull on one thread or strand of the fabric.

Similarly, decrease the length of each row as you work over the second half of the hole.

In a knitted garment, take care to pick up all the loops, to prevent laddering.

Now begin crossing the darn at right angles to the first stitches, weaving under and over alternate threads. Try as far as possible not to pick up the fibres of the fabric itself when crossing the darn, but only the darning threads. This will give a neater, woven look. Try, too, not to split the strands as you pick them up. Turn to the back of the work, neaten any raw or ragged edges by securing them to the back of the darned patch.

Press the darn on both sides, using a damp cloth.

How to darn by machine

This will depend on the type of machine you have. With a straight-stitch machine, darning is done with a spring darning foot. The feed dog is disengaged, either by using a feed cover plate or making a simple adjustment to drop the feed teeth. If you have a zigzag machine, you again disengage the feed, but normally no foot attachment is required. In this case, darning involves making a series of zigzag stitches over the area. Three-step zigzag, where available, or the five-step serpentine stitch, which some machines offer, are both ideal for darning.

The work to be darned is fitted into a darning hoop – either an 8 in. hoop or a small hoop for darning socks. The hole may be backed with a piece of muslin to give added strength.

The instruction book with the sewing machine should give advice on the way to darn with the model you are using. If you do not find this information sufficient, it is worth writing to the manufacturers to see whether there is any additional literature which would help you.

FIRST-AID FOR FORTY FREQUENT STAINS

Keep a few stain-removal agents handy for immediate use on stains. You can buy various kinds of proprietary stain-removers; and if you follow the directions carefully, you will be able to remove most stains, provided you treat them speedily enough. A useful substance to keep in the house for removing grease stains is carbon tetrachloride. A little on a pad of cotton wool will freshen a collar extremely well, and grease or greasy food stains can be removed quickly and easily. Carbon tetrachloride is available from any chemist or drugstore. *Warning:* it is very important to take certain safety measures, as carbon tetrachloride, wrongly handled, can be very dangerous. Always have a window open when you are using it, for the fumes, though not flammable, are poisonous. Always keep it out of reach of small children. Never use it in a room where there is a fire but no ventilation, or the fumes may cause you to become unconscious. Never iron over a piece of fabric which you have just treated with carbon tetrachloride: wait until it has had time to evaporate completely. The last rule sounds faintly tongue-in-cheek, but I am assured it is textbook advice for dry-cleaning operatives: it is dangerous to use carbon tetrachloride if you have had anything alcoholic to drink (obviously this rule assumes an excess of one or the other–or both) and those who take sleeping tablets are also advised to treat carbon tetrachloride with particular caution.

Probably the most dramatic type of stain remover which has come on to the market for washable clothes is the range of enzyme products –the enzyme pre-soak powders such as Biotex, Big S and Luvil, and the enzyme detergents such as Ariel, Radiant and Drive. These are almost invariably effective in removing protein stains, and sometimes non-protein stains too, provided you use them intelligently. Never forget that most enzyme products will be ineffective at temperatures above 60°C (140°F)–normally the temperature of the water which comes out of your hot tap.

Alcoholic drinks. Sponge immediately with clear warm water, pat dry with a clean absorbent towel.

Ball point pen. Methylated spirits is the most effective, but not on rayons or Tricel which it might damage. Second bests include carbon tetrachloride or cleaning benzene.

Beach oil. Eucalyptus oil is undoubtedly the finest for removing this black oil from clothes, shoes and body. Use it in the open air if possible–it is very pungent in a small room. An alternative is lighter fuel–useful if you are on a beach with no likelihood of obtaining eucalyptus oil that day.

Beer. Sponge with clear water, pat dry. Neglected stains may come out gradually after several machine-washes, or you can try soaking the mark in warm water with ammonia (1 tsp. to 1 pint water). For unwashable garments where home treatment proves ineffective, dry-cleaning will be the best answer.

Black grease. Grease from a car axle or a bicycle or a lawnmower presents two problems. You have to remove the grease, which is relatively easy with carbon tetrachloride which you can purchase from your chemist. Then there's the black stain which will probably linger on. Remove this by thorough washing if the fabric is washable, using water as hot as the fabric will allow, plus a light nailbrush.

With unwashable fabrics sponge with the grease solvent, then if the stain remains, sprinkle the area with french chalk, talcum powder or fuller's earth. Rubbing well with the fingertips, sprinkle on a little solvent, and when it has finally evaporated brush off the powder.

Blacklead. Use turpentine on a clean cloth.

Blood. Only one treatment is worth pursuing these days: an enzyme powder such as Bio-Tex, Big-S or Luvil. Almost invariably effective, if used according to directions.

Car oil. As for black grease.

Cellulose paint. Sponge with acetone or nail varnish remover. Do *not* use either, however, if the fabric is an acetate or Tricel. For these fabrics, use amyl acetate.

Chewing gum. A cure for chewing gum stains seems to have been given in every stain-removal guide published since the stuff was invented! Perhaps modern chewing gum has changed since the 'old days' but personally I find it leaves not so much a stain as a sticky mess. I suppose if you left it there long enough it would 'magnet' in all the surrounding dirt and thus become a stain. In the event of your finding chewing gum stains, however, scrape and pull off as much as possible. If the article is small, for example, a child's dress or a cushion cover, put it in a polythene bag in the refrigerator to make the gum harder, more brittle, less clinging. Or try rubbing the area with an ice-cube–the time-honoured method which I can never make to work. Clear up the residue of the gum with carbon tetrachloride.

Chocolate. Scrape off any solid chocolate with a blunt knife, then treat as for the coffee stain below.

Cigarette burns. A light scorch mark may be improved by applying a thick paste of borax mixed with glycerine. Leave it overnight, then either brush off the paste or wash the article, depending on the fabric. If the fabric is not washable you should still sponge it, wringing out the cloth frequently in fresh warm water, to remove all traces of the borax and glycerine.

Bad burns will require invisible mending– you can use your sewing machine for this if it is suitable. If you have never tried darning before, put in some practice first on sample scraps of material. If the burning is extensive you may have to use a piece of the same fabric and apply a patch. If you have not kept left-over scraps, you may be able to cut a small piece out of one of the seam allowances.

Cocoa. As for coffee. See below.

Cod liver oil. This clings limpet-like if allowed to settle. Whisk off as much as possible with a cloth or tissue, wash immediately if the fabric is suitable, or use carbon tetrachloride on the dry fabric if it is not. If the stain is stubborn, re-treat; and if that is unsuccessful try having the garment dry-cleaned straight away, making sure to tell the assistant what the stain is.

Coffee. Tackle the stain immediately. Mop up the coffee with a dry, old towel, then with a clean cloth and warm water, sponge the fabric vigorously. If the article is washable, wash immediately, first in warm water only and then increasing the temperature, if the fabric can take it. Leave the mark soaking in a good solution of very hot water and washing powder. Neglected stains may require a visit to a dry-cleaner. Point out the stain and be prepared for the fact that it may now be indelible. A borax solution (1 level tablespoonful per pint of water) is often recommended as an alternative solution for soaking the stain, but I have derived very little benefit from this method. I prefer to soak overnight in enzyme wash powder suds.

Dandelion. Sponge with methylated spirits (not on acetates or Tricel). Wash if the article is washable.

Dye. If the article is white, or so badly streaked that total removal of its colour is the only answer, use a colour-stripper called Dygon.

Re-dye if necessary. If you are not going to re-dye, wash the article thoroughly in a hot, fairly strong detergent solution to remove the yellowish tinge. Leave it to soak in the suds if necessary.

Egg. I have never met an egg white or yolk that did not respond to the scrape/sponge/dab-dry treatment. A little liquid detergent added to the water used for sponging will help. If the garment is not washable, merely scrape and sponge well. A newer answer for washable fabrics is the enzyme type product (see under Blood) which will act on the albumen in the egg.

Emulsion paint. A pernicious enemy–so immediate treatment is absolutely essential; even then the colour may cling to some fabrics. You need masses of water, constantly changed, to soak the article. Do not use turpentine. If the stain has hardened before you can do anything about it, try sponging with methylated spirits. If that fails, take your problem to the dry-cleaner.

Enamel paint. Sponge with turpentine or turps substitute.

Eye make-up. A special product sold for removing eye make-up from your face can also, I have found, be used for washable articles. Be sure to wash the treated area thoroughly afterwards.

Food stains. Wash as normal if the fabric can be washed. Where there are protein or albumen stains (gravy, egg, etc.) use a proprietary enzyme product.

Fruit juice. Soak immediately in plain warm water, adding 1 level tablespoonful of borax if wished. Neglected stains need soaking in a solution of 20 vol. hydrogen peroxide–one part to five parts water.

Grass stains. Sponge with methylated spirits.

Gravy. See Food Stains.

Grease. Use carbon tetrachloride, changing the pad held behind the stain as it becomes dirty, and renewing the cloth also.

Indelible pencil. Use methylated spirits or acetone (except for acetates and Tricel fabrics, for which you use amyl acetate). Alternatively permanganate of potash ($\frac{1}{2}$ teaspoon crystals in

$\frac{1}{2}$ pint warm water) may be used on any white fabrics except acetates and triacetates.

Ink. If possible swamp the stained area with water until all loose ink has been rinsed away, then wash in hot soapy water. Allow the article to dry naturally, and if the stain still remains, professional treatment may be necessary. Tell the cleaner what kind of ink it is (e.g. whether it is washable ink, Indian ink, marking ink, etc.). The odd small stain may respond to a proprietary spot remover or ink eradicator. Or try dabbing with methylated spirits.

Latex adhesive. 'Copydex' provide their own antidote–a specially-formulated solvent which works. Nothing else in your stain-removal kit will have the same effect. Details on Copydex packs.

Lipstick. Scrape, then sponge with carbon tetrachloride or eucalyptus oil.

Mildew. Repeated soakings in a strong solution of soap powder such as Persil may work if you are patient. Between each soaking rinse and hang the article to dry to catch any sunshine, which will have a mild bleaching effect. Often mildew will fade after several normal hot machine washes. Or try diluted 20 vol. hydrogen peroxide (one part to four parts of water) if the fabric is white. Extensive mildew may need professional treatment.

Mud. The surplus mud is easily rinsed away–it is the discoloration that remains which is the problem. Wash immediately if the fabric is suitable, in water as hot as the fabric can stand. For non-washable articles the treatment is different: do not soak or sponge, simply allow the mud to dry and brush off the next day with a clean brush. Talcum powder rubbed in may help.

Nail polish. Sponge with acetone or nail varnish remover on pads of cotton wool. If the fabric is acetate rayon or Tricel, use amyl acetate instead to avoid damaging the fabric.

Oil paint. Oil paint needs turpentine, turps substitute or proprietary paint cleaner.

Perspiration. The enzyme type products mentioned above can help here. Soak the marked areas in a solution made up as directed. Wash the article thoroughly, and allow to dry. If any staining remains, or perspiration odour, soak the fabric again, in a solution of vinegar and water (one part vinegar to eight parts warm water).

Rust. The simplest and most effective is a proprietary rust remover. Other methods employ chemicals which are not particularly safe to have around the house.

Shoe polish. If the fabric is washable, wash in warm water with a detergent plus a little ammonia. Re-wash at the normal temperature for the fabric and allow to dry. If any staining remains, or if you cannot try this method because the garment cannot be washed, use carbon tetrachloride or turpentine.

Suntan oil. Sponge with carbon tetrachloride.

Tea. As for coffee. See above.

Wine. If you are at table, pour salt on the stained area and leave it to soak up the wine while you go to fetch clean cloths to sponge the stain. As soon as is practicable, put the stained cloth to soak in cold water, adding a little borax if wished. If the wine stain has dried and set, stretch the cloth over your washing-up bowl, hollow the centre of the stain lightly, sprinkle thickly with borax and then pour boiling water through. Alternatively, after soaking in cold water, put the article to soak in a strong solution of soap powder and hot water. Some people find that soaking in an enzyme product helps. If the article is a delicate tablecloth, the soaking will be far more effective than hard rubbing.

If the garment cannot be washed, try a proprietary spray-on product, which will probably remove the mark without harming the fabric.

INDEX

Abrasion of glass fibre, to avoid, 160
Acetates, as lining to counteract static, 157; fibre information chart, 150-1; iron setting for, 27, 151; overseas trademarks, 150; sewing notes, 151; removing stains from, 151, 189, 190; tests for, 174-5; to wash, 137, 151
Acetic acid, 150
Acetic anhydride, 150
Acetone, 151, 152, 154, 188; in fibre test, 175
Acrilan, *see* acrylic fibres
Acrylic fibres: fibre information chart, 156-7; iron setting for, 27, 157; overseas trademarks, 156; sewing notes, 157; tests for, 174-5; to wash, 137, 157
Acrylic/cotton mixtures, *see* acrylic fibres
Acrylic/wool mixtures, *see* acrylic fibres
Acrylonitrile, 156, 164
Adjustable hem measure, 18
Adjustable waistband, 109-10
Adjusting pressure on machine, 13, 75
Adjusting tension, 13, 41, 75
Adjusting the paper pattern, 61
Advantages of home dressmaking, 185
Advice from the store, 137
After-sales service, sewing machine, 38
Agilon, 166, 170
Agitation, washing machine principle, 136
Alastra, 152
Albene, 150
Albumen stains, to remove, 189
Alcohol, effect with carbon tetrachloride, 188
Alcoholic drinks stains, to remove, 188
Aligning buttons with buttonholes, 132
All silk, 146
Alteration marks, using tailor's chalk, 22
Altering the paper pattern, 63
Amilan, 166
Ammonia, in stain treatment, 188
Amyl acetate, 188, 189
Anti-freeze, in man-made fibres, 135
Antron, 166
Antung, 146

Appearance, personal, 185
Appliqué work, 43
Approximate ease allowance table, 61
Argentina as source of wool, 148
Ariel, 188
Arm, to measure, 57
Armhole, to increase size of, 63
Armhole seams, to neaten, 104
Arnel, 154
Arrowhead stitch, 176
Arrows for direction of grain, 75
Assembling garment for first fitting, 68
Attachments for seamlines, 41
Attachments for sewing machines, 37
Australia as source of wool, 148
Automatic buttonholers, 37
Automatic embroidery, 43
Automatic sewing machines, 36
Avisco, 152

Babies' garments, a seam for, 84
Baby's bib, 186
Back bodice length, to measure, 56
Back waist length: ease allowance, 61; to measure, 56
Back width, to measure, 57
Background of fibres, *see* fibre information charts, 141-73
Backstitch, 177
Badly-finished seams, importance of avoiding, 74
Ball point pen stains, to remove, 188; marks on handbag, 185
Ban-Care, 172
Ban-Lon, 166, 168
Bar tack, 89
Barathea, 146, 148
Basting (tacking) stitch on sewing machine, 68, 75, 86
Basting (tacking) stitches by hand, types of, 72
Batiste, 142
Beach oil stains, to remove, 188
Bed-linen, 144

Bedding, cotton, 142
Bedford cord, 148
Beer stains, to remove, 188
Beginners sewing course, Chapter 4, 55
Beginning to stitch, 41
Belgium as source of flax, 144
Belgium as source of man-made fibres: Alastra, 152; Veranne, 160
Belts, 110; turning belts, 20
Bemberg, 152
Bernina machines, 35; *see also* sewing machine photographs between 40 and 41
Bias binding: for hem finishing, 121; where to avoid using, 186
Bias braid, 84
Bias strips: scissor gauge for, 25; to cut, 84
Bias tape to neaten underarm seam, 108
Bias-bound hems: 121, 123, 124
Bias-bound seam edges, 77
Bicycle grease stains, to remove, 188
Big S in stain treatment, 188
Biotex in stain treatment, 188
Black grease stains, to remove, 188
Blacklead stains, to remove, 188
Blackmore Pattern Service, 50
Blanket stitch, 177
Bleached calico or strong cotton, for pressing aids, 31
Blend, meaning of, 139
Blind-hemming, 35, 37
Blind-stitched hem, 121
Blind-stitched zip, 118
Blood stains, to remove, 188
Blue 'C' nylon, 166
Bobbin, non-jamming, 38
Bodice, 70; to measure, 56
Bodkin, 16
Body Measurement Chart, New Sizing, 51.
Body, restoring to fabrics after dry-cleaning, 185
Body, retaining through steam ironing, 27
Boiled water and steam irons, 28
Bonded interlinings: for buttonholes, 85; for linen, 145; for wool, 149; with acetate, 151
Borax, in stain treatment, 189, 190
Bouclé, 148
Bound buttonholes, 85
Bound pocket, 90
Bound seam edges, by machine attachment, 77
Bound seam edges, machined and hand-sewn, 77
Boys' trousers, 186
Brazil as source of man-made fibres: Grillon, 166; Rhodia, 150; Tergal, 168

BRI-NYLON, 166
British Celanese Ltd. (Courtaulds), 150, 154
British Enkalon Ltd., 166
British Man Made Fibres Federation, 139
British Standard 2747, 136
British Standard 3120, 164
British Standards Institution, 136
Broadcloth, 148
Brocade, 146; acetate brocade, 150
Bulked Terlenka, 168
Bulked yarns, 170; *see also* 156, 166, 168
Bulky seams, 42; pinking bulky seams, 24; trimming where seams intersect, 82. *See also* under grading, 80
Bullion stitch, 177
Burn marks, to treat, 189
Burning test, 174
Bust, ease allowance for, 61; to measure, 56
Butterick Publishing Co. Ltd., The, 50
Buttonhole scissors, 23
Buttonhole stitch (embroidery), 178
Buttonhole stitch for hooks and eyes, 133
Buttonhole twist, 21, 133
Buttonholer attachment, 35, 37
Buttonholes, 85: bound, 86; cutting open, 21; hand-worked, 88; machine-worked, 88; tailored, 89; to adjust size of, 86; to practise making, 66, 85; to re-space, 86
Buttons, 130
Buying the extras, 58
Buying your materials, 58

Caftan dress, zip for, 115
Calico or strong cotton, 142; for pressing aids, 31
Calico Printers Association Ltd., 168
Calpreta Carefree Wringable finish, 172
Calpreta Fixt Finish, 172
Calpreta Shrunk, 172
Cambric, 142
Canada as source of man-made fibres: Coloray, 152; Du Pont nylon, 166; Fiberglas, 160; Lycra, 158; Trilan, 154
Canada as source of wool, 148
Cantrece, 166
Cap sleeve, 109
Car axle grease stains, to remove, 188
Car oil stains, to remove, 188
Carbon paper, dressmaker's, 18, 22, 67, 68
Carbon tetrachloride, 157, 188, 189, 190; for hand-bag cleaning, 185; warnings, 187
Care and maintenance of the sewing machine, 44
Care for the clothes you have made, 185

Care labels, 137
Carpet wool fibres, 148
Case for sewing machine, 38
Casing, to thread, 16
Catch-stitched hem, 122
Catch-stitched hem, bias bound, 123
Cavalry twill, 148
Celafibre, 150
Cellulose, 150
Cellulose fibre, 152
Cellulosic fibres, information charts, 150–5: acetate, 150; rayon, 152; triacetate, 154
Cellulose paint stains, to remove, 188
Celon, 152, 166
Centimetre measurements, 41
Chain stitch, 178
Chalk, marking with, 68; chalk pencil, 15, 22; resin-based and wax-based chalk, 157; clay or limestone chalk, 157
Chalked thread, marking with, 68
Changing sewing machine needle, 41
Check-list when buying sewing machine, 38
Checking the grain lines, 65
Checking the measurements against each other, 62
Checking the seam allowance, 75
Chemstrand nylon, 166
Cheslene, 168
Cheslon, 166, 170
Chewing gum marks, to remove, 188
Chiffon, 146; rayon chiffon, 152
Chile as source of wool, 148
China as source of cotton, 142; as source of silk-worms, 146
Chintz, 142
Chlorine bleach and silk, 146
Chocolate stains, to remove, 188
Cigarette burns, to treat, 189
Circular skirt, hemline, 125
Classification of fabrics for ironing, 27; for washing, 137
Cleaning benzene, 188
Cleaning the sewing machine, 44
Clevyl T, 164
Cling, to lessen, 167
Clothes Care, Chapter 8, 184
Coat, zip for, 115
Coat buttons, 130
Cocoa stains, to remove, 189
Cod liver oil stains, to remove, 189
Coffee stains, to remove, 189
Coin-op dry cleaners, 185
Cold rinsing, 173

Cold water dye, 151
Collars, 95: distorted, to prevent, 97; points of, to trim, 98; rever, 99; soft, 101
Coloray, 152
Colour fabric, to choose, 53
Coloured cottons, to wash, 137, 143
Coloured linens, to wash, 137, 145
Coloured nylon, to wash, 137, 167
Colourfast rayons, 153
Colourfast wash, label for, 137
Colours which run, 186
Colva, 152
Commercial patterns, 11, see paper patterns
Concealed zipper, 111
Constructional seam, 74
Continuous filament yarn, 139
Conversion from Centigrade to Fahrenheit, 141
Copydex stains, to remove, 190
Cord, fine, to thread, 16
Corded buttonhole, 89
Corded seam, 83
Cording foot, 83
Corduroy, 142; to press, 29
Correcting figure faults, 63, 64
Cotton as lining to counteract static, 157
Cotton: fibre information chart, 142–3; iron setting for, 27; sewing notes, 143; tests for, 174, 175; to wash, 137, 143
Cotton, for sewing, see under Sewing Threads
Cotton flower, 142
Cotton lace, 143
Cotton-seed oil, 142
Cottons with special finishes: fibre information chart, 172–3; iron settings for, 27, 173; sewing notes, 173; to wash, 137, 173; when setting in sleeves, 105
Couching stitch, 178
Country wear, fabrics for, 53
Courtaulds Ltd., 152, 154, 156, 158, 164, 166
Courtelle, see acrylic fibres
Covers, ironing board, 29
Cracking of glass fibre, to avoid, 160
Crease-resist linen, 144
Crease-resisting finish, 172
Crêpe, 146, 148
Creslan, 156
Cretan stitch, 179
Crilenka, 156
Crimped Celon, 166
Crimped rayon, 152
Crimplene, see nylon (polyester), 168; also textured, bulk and stretch yarns, 170

Crochet hook, 16
Cross stitch, 179
Crossbred wool fibres, 148
Crylor, 156
Cuffs and sleeve edges, 127
Cupioni, 152
Cuprama, 152
Cuprammonium, 152
Cupresa, 152
Curling seam edges, one way to avoid, 84
Curtaining, cotton, 142; linen, 144
Curved hem, bias bound, 124
Curved seams, 80; to finish, 80; to press, 31, 81
Cutting gauge, 25
Cutting layouts, 59–60
Cutting needle, for sewing leather, 42
Cutting out shears, see dressmaker's shears
Cutting out the garment, 59, 66
Cutting tools, 15, 23–5
Czechoslovakia, as source of Silon, 166

Dacron, 168
Damask, 144
Damping down fabrics, 33
Dandelion stains, to remove, 189
Danufil, 152
Danulon, 166
Darning, 186; darning stitch, 179; darning mush-
   room, 16, 187; darning by machine, 187
Darts, 73: double-pointed, 74; on heavy fabric, 73;
   the right way to sew darts, 73; slashed edges of darts,
   to finish, 73; to mould, 31; to press, 73; to slash, 73
Day dresses, fabrics for, 53
Dealers' service, 38
Dealing with preliminaries, 58
Decorative garments, practicality of, 186
Decorative pincushions, 20
Decorative seam, to give line, 74
Decorative work with a sewing machine, 42
Deeglas, 160
Deeglas Fibres Ltd., 160
Delfion, 166
Delustrant, in fibre manufacture, 151
Demineralised water for steam irons, 28
Demonstration of sewing machine, 38
Demonstrators, sewing machine, 39
Denatured alcohol, in stain treatment, 185
Denim, 142
Depalene, 168
Depalon, 166
Depanyl, 166
Detergent, for wool, 149

Deterioration of cotton, a cause of, 142
Diagonal tacking (basting), 72
Diamond-shaped markings, 67
Dicel, 150
Dicel KN, 150
'Difficult fabrics', 42
Dimethyl formamide, in fibre test, 175
Dimity, 142
Diolen, 168
Direction of seams, 74
Directory of sewing processes, 72
Distilled water, 28
Dolan, 156
Dolman sleeve, 108
Domestic bleach on wool, 148
Double knitting wool, garments, making up, 19
Double top stitched seam finish, 78
Double v-notches, 66
Double-pointed dart, 74
Douppion, 146
Drafting paper patterns, 11
Dralon, 156
Dress designing, 11
Dress forms, 16, 17, 70
Dress linens, 144
Dress zipper, 111
Dressing, 185
Dressmaker's dummy, 16, 17
Dressmaker's shears, 23, 24: keeping sharp, 24;
   misuses to avoid, 24; pinking shears, 24; trying
   before buying, 23; when to oil, 24
Drill, 142
Drill weave linen, 144
Drip-feed irons, 27
Drive, 188
Dry clean only labels, 136
Dry-cleanable garments, 136
Dry cleaning, 185; of acrylics, 157
Dry extrusion, in man-made fibre manufacture, 138
Dry irons, lightweight, 26
Du Pont nylon, 166
Du Pont (UK) Ltd., 156, 158
Ducilo, 166
Dulled fibre, 139
Durafil, 152
Duraglas, 160
Dye, stains to remove, 189
Dyeing, nylon, 167
Dygon, 189
Dynel, 164

Ease, points to check, 70

Ease Allowance Table, 61

Eased seams, 81

East Germany, as source of man-made fibres: Prelana, 156; Trilon, 166; Wolcrylon, 156; Zehla, 152

Edge-stitched seam finish, 78

Edge-stitcher attachment, 37

Efylon, 166

Egg stain, to remove, 189

Egypt as source of cotton, 142

Egypt as source of Misr nylon, 166

Eight washing processes, 136, 137

Elastic, to thread, 16; for waistband, 110

Elastofibres, *see* Elastomerics

Elastomerics: fibre information chart, 158–9; overseas trademarks, 158; sewing notes, 159; tests for, 174–5; to wash, 159

Electric scissors, 24

Electrostatic properties of fibres, *see* fibre information charts, 141–73

Embossed finishes, 172

Embroiderers' Guild, 44

Embroiderers' Guild American Branch Inc., 44

Embroidery fabrics, linen, 144

Embroidery, hand, Chapter 7, 176

Embroidery frames, 25

Embroidery scissors, 25

Embroidery silks, 21, 26

Embroidery stitches, Chapter 7, 176

Embroidery, using a sewing machine, 42

Emery bag or cushion, 20

Emulsion paint stains, to remove, 189

Enant, 166

Encron, 168

Ends of seams, to finish, 42, 76

Enka rayon, 152

Enka-nylon, 166

Enkalon, 166

Enkasheer, 166

Enkaswing, 158

Enzyme powders, 188

Equipment for hand embroidery, 15, 25, 26

Equipment for sewing, to choose, 13–33

Estron, 150

Eucalyptus oil, as stain remover, 188

Europe as source of wool, 148

Even tacking (basting), 72

Evening dresses, ease allowance, 61

Evening wear, fabric for, 53

Evlan, 152

Evlan M, 152

Examinations, sewing, 12

Extrusion, explanation of, 138

Eye makeup stains, to remove, 189

Eyelet holes, to make, 26

Fabric, choosing, 53

Fabric lengths, care labels for, 137

Fabric losing 'body' after dry cleaning, to cure, 185

Fabric losing 'body' after pressing, 27, 29

Fabric preparation, 58

Fabric test piece, 40

Fabric, type of for garment, 53

Fabric width, 59

Fabrics for the occasion, 53

Faced neckline, 95

Faced sleeve edge, 127

Faille, 146

False hem, 123

Faults in the sewing machine, 46

Features to look for in a sewing machine, 37

Felting, 148

Felts, wool, 148

Fergolin, 154

Fiberglas, 160

Fibre blend, meaning of, 139

Fibre information charts:

    Cellulosic fibres: acetate, 150; rayon, 152; triacetate, 154

    Man-made fibres: acrylics, 156; elastomerics, 158; glass fibre, 160; metallic fibres, 162; modacrylics, 164; nylon (polyamide), 166; polyester, 168; textured, bulked and stretch yarns, 170

    Natural fibres: cotton, 142; linen, 144; silk, 146; wool, 148

    Special finishes, 172

Fibre mixture, meaning of, 139

Fibreglass, 160; *see also* Glass fibre

Fibreglass Ltd., 160

Fibrenka, 152

Figure types, 13, 48

Filament, rayon, 152

Filaments, man-made fibre, 138

Filaments, silk, 146

Final adjustments before stitching a garment, 69

Finding actual measurement of pattern pieces, 62

Finishes, *see* Fabrics, Fibres and Finishes, 135

Finishes for seams, *see* Seams and Finishes, 74

Finishing touches, 71

First fitting, 68

First sewing stitches, 19

Flame-resistant fibre, nightwear, 164

Flange hemmer, 37

Flannel, 148
Flannelette, 142
Flat bed sewing machine, 36
Flat fell seam, 84
Flattened look in fabric, to avoid when pressing, 27, 29
Flattened look in fabric, to correct after dry cleaning, 185
Flax plant, *see* linen, 144
Flax, tests for, 174–5
Fleecy linings, 156
Flisca, 152
Floccal, 152
Fluflene, 168, 170
Fluflon, 166, 170
Fly stitch, 176, 180
Foam-back fabrics, 42
Fold-away ironing board, 28
Food stains, 189
Fortrel, 168
Foulard, 146
France as a source of flax, 144; as source of silk-worms, 146
France as a source of man-made fibres: Clevyl T, 164; Crylor, 156; Floccal, 152; Rhodia, 150; Rhodiaceta, 166; Veranne, 160
Fraying, seam edges, the way to avoid, 84
Free-arm sewing machine, 36
Free-hand embroidery, sewing machine, 43
French chalk, in stain treatment, 188
French knots, 176, 180, 182
French seam, 84
Frequently-washed garments, 186
Front bodice length, to measure, 56
Fuller's earth, in stain treatment, 188
Fulling, 148

Gaberdine, 142; wool gaberdine, 148
Gathering foot, 37
Gathers, to press, 31
Gauge presser foot, 37
General equipment for sewing, 15
Germany as source of Rhodia, 150
Georgette, 146; wool georgette, 148
Gevetex, 160
Gingham, 142
Girl's overall, 186
Girls' sizes, Measurement Chart, 51
Glass cloths: cotton, 142; linen, 144
Glass fibre: fibre information chart, 160–1; tests for, 174–5; to wash, 137, 161
Glazed cottons, dealing with sleeves, 105
Glazed finishes, 172

Glospan, 158
Glycerine, in stain treatment, 189
Gosamer thread, 171
Grading a seam, 80
Grain of fabric, for direction of seams, 74
Grain lines, checking with yardstick, 23, 65
Grass stains, to remove, 189
Gravy stains, to remove, 189
Grease stains, to remove, 189
Grease-based stains, when using coin-op machines, 185
Grillon, 166
Grilon, 166
Grooming, 185
Guarantees for sewing machines, 38
Guide lines, for seams, 41

H.L.C.C., *see* Home Laundering Consultative Council
H.L.C.C. Classification of fibres for ironing, 27; for washing, 136
Half-sizes, 51
Ham, tailors, 31
Hand-embroidery, equipment for, 15, 25, 26
Hand-finishing seams, 78
Handbag, tidiness, to clean, to polish, 185
Hand-sewn hems, 126
Hard water and steam irons, 27–8
Hard water and wool washing, 149
Hard water deposit, 27
Hat felts, wool, 148
Heat settings for irons, 26, 27
Heavy-duty hook and eye, 132
Heavy fabrics, whether to pink, 24
Helanca, 166, 168, 170
Helion, 166
Hem to allow for growing, 124
Hem gauge, 18
Hem marker, 18, 119
Hemline, to measure, 18, 119; to stitch, 120
Hemmer attachment, 37
Hemstitching in embroidery, 180
Herringbone-finished seam, hand-sewn, 78
Herringbone stitch, 181
High bulk Tricel, 170
High bulking, 170
Hips, ease allowance, 61; to measure, 56
Holbein stitch, 181
Holland as source of flax, 144
Holland as source of man-made fibres: Enkaswing, 158; Fibrenka, 152; Lycra, 158; Nyma, 152; Nymcrylon, 156; Orlon, 156; Silenka, 160

Home dyeing of fibres, *see* fibre information charts, 141–73

Home laundering, 135

Home Laundering Consultative Council (formerly Committee), 27, 136, *see also* fibre information charts, 141–73

Home-made look, to avoid in curved seams, 80

Home-made look, to avoid when pressing, 27, 29

Hooks and eyes, 132

Household linens, darning, 186

Huckaback weave linen, 144

Hungary as source of man-made fibres: Danulon, 166; Efylon, 166

Hydrochloric acid in fibre test, 175

Hydrofluoric acid and glass fibre, 160

Hydrogen peroxide in stain treatment, 190; for handbag stains, 185

Identification of textile fibres, *see* fibre information charts, 141–73

'Identification of Textile Materials', publication, 174

Imitation leather, 42

Important measurements (bust, waist, hips, back waist length), 52

Indelible pencil, to remove stain, 189

India as a source of cotton, 142; as source of silkworms, 146

Ink stains, to remove, 190

Instruction book with sewing machine, 36, 39

Instruction literature for washing machines, 136

Instruction sheet in paper pattern envelope, to make clear, 59

Insulation value of fibres, *see* fibre information charts, 141–73

Interfacings: layout for, 59; for buttonholes, 85; to tack, 72; to trim or grade, 80

Interlinings, suitable choice for washing, 138

International Wool Secretariat, 149

Intersecting seams, 82

Inward curve, to clip, 81

Irish linen, 144

Iron settings, H.L.C.C., 27, 141

Iron-on interlining, with necklines, 95

Ironing board covers, 29

Ironing boards, 28

Ironing equipment, 15, 26–33

Ironing of fabrics, 27, *see also* Chapter 6, Fabrics, Fibres and Finishes, 135

Irons, 26, 27, 28

Irons, numbered heat settings for, 27

Italy as source of man-made fibres: Albene, 150; Delfion, 166; Ducilo, 166; Helion, 166; Nailon, 166; Lilion, 166; Ortalion, 166; Rhodia, 150; Silene, 150; Terital, 168

Italy as source of silkworms, 146

Jacket zipper, 111

Jacquard weave linen, 144

Japan as source of man-made fibres: Amilan, 166; Grilon, 166; Kanekalon, 156; Nipolon, 166; Tetoron, 168

Japan as source of silkworms, 146; as source of wool, 148

Jersey, 146; acrylic fibre jersey, 157; wool jersey, 149

Joining bodice to skirt, 71, 109–10

Jumper, mending, 16

Junior Petite sizes, Body Measurement Chart, 51

Kanekalon, 156

Kapok, for pressing aids, 31

Kapron, 166

Kimono sleeve, 109

Kirkpatrick process, 144

Knitted nylon, 167

Knotting ends of thread, 76

Kodel, 168

Labels, on fabrics by the yard, 27, *see also* Chapter 6, Fabrics, Fibres and Finishes, 135

Labels on ready-made garments, 27

Labels on washing powder packs, 136

Labelling and the home dressmaker, 137

Lace, 142, 146

Lamonyl, 166

Lancola, 150, 170

Lanolin, 148

Lansil, 150

Lansil Ltd., 150

Lapped seam, 82

Lapped seam zip, closed at both ends, 115

Large-eyed needle (bodkin), 16

Latex adhesive, stains, to remove, 190

Launderettes, 185

Launderettes and washing labels, 136

Lawn, cotton, 142

Lazy-daisy stitch, 181

Le Roy/Weldon Pattern Service, 50

Leather, to stitch, 42

Leisure wear, fabrics for, 53

Length of skirts, 57; to mark out, 119

Left-handed embroiderers, how to reverse embroidery instructions, 176

Light fabrics, preventing facing from riding up, 95
Light on sewing machine, 38, 45
Lilion, 166
Lillikins, 20
Linen drill, 144
Linen: fibre information chart, 144–5; iron settings for, 27; tests for, 174–5; to mark, 68; to wash, 137
Lingerie: hook and eye for, 132; seam for, 84
Lining of acrylics, 157
Linron, 144
Linron and cotton, 144
Linron and Courtelle, 144
Linseed oil, 144
Lint brush, to clean machine, 44
Lipstick stains, to remove, 190; marks on handbag, 185
Loft, in fabrics, 170
Long and short stitch, 176, 181
Low gear speed for sewing machines, 37
Lubrication of the sewing machine, 45
Lurex, 162
Lurex Co. Ltd., 162
Lurex 500, 162
Lustre finishes, 172
Lustrous fibre, 139
Luvil, in stain treatment, 188
Lycra, 158

McCall Publishing Co. Ltd., 50
Machine attachment for binding, 77
Machine darning, 186
Machine embroidery, 42
Machine embroidery thread, 21
Machine sewing, see Chapter 2, Sewing Machines, Their Selection, Use and Care, 34
Machine tacking stitch, 68, 75, 86
Machine-washable wool garments, 149
Machine-worked buttonholes, 88
Magnet, 19
Maintenance of the sewing machine, 44
Making up the garment, 70
Man-made fibres, see Chapter 6, Fabrics, Fibres and Finishes, 135 (man-made fibre tables, 156–71)
Man-made fibres, manufacturing process and raw materials for, 138
Marglass, 160
Marglass Ltd., 160
Marquisette, 146
Marking the instruction sheet, 60
Marking the pattern envelope, 60
Marking with chalk, 68; with chalked thread, 68

Maudella Pattern Co. Ltd., 50
Maximum machine wash, definition, 136
Measurement Standard Committee of the Pattern Fashion Industry, 50
Measurement Chart, New Sizing, 51
Measurement, to assess, 55
Measurements: your personal measurement chart, 56–7
Mechanically pre-shrunk finishes, 172
Medium machine wash, definition, 136
Mending, see darning
Mending with darning mushroom, 16
Melt extrusion, in man-made fibre manufacture, 138
Mercerised cotton fabrics, 143, 172
Mercerised cotton thread, 21, 143
Mercerising, 142, 172
Merino wool, fibres, 148
Metal shank buttons, 131
Metallic fabrics: fibre information chart, 162–3
Methylated spirit, for stain treatment, 188, 189; for handbag care, 185
Methyl chloride, in fibre test, 175
Metlon, 162
Microscopic view of fibres, see fibre information charts, 141–73
Mildew, 142, 154, 190
Milled cloths, wool, 148
Minalon, 150
Minimum iron finish, 172
Minimum machine wash, definition, 136
Minor breakdowns, 45
Miralene, 170
Miralon, 170
Mirror: full length for sewing area; 14; for left-handed embroiderers, 176; in grooming, 184
Misr nylon, 166
Misses' sizes, 51
Mitt, pressing, 31
Mixtures and blends, definitions, 139
Modacrylic fibres: fibre information chart, 164–5; tests for, 174–5
Modified rayons, 152
Moire, 146
Moire, acetate, 150
Molony Report, The, 136
Monsanto Textiles, 156, 166
Moulding darts, aids for, 31
Moureu, 156
Mud stains, to remove, 190
Multi-slotted binder, 37
Muslin, 142

Nail polish, 190
Nail polish remover, 151
Nailon, 166
Nap, on silk, 147
Napping, 148
Natural fibres, fibre information charts, 142–9:
    cotton, 142; linen, 144; silk, 146; wool, 148
Natural fibres, threads for sewing, 21
Neatening seam edges, main ways, 77
Neckline, see Necklines and Collars, 95; if it fits
    badly, 69; points to check, 70
Neckline zipper, 111
Needle board, 29
Needle for threading tape (bodkin), 16
Needle, importance of fitting right size, 13
Needle, sewing machine, is it suitable?, 41
Needle marks, to avoid, 75
Needle threader, 19
Needlecase, 19
Needles for hand-sewing, 19
Needles for small girls, 19
Needles, rusty or sticky, to cure, 20
Needles, to pick up easily, 19
Net, rayon, 152; silk net, 146
Netherlands, as source of Nyma, 152; see also under
    Holland
Nett silk, 146
New Sizing, a guide, 50
New Zealand as source of wool, 148
Nipolon, 166
Noil, 148
Non-jamming bobbin, 38
Non-iron finish, 172
Non-protein stains, 188
Notches, to cut, 81
Nun's veiling, 142
Nylon: fibre information chart, 166–7; iron setting
    for, 27, 167; overseas trademarks, 166; tests for,
    174–5; to wash, 137, 167
Nylon net, 143
Nylon sewing thread, 21, 171
Nylon whitener, 167
Nyma, 152
Nymcrylon, 156

Office wear, fabrics for, 53
Oil paint, stains, to remove, 190
Oiling your machine, 13, 45
One-piece sleeve, 102
Open top zip fastener, to insert, 110
Open weave wool, to treat, 149
Orange stick, 20

Order of making up a garment, 70, 72
Organdie, 35, 43, 142
Organza, 146
Orlon, see acrylic fibres
Ortalion, 166
Outward curve, to notch, 81
Overcast running stitch, 182
Overcast seam edges, by hand, 78
Overcast seam edges, by machine, 79
Overlock stitch, 36
Overpressed look, to avoid, 27, 29
Overseas trademarks, 150, 152, 154, 156, 158, 160,
    162, 164, 166, 168
Owens-Corning Fiberglas Ltd., 160

PVC (vinyl) to stitch, 42; see also polyvinyl chloride,
    164
Paint cleaner, 190
Paper pattern manufacturers, 50
Paper patterns: choosing, 47; opening the pattern
    envelope, 59; checking actual measurements of
    pattern, 62; pattern adjustments, 61; pattern
    pieces, altering, 63–4; pattern cutting, 11; pattern
    markings, to transfer, 22, 66; pattern, taking
    trouble with, 13; pattern drafting, 11; pattern for
    press mitt, 30; pattern for seam roll, 33; pattern
    for tailor's ham, 32
Paper, to protect seams when pressing, 151
Patch pocket, 89
Patching, 186
Patterns, see paper patterns
Pellon, 95
Perchlorethylene, 157
Perivale Spun Terylene, 171
Perlofil, 166
Perlon, 166
Permanent press finishes, 172
Permanently crisp finishes, 172
Permanganate of potash in stain treatment, 189
Persil, in stain treatment, 190
Perspiration stains, to remove, 190
Peru as source of wool, 148
Peter Pan collar, 95, 96
Petit point, see Tent Stitch, 183
Petrochemical industry, 158.
Petroleum, 135, 156
Pfaff, 38, see also sewing machine photographs
    between pages 40 and 41
Phrix, 152
Pile fabrics, to press, 29
Pincushion, 20
Pinking shears, 24, 79

Pinning pattern pieces, 65
Pinning: planning and pinning the pattern layout, 65
Pinning seam, 75
Pins, 19, 20; sizes of, 20; to pick up easily, 19
Piped seam, 83
Piqué, 142
Plaids and stripes, 58
Plain collar, 95, 96
Plain hem, 120
Plain materials, to mark, 68
Plain sleeve, 102
Plain weave, linen, 144
Plait stitch, 126
Planning the pattern layout, 65
Pleated garments containing man-made fibres, to wash, 137, 155, 157, 167, 169, 173
Pleated skirt, hemline, 125
Plissé, 142
Pockets, 89
Pointed collar, 95, 96
Pointed scissors, 24, 25
Points of collar, to trim, 98
Poland, as source of Stilon, 166
Polyamide: fibre information chart, 166–7; iron setting for, 27, 167; overseas trademarks, 166; tests for, 174–5; to wash, 137, 167
Polyester: fibre information chart, 168–9; iron setting for, 27, 169; overseas trademarks, 166; tests for, 174–5; to wash, 137, 169
Polymer, 156
Polynosic fibre, 152
Polyurethane synthetic elastomer fibres, see Elastomerics, 158–9
Polyvynylchloride, 164, see also PVC (vinyl) 42
Pongee, 146
Poplin, 142
Porth Textiles Ltd., 162
Practical Fashions Ltd., 50
Practice sheets for machine stitching, 39, 40
Prelana, 156
Pre-shrinking fabrics, 58
Press fasteners, see snap fasteners
Press mitt, 30; to make, 31; using for sleeves, 105; using for rayon, 153
Presser foot, 41
Pressing aids, a set to make yourself, 15, 30–3
Pressing cloths, 26, 27, 29
Pressing cloths, paper, 29
Pressing curved seams, 31
Pressing equipment, 15, 26–33
Pressing intricate gathers, 31

Pressing open a seam, 76
Pressing small sleeves, 31
Pressure marks, iron, to avoid, 151
Pressure on sewing machine, 41; adjusting, 75
Professional launderer, 136
Protein stains, 188
Puckered dart, reason for, 73
Puckered seams, possible reason for, 21; the importance of avoiding, 74
Puckers, to avoid in sleeves, 102
Puff sleeve, 106, 173
Pulsator washing machine action, 136
Pure dye silk, 146
Pure new wool, 148
Purified cellulose, 150

Questions and answers on New Sizing, 50
Questions to ask before buying a sewing machine, 38
Quilting attachment, 37

Radiant, in stain treatment, 188
Raglan sleeve, 107
Raycelon, 152
Rayon: fibre information chart, 152–3; as lining to counteract static, 157; iron setting for, 27; tests for, 174–5; to wash, 137, 153; where using steam-or-spray iron, 28
Raw materials for man-made fibres, 138
Re-texturing, 185
Ready-made garments, labels for, 27, 136
Rechecking your equipment, 58
Redon, 156
Reducing bulk, zips, 115; collars, 80
Refrigerator, hardening chewing gum for easy removal, 188
Regenerated fibres, see under Cellulose fibres
Reinforced buttons, 131
Repp, 142
Reproducing pattern markings, tools for, 22; transferring from pattern to fabric, 66
Resilience in clothes, 185
Resilience of man-made fibres, see fibre information charts, 141–73
Resins, in fabric finishes, 172
Respacing buttonholes, 86
Restricting dolman sleeve, to cure, 108
Rever collar, 95, 99
Reversing to finish seam, 41, 42
Rexor, 162
Rhodia, 150
Rhodiaceta, 166

Rhonel, 154
Ribbon binding, used to reinforce neckline, 96
Ribbon, threading, 16
Ribbon to neaten underarm seam, 108
Ribbon to reinforce kimono sleeve, 109
Richelieu embroidery, 178
Rigmel, 172
Ring zip, 114
Ripping scissors, 25
Rolled and overcast hem edging, 126
Rolled hem edging, plait stitch, 126
Roly poly stitch, 182
Rope or tow, in man-made fibre manufacture, 139
Rotproofing, treatment for cotton, 142
Round neckline, 95
Rounded collar, 98
Rulers, 20: for buttonhole markings, 86; in transferring marks, 68
Running stitch, 182
Russia as source of cotton, 142; as source of flax, 144, *see also* USSR
Rust, 190
Rusty needles, to cure, 20
Rusty pins, to prevent, 20

Saddle-stitched seam, hand finished, 84
Sailcloth, 142
Sanforized, 172
Sarille, 152
Sateen, 142
Satin, 142, 146; acetate satin, 150
Satin stitch, by machine, 35; by hand, 182
Savings made through home-sewing, 15
Sawdust, as filling for tailor's ham, 32
Schappe-spun Terylene sewing thread, 171
School darning lessons, 186
Scissor cutting guage, 25
Scissors, 23-5: keeping sharp, 24; misuses to avoid, 24; pointed, 24, 25; ripping, 25; when needing sharpening, 24; when to oil, 24
Scissors, electric, 24
Scorch marks, to treat, 189
Scottish linen, 144
Scouring of wool, 148
Scrapbook of sewing, 55, 62
Scroop, 146
Seam allowance, to check, 75
Seam allowance on collar, to clip, 97
Seam allowance on curved seam, to clip or notch, 81
Seam edges, to grade or trim, 80
Seam guide attachment, use with curved seams, 41, 76, 80

Seam roll, 33, 76, 151, 153
Seam unpicker, 21, 25
Seams and finishes, 74
  bias-bound seam finish, 77
  constructional seam, 74
  curved seam, 31, 80
  decorative seam, 74
  double top-stitched seam finish, 78
  eased seam, 81
  edge-stitched seam finish, 78
  flat fell seam, 84
  French seam, 84
  herringbone-stitched seam finish, 78
  intersecting seam, 82
  lapped seam, 82
  saddle-stitched seam, 84
  seam edges bound by machine and by hand, 77
  seam edges bound by machine attachment, 77
  seam edges overcast by hand, 78
  seam edges overcast by machine with zigzag stitch, 79
  seam ends, to finish, 41, 42, 76
  seam on a corner, 83
  seam on the cross, 68
  seam with welt finish, 79
  some special ways with seams, 79
  stayed and pinked seam finish, 79
  to grade or trim, 80
Seed stitch, 183
Seersucker, 142
Segmented polyurethane, 158
Semi-automatic sewing machines, 34, 37
Sequence of dressmaking, 72
Serge, wool, 148
Sericin, 146
Serpentine stitch, 35
Servicing of sewing machines, 38
Setting for irons, 27
Setting in sleeves, 102
Sew a fine seam, some simple rules, 75
Sewing areas, 14
Sewing boxes, budget type, plastic and wicker, 14
Sewing cards for small girls, 19
Sewing corners, 14
Sewing course for beginners, Chapter 4, 55
Sewing equipment, 15-33
Sewing in reverse, 41, 42, 76
Sewing machine attachments, 37
Sewing machine tables, 38
Sewing Machines, Their Selection, Use and Care, Chapter 2, 34
  automatic type sewing machines, 36

Sewing machines—*cont.*
  basting (tacking) stitch on, 68, 75, 86
  buttonholer feature, 37
  demonstrations of, 38
  desirability of, 15
  embroidery thread for, 21
  embroidery with, 42
  features to look for, 37
  flat bed or free arm type, 36
  guarantees, 38
  instruction book, 39
  keeping ready to use, 14
  learning to use a new type, 38
  needles for, 41
  pressure to select, 41, 42
  reversing for seams, 76
  semi-automatic, 34
  service for, 38
  sewing table for, 38
  stitch length, 41
  storing, 14, 38
  straight-stitch machines, 34
  swing-needle machines, 35
  tacking (basting) stitch on, 68, 75, 86
  tension, 41
  types of, 34
  where to use and store, 14, 38
  zigzag-type machines, 35
Sewing notebook, 55, 66
Sewing notes for natural and man-made fibres, *see*
  fibre information charts, 141–73; *also* 42
Sewing notions, 58
Sewing on the buttons, 130
Sewing processes, a directory, 72
Sewing room, 14
Sewing straight, 39
Sewing threads, 21; for man-made fibres, 171; for
  tacking, 21, 67, 75
Shank for button, to make, 130
Shantung, 146
Shaped skirt, 124
Sharp-pointed collar, turning, 20
Sharpening scissors, 24
Sharps, types of needle, 19
Shawflex, 166, 168
Shears, dressmaker's, *see* Dressmaker's shears
Sheen on silk, 147
Sheer fabrics, pins for, 20
Shell edging by hand, *see under* Plait stitch
Shell edging by machine, 35
Shiny look, avoidance when pressing, 27, 29
Shirtwaist sleeve, 128

Shoe buttons, buckles, thread for, 21
Shoe polish stains, to remove, 190
Short sleeve, 106
Shoulder seams, point to check, 70; to measure, 57
Shrink test, 58
Shrinking fabrics, 59
Side seams, to measure, 56
Silene, 150
Silenka, 160
Silk: fibre information chart, 146–7; iron setting
  for, 27, 147; sewing notes, 147; tests for, 174–5;
  to wash, 137, 147
Silk cord for buttonholes, 89
Silk finishes, 146
Silk thread, 21, 147
Silk velvet, 146, 147
Silks for embroidery, 21, 26
Silkworms, 138, 146
Silon, 166
Simplicity Patterns Ltd., 50
Simplified stitch selection on sewing machines, 37
Simplified threading system on sewing machines, 37
Size of pattern, 49
Sizing of silk, 146
Skirt length, to measure, 57
Skirt pocket, 93
Skirt zipper, 111
Skirts, waistline to treat, 110
Slacks, waistline to treat, 110
Sleeve board, 33
Sleeves, 102:
  cap sleeve, 109
  cuffs and sleeve edges, 127
  dolman sleeve, 108
  kimono sleeve, 109
  plain sleeve, 102
  pre-shrinking excess fulness, 105
  puff sleeve, 106
  raglan sleeve, 107
  shirtwaist sleeve, 128
  sleeve edge turned and stitched, 127
  sleeve, small, to press using pressing aids, 31
  to set in, 102
  using sleeve board to press, 33
  where using a specially-finished fabric, 105, 173
Slip basting (tacking), 72
Slippery fabrics, to prevent facing riding up, 95
Slow speed for sewing machines, 37, 41
Slub silk, *see* silk, 147
Snap-fasteners, 134
Snap-on presser foot, 37; for foam-back fabrics, 42
Snipping off loose ends, 42

Snipping thread, pointed scissors for, 24
Socks, to darn, 186
Soft collar, 101
Soft water, 28
South Africa as source of wool, 148
South America as source of cotton, 142
Space for sewing, 14
Spain, as source of man-made fibres: Crilenka, 156; Lilion, 166; Perlofil, 166; Tergal, 168
Spandex yarns, 158
Spanzelle, 158
Special finishes: fibre information chart, 172–3; sewing notes, 105, 173; to wash, 173
Specially-finished cottons, dealing with sleeves, 105, 173
Specially-finished cottons, *see* Special Finishes, 172–3
Specially-finished linens, *see* Special Finishes
Specially-finished rayons, 153, 172–3
Speed, slow, for sewing machines, 37, 41
Spinnaret, 138
Spinning gel, 150
Spinning the filament fibre, 138
Spirit cleaner, for handbags, 185
Split underarm, to prevent, 108
Sponge for pressing, 33
Sportswear, fabrics for, 53
Spray-on stain treatment, 190
Spun fibres, 139
Spun silk, 146
Spun-dyed fibre, 139
Spun-dyed yarn, 138
Square neckline, to reinforce, 96
Stab needle, 35
Stain removal guide, 187
Stain repellent finishes, 172
Staining brown when ironing, cause, 27
Standard measurements, 61
Standard rayon, 152
Standardization of iron temperatures, 27
Standardized iron heat settings, 27
Staple fibre, 152
Staple yarn, 139
Starlene, 168
Static, 151, 155
Stayed and pinked seam finish, 79
Steam gun, 185–6
Steam iron, 27
Steam treatment for dry cleaned garments, 185
Steam-or-spray irons, 26, 28
Stem stitch, 183
Stiletto, 26, 89
Stilon, 166

Stitch length, choosing correct, 41, 75
Stitching a hem, 120
Stitching a seam, way, 75
Stitching correctly, sewing machine, 41
Stitching straight, 39–40, 75
Stitching, turning a corner, 83
Stitches, embroidery, 176
Stock size, 47
Storing the garment you are making, 14
Storing the sewing machine, 38
Straight machine stitching, way to achieve, 39
Straight skirts, 120
Straight stitch (embroidery), 183
Straight-stitch sewing machine, 34
Strapless dress, ease allowance for, 61
Stretch fabrics, 36, 42, 158, 170. Fibre information charts:
    Elastofibres, 158–9
    Textured, bulked and stretch yarns, 170–1
Stretch fabrics and the automatic sewing machine, 36, 140
Stretch stitch, 36, 140, 167
Strip lighting for sewing cupboard, 14
Stripes and plaids, 58
Style patterns Ltd., 50
Sudan as source of cotton, 142
Suede, 42
Suitings, linen, 144
Sulphuric acid, 150; in fibre test, 175
Suntan oil stains, to remove, 190
Surah, 146
Sweden as source of Tacryl, 156
Swing-needle machine, 35
Switzerland as source of Flisca, 152; Grilon, 166; Lamonyl, 166
Synthetic elastomers, 158
Synthetic fabrics, importance of avoiding need to unpick, 75; thread for, 21, 171
Synthetic fibres, 156–70; *see* Chapter 6, Fabrics, Fibres and Finishes, 135
Synthetic resins in fabric finishes, 172
Synthetic rubber, 156

T-squares, 20
Table for sewing machine, 38
Table linen, 144
Tablecloths: cotton, 142; stains to remove, 190
Tacking, 75
Tacking main sections for first fitting, 68
Tacking stitch on sewing machines, 68, 75, 86
Tacking stitches, thread for, 21
Tacking stitches, types of, 72

Tacking thread, 21, 67, 75

Tacryl, 156

Taffeta, 146; acetate taffeta, 150; to mark taffeta, 68

Tailored buttonholes, 89

Tailoring, 11

Tailor's chalk, 22

Tailor's ham, 31, 32; to make, 31; for rayon, 153; for acetate, 151

Tailor's hem, 120

Tailor's mitt, to make, 30-1; for pressing wool, 149

Tailor's tacks, 18, 21, 22, 23, 67; how to make, 67

Talcum powder: as stain treatment, 188; in sewing foam-back fabrics, 42

Tank-type steam irons, 27

Tap water, inadvisability for steam irons, 28

Tape measure, 21, 22

Tape, threading, 16

Tapestry needles, 19

Taping bias edges, 68

Taslan, 170

Tea, stains, to remove, 190

Tea towels, linen, 144

Teen sizes, 51

Teklan, 164

Temperature of water, conversion from Centigrade to Fahrenheit, 141

Temperature of water, with enzyme products, 188

Temperature setting, irons, 27

Template for pocket, 89

Temporary folds, to tack (baste), 72

Temporary pleating, to tack (baste), 72

Tension, 13, 41, 75

Tent stitch, 183

Tergal, 168

Terital, 168

Terlenka, see polyester fibres

Terry towelling, 142

Terylene, see polyester fibres

Terylene sewing thread, 21, for man-made fibres, 171

Terylene/wool blends, 137, 169

Test pieces for straight stitching, 40; for practice zips, 110

Testing fabric for stitch length, tension, 41

Testing stitching before sewing, 75

Tests for fibres, 174-5

Tetoron, 168

Textile industry, 139

Textile Institute, The, 174

Textrallized, 166, 170

Textured, bulked and stretch yarns; fibre information chart, 170-1

Thermostatically-controlled irons, 26, 27, 28

Thimble, 22

Thread, sewing, 21; for man-made fibres, 171

Thread, tacking, 21, 67, 75

Threading a needle easily, 19

Threading elastic, tape and ribbon, 16

Threading systems on sewing machines, 37

Three-position needle, 35, 44

Three-step zigzag, 35

Throatplate on sewing machine, 41

Tissue paper when pressing rayon, 153; when sewing silk, 147

To correct figure faults, 63, 64

Tools for dressmaking and needlework, 13-33

Tools for sewing, redeeming the cost of, 15

Topel, 152

Tow, in man-made fibre manufacture, 139

Towelling, cotton, 142

Town wear, fabrics for, 53

Toy pile fabrics, 152

Tracing wheel, 18, 22; to use, 68

Transferring markings from pattern to fabric, 66

Trevira, 168

Triacetate fibres: fibre information chart, 154-5; iron setting for, 27, 137; removing marks from, 188, 189, 190; sewing notes, 155; tests for, 174-5; to wash, 137, 155

Tricel, see triacetate fibres

Tricel-and-rayon, see triacetate fibres

Tricel/Sarille, see triacetate fibres

Tricelon, 154

Trichlorethylene, 154

Trilan, 154

Trilon, 166

Trimming a seam, 80

Trimming points of a collar, 98

Triple lock stretch stitch, 36

Trouser zipper, 111

Trying on a garment for first fitting, 68

Trying on the pattern pieces, 64

Trylko thread, 171

Tucker attachment, 37

Tuition, new sewing machine, 38

Tulle, 142, 146

Turkey, as source of cotton, 142

Turner Bros. Asbestos Co. Ltd., 160

Turpentine in stain treatment, 188, 190

Turpentine substitute in stain treatment, 190

Tussah, 146

Tussore, 146

Tweed, 43, 148; silk tweed, 146

Tweezers in the sewing box, 23

Twill weave linen, 144

Twin-needles, 35
Twist, buttonhole, 21, 133
Twist, to avoid in sleeves, 102
Twisted collar, to avoid, 98
Two-piece sleeve, 102
Two-position needle, on sewing machine, 35
Tycora, 170

USA as source of cotton, 142
USA as source of man-made fibres: Antron, 166; Arnel, 154; Avisco, 152; Cantrece, 166; Chemstrand nylon, 166; Coloray, 152; Creslan, 156; Dacron, 168; Du Pont nylon, 166; Dynel, 164; Encron, 168; Enka nylon, 166; Enka rayon, 152; Estron, 150; Fiberglas, 160; Fortrel, 168; Glospan, 158; Kodel, 168; Lycra, 158; Metlon, 162; Orlon, 156; Topel, 152; Verel, 164; Vycron, 168; Vyrene, 158; Zefran, 156
USSR as source of silkworms, 146
USSR as source of man-made fibres: Enant, 166; Kapron, 166, see also under Russia.
Unbleached calico, 142; for pressing aids, 31; as interlining, 149
Underarm seam, to measure, 56
Unpicking, to avoid need for, 75
Unpicking tool, for seams, 21, 25; using after first fitting, 69
Upholstery cotton, 142
Upholstery pins, 20
Upholstery zipper, 111
Upright basting (tacking) 72
Uruguay as source of wool, 148

V-neckline, to reinforce, 96
V-notches, 66
Vaseline, 42
Velour, wool, 148
Velvet, 142; needle board for pressing, 29, 147; silk velvet, 146; rayon velvet, 152
Velveteen, 142; needle board for pressing, 29, 147
Veranne, 160
Verel, 164
Viking Husqvarna sewing machine, 35, 39; see also sewing machine photographs between pages 40 and 41
Vilene, 95
Vincel, 152
Vinegar, in stain treatment, 190
Vinyl, 37, 42
Vinylidene chloride, 164
Viscose rayon, 152
Viscous liquid in fibre manufacture, 138

Vogue Pattern Service, 50
Voile, 142
Vycron, 168
Vyrene, 158

Wadding, acetate, 150
Waist, ease allowance, 61; to measure, 56
Waistband mounted on elastic, 110
Waistlines, 109; if too loose, 69; to measure, 56
Waistline seam, point to check, 70
Warnings: for carbon tetrachloride, 187; for plastic bags, 70; when testing fibres, 174
Warp knit polyester, 168
Wash care labels, 137
Washable pleated garments, see pleated garments
Washing of fabrics and fibres, see Chapter 6, Fabrics, Fibres and Finishes, 135
Washing processes, 136
Washing product packs, labelling, 136
Washing temperature agreement, 136
Waste wool, 148
Water, hard, 28
Water, soft, 28
Water-repellent finishes, 172
Water-soluble particles, 185
Waxed thread, for buttonholes, 89
Weight, if fluctuating, 55, 110
Welt pocket, 92
Welt seam, 79
West Germany, as source of man-made fibres: Bemberg, 152; Colva, 152; Cupioni, 152; Cuprama, 152; Cupresa, 152; Danufil, 152; Diolen, 168; Dolan, 156; Dralon, 156; Gevetex, 160; Perlon, 166; Phrix, 152; Redon, 156; Trevira, 168
Wet extrusion, 138
Whipcord, wool, 148
White spirit, 157
Width of fabric, 59
Wild silk, 146
Wild silkworms, 146
Winceyette, 142
Wine stains, to remove, 190
Wolcrylon, 156
Women's sizes, 51
Wood pulp, 152
Wood pulp in triacetate, 154
Wool: fibre information chart, 148–9; iron setting for, 27, 149; sewing notes, 149; tests for, 174–5; to wash, 137, 149
Wool garments, to cure flat look after dry cleaning, 185

Wool mixtures, 137, 148–9
Wool/cotton mixtures, 137, 149
Wool/rayon mixtures, 137, 149
Woollen process, 148
Worked buttonholes, 85
Worsted process, 148
Wrist, to measure, 57

Yardstick, 21, 23; to measure hems, 119

Young Junior/Teen sizes, 51

Zefran, 156
Zehla, 152
Zigzag sewing machines, 35
Zigzag stitch in seam finishing, 79; to reinforce hem, 122; on towelling, 186
Zip fasteners, 71, 110; ways to insert, 110–18
Zipper foot, 37